HAUNTED BY THE CIVIL WAR

Haunted by the Civil War

CULTURAL TESTIMONY IN THE NINETEENTH-CENTURY UNITED STATES

Shirley Samuels

PRINCETON UNIVERSITY PRESS
PRINCETON & OXFORD

Published by Princeton University Press
41 William Street, Princeton, New Jersey 08540
99 Banbury Road, Oxford OX2 6JX

press.princeton.edu

GPSR Authorized Representative: Easy Access System Europe - Mustamäe tee 50, 10621 Tallinn, Estonia, gpsr.requests@easproject.com

ISBN 9780691248578
ISBN (e-book) 9780691248646

Library of Congress Control Number: 2025934810

British Library Cataloging-in-Publication Data is available

Editorial: Anne Savarese and Emma Wagh
Production Editorial: Theresa Liu
Jacket/Cover Design: Haley O'Neill
Production: Erin Suydam
Publicity: William Pagdatoon
Copyeditor: Jennifer Harris

Jacket image: Winslow Homer, *Camp Fire*, 1880, oil on canvas. Gift of Josephine Pomeroy Hendrick, in the name of Henry Keney Pomeroy, 1927 / The Metropolitan Museum of Art.

This book has been composed in Miller

Printed in the United States of America

10 9 8 7 6 5 4 3 2 1

CONTENTS

ILLUSTRATIONS

HAUNTED BY THE CIVIL WAR

Introduction

Men at War

On the fourteenth anniversary of Abraham Lincoln's death, the poet who had famously mourned his absence delivered a lecture in Philadelphia declaring that the "secession war" was too recent to describe. Although he had previously written about the war in the poems of *Drum-Taps* (1865), on this day Walt Whitman announced that "A great literature will yet arise out of the era of those four years" because they offer "an inexhaustible mine for the histories, drama, romance, and even philosophy of peoples to come."[1] Whitman ended his eulogy by noting that the "grand deaths of the race . . . are its most important inheritance-value—in some respects beyond its literature and art."[2] The importance of such an inheritance, the charge that the greatness of literature or art would continue to pale before the quest to make such deaths significant, presented many challenges for the writers and artists who depicted the emotions, the bodies, and the landscapes left as a residue from this absorbing war. Developing a cultural legacy out of the grimy fabric of war became a greater challenge when the corpses—whether celebrated, claimed, or abandoned—proliferated across thousands of miles. Definitely haunted by Lincoln's death, Whitman, who has in turn haunted readers with poems like "When Lilacs Last in the Dooryard Bloomed," eerily proposes that death outweighs both literature and art.

The question remains: Why does the Civil War continue to haunt America? In other words, why does a series of often inchoate battles fought more than 160 years ago continue to be debated as though the victory or the loss contained something like the soul of the country?[3] The origin tales of Civil War haunting have been traced back to 1619 with the arrival of the first ships that came from England to Virginia carrying humans catalogued as cargo.[4] They might also be traced to the seventeenth-century silencing of women, such as Anne Hutchinson, banished by her minister John Cotton after she dared to claim access to the voice of God.[5] This book focuses on the nineteenth century, yet the writers and artists of that century were haunted by earlier histories. These include the violence of not only the American Revolution, that much celebrated "birth" of the codified nation-state, but also the almost numberless small battles that led up to the defining moments of the Civil War. Crucially and tragically, the soldiers who emerged to fight on both sides included veterans from nearly forgotten wars, such as the Cherokee Wars that lasted, conservatively, from 1776 until 1795, and the Seminole Wars that resumed in the early nineteenth century, influencing national policy for decades.

Such armed conflict continued in the West in such places as "Bleeding Kansas" and the Dakota territory, even as contemporary reenactments commemorate the Civil War battles that haunt the landscapes of the eastern United States.[6] The concept of democracy remains haunted in this country because of its dual attachment to the legacy of slavery and the rift between North and South remaining from the war. In the abstract, the idea that democracy means access to participation in government adheres to the usual phrasing of participatory democracy.[7] Yet such a concept of democracy has always involved exclusions, and in the United States these date from the earliest debates over how to count citizens, debates that arose among signers of the Declaration of Independence and resulted in counting enslaved human beings as fractions. Those excluded have witnessed their exclusion more vividly than those included have witnessed that privilege.

One of the most painful literary accounts of such exclusion during the nineteenth century appears in the emancipation narrative *Incidents in the Life of a Slave Girl* (1861). When Harriet Jacobs wrote about hiding in her grandmother's house from the confinement of her enslaved status, she described looking through the small hole she named the "loophole of retreat," eager for fresh air and a glimpse of her children. What she witnessed—a woman fleeing down the street, for example, from those who wished to claim her body as property—resulted from the operations of a democracy whose laws both excluded and confined her. This book bears witness to such exclusions while testifying about the desire for freedom that ideas about democracy still convey. This introduction examines some of these terms and the sensations they arouse.

To witness the history of democratic yearning in the nineteenth-century United States is to observe and testify about a vivid landscape with sometimes competing languages. That testimony can evoke, sometimes simultaneously, the pleasure of belonging and the pain of alienation. For Walt Whitman, looking back on the war in his reflective *Democratic Vistas* (1871), the success of democracy is certain, but he also saw a "battle" raging "between democracy's convictions, aspirations and the people's crudeness, vices, caprices."[8] The image of people's "crudeness" at war with democracy's "aspirations" persists through the nineteenth century. The action of witnessing presents connotations at once of attesting to faith and giving testimony in a court of law. Although they literally fought for it, citizens who express faith in democracy often articulate something fragile or misplaced in the face of the challenges brought by war, slavery, genocide, and territorial imperialism. To bear witness in relation to the testimony of such voices is to convey the charge of competing words, to observe how pictures work as propaganda and illustration, to see what images the speakers use to testify—and to be haunted by death.[9]

Writers from the nineteenth century repeatedly display faith in testimony while they also exhibit uncertainty about the possible consequences of the act of looking. Fiction and poetry dominate this book's choices of bearing witness, yet throughout this book I look for visual productions to complement a cultural understanding of political consequences. As I investigate forms of devotion to democracy, my witnessing stops short of the zeal and determination that drove the production of a book such as *American Slavery as It Is: Testimony of a Thousand Witnesses* (1839). When the Southern sisters Angelina and Sarah Grimke, intimately familiar with the legacy of the Southern "peculiar institution" because they grew up in the midst of it, worked with their Northern abolitionist friend Theodore Weld to produce that book, they used the testimony of Southern newspapers to expose the practices of slavery, because such newspapers routinely described the wounds, scars, and brands that identified brutal practices as a form of identification.[10] The introduction to that book evokes a court proceeding in which "the case of Human Rights against Slavery" will be "adjudicated in the court of conscience."[11] The ambiguous status of a "court of conscience" rarely appears in the legal testimony that determined federal policy toward either slavery or what became known as "domestic dependent nations." Such invocations of domesticity and dependence declared an impossibly fraught relation to nationalism within the first decades of the nineteenth century.[12]

When Whitman writes about democracy he references faith in a democratic vision that appears at once intimate and national. Absurd as his declarations of faith might appear—and they can definitely appear absurd in Whitman—the very love that he promotes becomes an essential part of his witnessing. For Whitman to address "Democracy!" is almost always to use an exclamation mark, and often to exclaim further, "Near at hand to you a throat is inflating itself and joyfully singing!" That joy can seem presumptuous, as when he asserts of "my nations" that he will "include you all with perfect love!" Yet he made it his life's work to embrace that love, while mixing it with the details of war, of landscapes, of the particularities of the states from which came the young men that he loved so well. Exceptions occur. When Whitman offers a "Glimpse of War's Hell Scenes" in *Specimen Days* or shows the "monkey-looking dwarfs" that have returned barely alive from prisoner of war camps, he turns to grim pondering. Even then, through suffering that raises doubts concerning the human capacity to offer testimony about such deeds, it bears repeating that the "kelson of creation" for Whitman is love.[13] As a witness, Whitman testifies to a democracy perpetually unavailable, although he repeatedly celebrates that the bodies it contains can be embraced.

The onset of the war had a correlation in the development of photographic techniques; the covered wagons of photographic darkrooms trundled along to battlefields as the studios they left behind in cities like New York or Washington, DC, sought to sell images from the front. An appetite for visual representations of the blistering devastation to both bodies and landscapes recorded in photographs such as those later republished in Alexander Gardner's *Photographic Sketchbook of the Civil War* (1865–1866) meant that such photographs could be seen in city streets far from the front. These images, merging stones and bones, have a technical corollary in the detail that the exposure times of cameras conveyed the stillness of ruined landscapes and corpses more easily than they could portray living bodies. The captions for the photographs that Gardner provides are famously inaccurate, as they distort how both bodies and weapons arrived at the locations he shows. The attention paid to the bones that littered those landscapes includes an implicit analogy that the rocks among which they appeared seem to have swallowed them. Gardner comments of his image "Home of a Rebel Sharpshooter" that the soldier's "bones lie bleaching . . . between the rocks at Gettysburg.[14] The thin line between bones and rocks appears in the notations made by Walt Whitman in *Specimen Days* when he observes how many bodies were swallowed up by the land and remain in "secluded spots" as "skeletons."[15] These skeletons at once merge with the landscape and linger, as Whitman later notes, as dust.

Writers such as Stephen Crane and Ambrose Bierce might initially appear to endorse remembering the war as a crisis about masculinity and the bodies of white men. Such a condition of understanding the war appears in the literature of both the North and the South. Troubling these persistent implications, this book first considers the effects of the environment and then turns to other forms of witnessing. The language of Crane's famous opening to *The Red Badge of Courage*—"The cold passed reluctantly from the earth"—gives the landscape an active presence.[16] The "retiring fogs revealed an army stretched out on the hills, resting" and yet the landscape seems to be seeking to end its rest as the "low brows of distant hills" contain "the red eye like gleam of hostile camp fires" (3). More disturbing eyes appear in corpses. Henry Fleming, the "youth" who has come to fight as a heroic investment, finds himself first running from battle and then encountering a corpse: "he was being looked at by a dead man" (41). To encounter either landscapes or corpses in this novel is to find yourself being watched (figure I.1). And the watching, as in Winslow Homer's sketch, *Sharp-Shooter on Picket Duty*, carries the threat of death.

The look of death in the landscape that the writer Ambrose Bierce presents through stories such as "The Affair at Coulter's Notch" (1889) introduces gender to the matter of political loyalty. Captain Coulter, the eponymous Union soldier, has been ordered to fire on his own house, located in a "notch" between warring parties, where his wife and son are sheltered. At the end of the story, after the house has collapsed, Coulter is found cradling the corpse of his Confederate wife so closely that observers cannot at first distinguish between Coulter's beard and his dead wife's hair. The notoriety of such horror in Bierce's writing overshadows the extent to which it might be realistic reporting, and even possibly understatement. In "Chickamauga" (1889), for instance, the "inarticulate and indescribable cries" of a mute child who finds his mother apparently raped and definitely murdered after he has been wandering in the woods and trying to ride on the backs of injured crawling soldiers might also show the mute need to cry a language that cannot be uttered, to speak words that cannot be spoken.[17] When the body subsides into the landscape, language subsides as well.

Women and landscapes, women and tears—the back story of war often seems to involve the soldier's desire to return home to a mother, a wife, a sister. What history adheres to such locations? The home might have been burned. Or shelled. Or abandoned. What became of the women and children who lived in that home, asks Ambrose Bierce's story. Yet the homes that appear in these short stories, however shattered and violated, are still the homes of white people. The confusion caused by seeing the beard of Captain Coulter draped over the long hair of his dead wife seems to blur the relation between the male Union soldier and the dead female

FIGURE I.1. Winslow Homer (1836–1910). *Home, Sweet Home*, ca. 1863. Oil on canvas. Overall dimensions: 21 1/2 in. × 16 1/2 in. (54.6 cm × 41.9 cm). Two Union soldiers (infantrymen, according to the insignia on their caps) listen to the regimental band play "Home, Sweet Home." Patrons' Permanent Fund (1997.72.1). Courtesy of the National Gallery of Art, Washington.

Southern sympathizer to whom he has been married and against whom he has been directed to fire cannonballs.

The haunting evoked by the sight of corpses in such a short story finds a corollary in the haunting provoked by the photographed faces of the wounded. It remains unnerving to open the pages of the photographic notebooks kept by Reed Bontecou, a medical surgeon during the war who wanted to document the results of the treatments he carried out after battles. The discomfort caused by looking at the faces of the young boys whose bodies have been torn engages the archival difficulty in understanding that surveillance is at once medical and political, at once personal and cultural. The spectacle of these faces set into the pages of an album makes them specimens of treatment, but also specimens of war. The idea of producing such albums as though they belonged in parlors introduces an aspect of war as uneasy vigilance and even an uncomfortable tourism as Northern soldiers took trains to the South and tried to figure out landscapes that became unrecognizable as trees were felled and bodies took the place of boulders.[18]

Encounters with the landscape suffuse literary and artistic imagination in the nineteenth-century United States before and after the war. The postbellum turn to celebrating Western landscapes shows the West pulling against the difficult maneuvering of urban populations and industrialization in the Eastern United States. That thread pulling cultural and political energies westward was enhanced by the railroad. The "golden spike" was driven into the landscape of the West just after the war ended, a reminder that the war took place against a background of commerce and mobility. The transcontinental railroad project that was begun in the earliest days of 1863 was proposed as a means to reach markets in Asia. It reached a ceremonial end just after the war, on May 10, 1869.[19] The railroad mobilized art as well as commerce: able to reach Western landscapes more quickly, the photographers who had followed troops across stony landscapes to find dead bodies now turned to the stony sublimity of Yosemite. Their images were echoed in the large landscapes of painters like Albert Bierstadt, whose vast mountains drew the eye away from small bodies in the foreground and reinforced the shift in popular attention from the loss of bodies in landscapes to landscapes that dwarfed bodies.

Witnessing

To declare that the Civil War haunts America is also to note that the disunified nation still called the United States persists as a haunted house, with ghosts as a legacy of its foundation. Abraham Lincoln, considered during his lifetime as divisive and controversial, famously issued a warning about a "house divided"[20] that persists. The color-coded maps showing political disagreements in the current century—disagreements nurtured by the violence surrounding legislation about education, race, abortion, or immigration—resemble the maps that showed states splitting from the Union over the matter of slavery.[21] In referring to Lincoln's apocalyptic warning, I engage with the present while looking backward; by the time you read these words, the daily moments of crisis will have moved inexorably into the past.[22] But the haunting will continue.

To observe how the Civil War haunts America, this book examines not only ghosts that cannot rest but also the cultural practices that invoke them as persisting.[23] These ghosts have been named, remembered, celebrated, or shamed according to the regions of the United States where they carried out their deeds when alive. In the West, the displacements of officially sanctioned genocide persist as controversies about Indigenous land rights in places like Oklahoma.[24] In the North, the history of racial strife persists as a controversy about police tactics. Southern celebrations, commemorations, and reenactments continue to produce a vision of the "war between the states," but the concept of a unified nation becomes ever more elusive. My project seeks neither to compete with particular stories of battlefield remembrance nor to embrace a resistance founded in ideology. Rather, by tracing ceremonies, rituals, reenactments, and memorials in both literature and art, I propose that how often we look at the dead ties us to a history that has no end.[25]

To remember the Civil War through such visible emblems of a heroic but lost identity as statues for fallen heroes continues to invoke controversies over what was lost. For example, Augustus Saint-Gaudens created the much-admired Robert Gould Shaw memorial (1897) in Boston Common to depict the doomed advance of the Massachusetts Fifty-Fourth Infantry at Fort Wagner.[26] While the memorial honors the heroic sacrifice by newly enlisted African American soldiers, in visual terms it celebrates white sacrifice: the doomed marching men are led by a white man on horseback. On the opposite side, certain statues in southern cities such as New Orleans, until recently, commemorated Southern generals. The statues don't hold still: in places like Charlottesville, Virginia, their proposed removal generated violent protests from groups that represented both the North and the South. After toppling a statue in North Carolina, protestors kicked at its inert form in the grass.[27] These monuments often represent the groups that sought political or cultural power by erecting them decades after the war ended, including nostalgic lobbying groups such as the

Daughters of the Confederacy. Understanding this history reveals a haunting that has emerged repeatedly in the more than 160 years since the war officially ended. In arguing that the United States has been haunted, I also assert that the Civil War is still alive.[28]

Talking about ghosts—both warding them off and inviting their return—has always been attractive as a mode of storytelling. The "frisson" of hearing or seeing a ghost mingles with the desire to know the story behind the fear, and both the story and the fear enact a kind of pleasure.[29] In naming ghosts I share the concern embedded in figures like the "crawling already? baby" in Toni Morrison's *Beloved*. This two-year-old, killed by her mother Sethe, who pays for a tombstone with her body, haunts a house and a family that both contain and resist the memories of the house divided.[30] The ambiguity of the injunction in the novel's final pages—is this really "not a story to pass on"?—might also haunt the telling here. In the pages that follow, I describe many historical ghosts.[31] Each violent death that reflects the legacies of policing race and identity revives the historical shame of haunting.

To be haunted by the Civil War does not mean that an exorcism is in the future. Citizens of the United States will continue to live with these ghosts. The collective voices at the end of *Beloved* raise a wordless chant that brings peace for the house. Still trying to use our words to articulate what has happened, we develop stories to pass on, whether we believe them or not.[32]

The first chapter of this book, "Visions of Democracy," discusses early deliberations about the racialization of an ideal democracy and includes a more detailed account of how the violent debates about land ownership and slavery that led to the Civil War challenge democratic ideals. The second chapter, "Poetry and War," examines the language of sensation in the war poetry of Herman Melville, Emily Dickinson, and Walt Whitman as well as in Lincoln's relation to the poetic and visual culture of his time.[33] In "Democratic Mourning," the third chapter, I turn to the haunted aftereffects of war. Here I focus on Elizabeth Stuart Phelps, who wrote some of the most popular inspirational fiction of the nineteenth century, as well as writings by Louisa May Alcott and Harriet Beecher Stowe. Women in Phelps's postbellum sentimental novel *The Gates Ajar* (1868) confront the boundary between heaven and earth. Mourning lost loved ones, they live in an emotional border territory that alludes to the violent skirmishes and deadly betrayals taking place in border territories along the Mississippi River.

The fourth chapter, "The Republic of Men at Sea," turns to both rivers and the sea. It sets in motion a comparison of travel along the Mississippi

River in the writings of Herman Melville and Mark Twain. For each writer, rivers become porous boundaries between territories considered free and places of bondage, a contrast considered here in relation to the numerous crossings of the Atlantic Ocean that conveyed enslaved bodies. Today's readings cannot be landlocked; they incorporate the expanding geographical boundaries of the nineteenth century and make a circuit from the westward expansion toward markets with China to the southern frontier with the Caribbean. For these modes of transit, the hauntings that accompany the often-lethal practices of enslavement and the simultaneous genocides of the Western United States emerge as key elements while considering the mythology of men set free on the water. In the fifth chapter, "Women at Home," I look at feminism with respect to labor in late-nineteenth-century productions by Charlotte Perkins Gilman, Lucy Larcom, and Frances Harper, and ask about the relation of their feminism to the casualties of the war. The afterword looks at the invocation of wartime stories in the work of contemporary playwrights such as Suzan-Lori Parks.

Women at War

The organization known since the nineteenth century as the United Daughters of the Confederacy (UDC) states on its website that it most emphatically does not support white supremacy. At the same time, the website expresses regret about the desecration and removal of Confederate statues, many of which its past members worked to install, because the men honored by these monuments were all "American." Yet the membership page explicitly forbids extending membership to descendants of any member of the Confederate States of America (CSA) who signed the loyalty oath before April 9, 1865.[34] That is, they do not welcome descendants of soldiers who turned their backs on the Confederate nation they had sworn to defend before the war had officially ended.

It seems emphatically strange that there is no equivalent postbellum organization for the Daughters of the Union Army. Perhaps women in the nineteenth-century Northern states were too exhausted from the work of the so-called sanitary commissions that provided support for the Union Army and too distracted by counting their losses. Raising funds for Union soldiers while knitting socks, picking lint for bandages, and hosting fundraising fairs that featured fabrics and board games with political motifs, the Northern women who supported the Union Army seem to have felt no need to commemorate the sacrifices made by their husbands, sons, fathers, and brothers beyond their support for what was then called Decoration Day. Or maybe they already had an awkward sense of kinship. Before naming such an organization, both groups might have had to consider themselves as descended from the implicitly racialized organization known as the Daughters of the American Revolution. (The DAR emerged slightly earlier than the Daughters of the Confederacy, and was founded in 1890.) The oddity of all these organizations is that they proceed as though it's not possible to remember your place in the national order unless you name it with a familial order. Still, among the Sons of Confederate Veterans, the Sons of Union Veterans, the Children of the Confederacy, the Daughters of the Confederacy, why were there no daughters of the Union? Certainly we see one in photographs like the one here (figure I. 2) that shows a daughter mourning a lost soldier father. The badges that mark her small body as grieving are overridden by the haunting in her eyes.

What, then, does it mean to be a daughter of war? The organization set up as the UDC, honoring both the veterans and the women of the Confederacy, was founded in 1894. Still active, the UDC offers a sense of belonging that almost mocks citizenship in the "United States." In the felt relation between kinship and national belonging, the current website conceals the organization's previous relations with the Ku Klux Klan to which members contributed a memorial in 1926. The controversial Confederate memorial at Arlington National Cemetery, commissioned by the UDC, centrally featured the statue of a white woman and included images of enslaved persons expressing support for Confederate soldiers. Commissioned in 1910, its dedication was attended by President Woodrow Wilson in 1914. After repeated appeals protesting its presence on what some consider the hallowed ground of a national cemetery, it was removed only recently, in December 2023, and put into storage.

Promoting a form of reverence for mythical fathers, the group also founded the Children of the Confederacy (more formally "The Children of the Confederacy of the Daughters of the Confederacy") to take the legacy forward. The results persist: a number of Southern states encourage attention to the mythology of the lost Confederacy not only by resisting the removal of Confederate memorial statues but also, far more significantly, by increased attention to how the history of the United States, including the Civil War but also the struggles over Civil Rights or Brown v. Board of Education, will be presented in schools. That struggle involves colleges and universities and libraries—what material can be made available to the young is essentially a struggle over the Children of the Confederacy and what they can learn in Southern schools.

FIGURE I.2. Unidentified girl in mourning dress holding framed photograph of her father as a cavalryman with sword and Hardee hat. Photograph: sixth-plate tintype, hand-colored. Case: 3.7 in. × 3.3 in. (9.5 cm × 8.4 cm). Liljenquist Family Collection of Civil War Photographs. Courtesy of Library of Congress Prints and Photographs Division.

Haunted Bodies

Beginning with haunted bodies and an affective inquiry into witnessing and democracy, this book explores alternative cultural histories in the paths to and from the trauma of war. To attempt such cultural history within the context of extraordinary changes—such as the end of slavery, the emergence of feminist politics, the industrial revolutions, the growth of cities, and the expansion of geographical claims to national boundaries—is to make selective choices about the volatile nineteenth-century United States. The chapters thus sample artistic and literary expressions in a historical context that saw a dramatic increase in magazines, newspapers, gift books, and cultural borrowing resulting from lax international copyright protection. Invoking declarations, from the "original" declaration of national identity to the "Declaration of Sentiments and Rights," *Haunted by the Civil War* presents sometimes competing political and cultural testimony about national belonging in the nineteenth-century United States.[35]

Using both symbolic and actual bodies as it interrogates the relation of witnessing to war, this book presents salient stories and images from the nineteenth century to challenge readers as well as to provoke further research. Telling stories about different cultural understandings of history, the book includes the staging of popular responses and the juxtaposition of texts and authors. Throughout, its attention to cultural moments engages the challenge of how to combine the visual texture, the political decisions, and the historical context into a narrative. My story encourages both historical and aesthetic understandings of genres: I tell the story mostly by interpreting literary expressions such as drama, fiction, poetry, and legal discourse, but I also look at the arts with which these genres intersect, such as painting, sculpture, and photography. To note the interpenetration of such genres with the history of conflict encourages a reading practice that involves at once an overview and the specific intimacy of coming to know an author, an image, a statue, a poem, a story, a performance.

The battles that predate the Civil War in addition to those that followed often began in reaction to legislative decisions as well as armed uprising. Historians have marked certain armed conflicts from the nineteenth century as turning points of violent response. These include responses to the Alien and Sedition Acts of 1798, the tragic displacements of the Cherokee Removal Act of 1830, the Astor Place Riots of 1849, the raid on Harper's Ferry in 1859 (and the subsequent hanging of John Brown), and the miserable fate met by George Armstrong Custer's troops at Little Big Horn in 1878.[36] To these dates we might add the militarized boundary disputes known as the Mexican–American War (1846–1848) as well as the quarrel over shipping that came to be known as the War of 1812. These events appear as temporal markers etched in blood: they insert codified violence into both urban spaces and the marginal spaces at the edge of territorial claims.

The violence that seems endemic to expanding the territorial limits of the United States marks both dramatic and incremental shifts in the locations of national identity. That is, if we consider the large expansions

FIGURE I.3. Winslow Homer (1836–1910). *The Army of the Potomac—A Sharp-Shooter on Picket Duty*, published in *Harper's Weekly*, November 15, 1862. Wood engraving based on painting by Homer. Sheet: 10 13/16 in. × 19 in. (27.5 cm × 48.3 cm). Gift of Peggy L. and Harold L. Osher (Peggy Liberman, Class of 1951). 1996.7.25. Courtesy of Davis Museum, Wellesley College.

that forcefully incorporated Texas, New Mexico, Arizona, and most of California, the violence that accompanies the very geographic placing of the nation's borders shifts during the nineteenth century. As historians and artists visualize such moments, they rewrite the landscapes and populations of North and South, East and West. For a visual example, the widely viewed nineteenth-century engraving of Winslow Homer's painting *Sharp-Shooter*, showing a man in a tree with a gun (figure I.3). He appears at first glance to invoke the overlap of nature and violence, almost making killing seem natural as his left hand grasps the branch to steady the overlapping "X" of the rifle in his right hand. The young man could be perched in a tree looking to shoot a deer, but, as a Civil War marksman, he waits in the tree to shoot a person. The canteen dangling below the mouth of the rifle reminds the viewer that it can be thirsty work.[37]

Political changes arrived not only through violence, however, but also through the quiet meetings of groups who met to propose or rewrite legislation: the women who gathered to write a "Declaration of Sentiments" at Seneca Falls in 1848, the soldiers who surrounded George McClellan and Abraham Lincoln as they met after the battle at Antietam in 1862, and, notwithstanding the genocidal violence that preceded and accompanied them, the strategies that drove the Homestead Act and the transcontinental railroad launched during the war and memorialized by the men who met to drive the ceremonial "golden spike" in 1869.[38] These ceremonies engage forms of witnessing that involve contracts not always commemorated by photographs. Yet the women who signed the "Declaration of Sentiments," the men gathered by a military tent, the men who gathered by the railroad, were all met by forms of violence as well as celebration. As the British cultural theorist Stuart Hall once observed, "I simply want to say that in the histories of the migration, forced or free, of peoples who now compose the populations of those societies, whose cultural traces are everywhere intermingled with one another, there is always the trace of historical violence and rupture."[39] The archives of the nineteenth century make it possible to observe such traces of "historical violence and rupture," while embracing the wonders of natural phenomena, the intimacy of loving relationships, and the extraordinary power of language.

Through the advent of photographic reproductions, historical witnessing became something that could be visually reproduced and preserved in an archive of historical memory. For example, when Abraham Lincoln was photographed at Antietam with General McClellan, it was unpreccdented to see a president on the battlefield.[40] Surrounded by men in uniform, Lincoln towers above them but also seems distracted (figure I.4). Historians have noted that the Emancipation Proclamation was first drafted after this victory at Antietam. Such markers of temporal significance have become so commonplace that we no longer notice that we hold Lincoln's face between our fingers and spend it as currency; the once revered "father of our country," George Washington, stands by in our pockets. The literal currency of their faces keeps them alive in popular consciousness, yet the currency itself still has a political valence as the lingering controversy over the replacement of Andrew Jackson with Harriet Tubman on the twenty-dollar bill demonstrates.

The war persists in popular culture to invoke an idealized national mourning. One movie about Abraham Lincoln, for instance, opens with Black soldiers reciting the Gettysburg Address.[41] Such recitals of momentous words from a singularly divisive event—mourning the dead from the Battle of Gettysburg—sometimes bookend the combinations of integrity and compromise that led up to the Civil War. The address, engraved in stone at one end of the National Mall, remains a speech to memorize. The cemetery itself remains politically controversial as the size of monuments commemorating the Confederacy in relation to the monuments for Union soldiers can still spur arguments. The volatile symbolism of

FIGURE I.4. Alexander Gardner (1821–1882). "President Lincoln on Battle-Field of Antietam," 1862. Albumen silver print. 6 5/8 in. × 8 15/16 in. (17 cm × 23 cm). Reprinted in Gardner's *Photographic Sketch Book of the War* (1866). As the only man out of uniform, Lincoln's tall hat makes him rise above the military men who surround him. (See figure I.2.) Courtesy of Amon Carter Museum of American Art, Fort Worth, Texas. P1984.30.A.23.

such nineteenth-century monuments—specifically Confederate statues—continues to provoke violence in the twenty-first century. Such violence at once commemorates and reenacts how the first half of the nineteenth century existed on a political stage that could include a senator bludgeoned almost to death on the floor of the US Senate (Charles Sumner attacked by Preston Brooks) and President Lincoln collapsing in his own blood at the theater where he had gone to unwind after the tumultuous conclusion of war.[42]

A few writers resisted war. Some, like Nathaniel Hawthorne, seemed indifferent. Overt resistance appears in the nuanced politics of a writer such as Henry David Thoreau, whose essay "Civil Disobedience" reflected anti-war sentiments—in his case, resistance to the war with Mexico—that led to a short stint in prison.[43] The resistance to war on religious grounds paled in comparison to the religious justifications that appeared on both sides of the conflict. In particular the rage directed against the biblical justification for slavery that appears in Frederick Douglass has an uneven counterpart in the Southern fictions that proffered a view of benevolent enslavement in line with biblical scripture.[44]

Women in both the North and the South wrote in support of the war. Sometimes they put their bodies on the front lines, something that appears occasionally in the examples of cross-dressing soldiers.[45] Polemical writing about gender norms more often appeared as part of abolitionist propaganda designed to encourage sympathy for the threats to women and families under the conditions of enslavement. While this book most often engages with prose, I definitely value poetry, and want to note especially the sentimental poetry written in the decades before the war to support political causes such as abolition or to protest working conditions in factories.[46] The project engages the political quandaries of abolition, but it also seeks to investigate further the relationship between oratory and autobiography in places such as the writings of Frederick Douglass.[47] Attention to shifts in poetic style—for instance, in the challenges to the lyric form that appear in Walt Whitman and Emily Dickinson—has sometimes drawn critical attention away from how their writing at once challenged existing poetic norms and displayed their reactions to war.

The increased distribution of newspapers, magazines, and gift books, along with increasingly mobile populations, changed how diverse populations absorbed culture in the nineteenth century.[48] As advances in railroads and canals during the early part of the century made travel from the Eastern states easier, the role of the travelogue by authors as diverse as Margaret Fuller and Charles Dickens changed the landscape as they invented forms of cultural tourism.[49] Within cities, new audiences appeared for the conversation, the musical ditty, the minstrel performance, and the "low" cultures of the moment. Thinking in geographical terms, such writers as Maria Amparo Ruiz de Burton and John Rollin Ridge wrote vividly about the crises affecting and sometimes precipitated by the diverse populations negotiating the changed borders between the United States and Mexico.[50] The concept of national boundaries was challenged by international perceptions: in addition to the Mexican–American War and its territorial invasions, and the violence surrounding the Fugitive Slave Law that provoked the writing of *Uncle Tom's Cabin* (1852), writers reacted to the European revolutions of 1848.

Given the repeated violence around citizenship and national belonging, it might come as no surprise that the writers and artists I discuss in this book express an uneasy relation to displacements in the American landscape.[51] A tension persists between celebrating democratic ideals and describing the failures of democracy in the face of legal slavery and genocidal slaughter, while exposing the less dramatic daily oppressions of immigrants, laborers, and women. For Whitman, the problems of democracy could be solved by literature: "a great original literature is surely to become the justification and reliance, (in some respects the sole reliance,) of American democracy." Even as he celebrates "rivers and bay, sparkling sea-tides, costly and lofty new buildings, façades of marble and iron, . . . the flags flying, the endless ships, the tumultuous streets," Whitman thinks that only poetry can hold the nation together.[52]

To encourage readers to engage with a time that might seem remote and with items that have become increasingly remote—a book, a painting, even a photograph—is to find ambiguity about how representation reveals itself in a time when novels were published with subtitles such as "founded in fact" or "a true tale." The testimony included in this book inversely reflects on the variant forms of desire and longing for an idealized form of democracy, while it occasionally displays nostalgic mourning for the sensation caused by the shattering of such ideals. Such a cultural history draws on literature as well as "ekphrasis," the ways that words address images.[53]

The malleable margins of political strife during the war often kept populations uncertain about whose guns might have been firing in the distance. Yet during the consuming years of strife many Northern city dwellers chose to ignore it, or, at worst, participated in events such as the New York City Draft Riots, seeking to ward off participation and at the same time punishing the most helpless inhabitants, such as the children in the so-called Colored Orphan Asylum.[54] Even as the announced teleology of war spoke to Christian beliefs and the rights of states to self-determination, the boundaries of what became North America had an elastic form before the Louisiana Purchase, before the Treaty of Guadeloupe Hidalgo. The landscape claimed as the nation changed through the enacting of many suspect treaties; the idea that the West was an available space for settler colonialism remains a legacy of the early-nineteenth-century journeys of Lewis and Clark.[55] The witnessing performed here emerges through many narratives, including interior ones that can only be guessed at, such as the emotions and longing that their companion and guide, Sacagawea, might have felt. What it means to be haunted by these voices becomes filtered through the vocabulary of war.

Living with Ghosts

Sensational images and the language of sensation retold the political business of the nineteenth-century United States. Often when political decisions were announced in a more somber way, reactions in the press expressed emotion. During the tense times of forcible Cherokee removal, the incursions of the Mexican–American War, the struggles over slavery, the convulsions of the Civil War, and the horrors of Reconstruction, politicians, writers, and artists used sensation to convey an affective relation to an emerging concept of the nation. How such visions of political struggle meet sensational language forms part of this account of what haunts the literature, art, and politics of the United States that emerged from and through the war.

I worked on this book during the years of the pandemic, and some of the writing took place while sitting alone in a house that feels haunted. That house, known as Quarry Farm, a property set up for scholarly retreats by the Center for Mark Twain Studies, sits on a hill above Elmira, New York, a place that has a vivid nineteenth-century history. Over almost twenty years, the Twain family traveled by train to summer there with Olivia Langdon's sister; Twain's children were all born there. Mark Twain was photographed in a rocking chair on the porch of that house, but the separate study built for him to write in was located on a ledge above, looking out over the valley where the Chemung River flows into the Susquehanna. As he sat there and smoked cigars (and petted his cats), Twain wrote his stories about rivers and the past, such as *The Adventures of Huckleberry Finn* (1884), stories that are celebrated (and sometimes spurned) for the conflicted way they remember a past before the war that still haunts the United States. At the same time, Twain listened to actual stories of those who had escaped conditions of slavery.[56] In his modest home on a strip of land adjacent to the cemetery in the river valley below Quarry Farm, a former freedom seeker named John W. Jones continued the work that he had begun before the war when he served as a conductor on the Underground Railroad.

Insofar as Twain's famous stories reflect a history of racial haunting, it might come as no surprise that they have been banned from schools and libraries in this country. That conflict between what it means to live in the current moment of crisis and a desire to celebrate a nostalgic sense of witnessing the past produces a haunted memory. The ways that Tom Sawyer and Huck Finn react to the dead while their journey south along the Mississippi River repeatedly places them in perilous proximity to scenes of death—from threats of murder to shootouts in the street, from the elegies contained in the poetry of Emmeline Grangerford to the feud between the Grangerfords and the Shepherdsons—stand among the oddest conversions of horrifying violence into a story for children. The ongoing controversy about what such books show—does the river represent freedom or danger?—has been submerged into a controversy about what books might be dangerous for children to read. In particular, no one can explain why it has become dangerous to talk about race, at its simplest a recounting of history through forms of witnessing that still exist across North America, in poems, stories, paintings, photographs, and statues.

But it also means that the commemorations even in a small town like Elmira have expanded to involve different ghosts. Recent work on the history of Elmira during the war has grown to include the relation of the town's prisoner of war camp, once known as "Helmira," to the legacy of the man who looked after corpses there, expanding his role as a conductor on the Underground Railroad to deliver bodies to their final resting places in Southern states. During and after the war John W. Jones was paid per burial to inter the bodies of Confederate prisoners of war as well as Union soldiers and townspeople. Joining the dust of soldiers from both sides of the war, both Twain and Jones are now buried in Elmira.[57] John W. Jones now has his own historical museum as the agency of those who were once held in bondage has increasingly come to be recognized.[58] While he leaves almost no written record, and a sparse visual record, his house has been preserved and the history of his involvement with what is now a national cemetery, called Woodlawn, has been recently expanding. In that cemetery, the rows of tombstones for Confederate prisoners of war with their pointed tops and the rows of tombstones for the Union soldiers with their rounded tops also buried there share vertical and horizontal lines.

The memorials most visible in small Eastern towns, including Elmira, are often statues erected long after the war, statues that show men standing erect in a public square holding a rifle. Their presence becomes almost invisible after many decades, but they have also evoked violent responses.[59] Such statues of anonymous standing soldiers that anchor public squares in small towns do not present the same challenge attached to the named statues of Civil War figures. These soldiers include General Ulysses S. Grant, whose mounted presence anchors one end of the National Mall in Washington, DC. At the other end of the mall sits Daniel Chester French's monumental Abraham Lincoln. That momentous presence appears removed from war, but the words inscribed to the left and right of Lincoln's seated gaze recollect the most violent times in the history of the United States. Yet statues of George Washington, once enshrined as "father" to the United States, and Thomas Jefferson have also been toppled in the ignominious fashion of dictators.[60] It seems unlikely that the Washington Monument standing between these solid figures along the parklike path between museums and government dwellings could meet the same fate, but sometimes I wonder.

FIGURE I.5. "Manacles." These manacles were a souvenir collected by Julia Wilbur from a local prison after the fall of Richmond, Virginia. Division of Rare and Manuscript Collections, #1543, Cornell University Library.

One goal of this book is to think about the stony glance of statues in relation to the words and images that surround commemorations of the war. To be haunted by these sites is also to bear witness. Throughout the book, cultural testimony bears witness to physical acts and acts of the imagination carried out by both men and women. These inhabitants were often haunted; they told haunting stories of the legacies of Civil War violence. The citizens of Elmira paid to observe prisoners from platforms erected on the walls surrounding the prisoner of war camp in their midst while listening to the tolling of bells for the burials.

A digression from this attention to violence might be useful here. As I study the nineteenth-century United States, I am sometimes most impressed by the stories that have left the least evidence, especially stories involving the courage and creativity of women who resist. Sometimes they resist slavery, as with the extraordinary story of Elizabeth Keckley, who became the dressmaker for Mary Todd Lincoln but began her life in slavery. In *Behind the Scenes, or Thirty Years a Slave and Four Years in the White House* (1868), she wrote of refusing to stand still for a vicious beating and wrestling with the man who held the stick. Sometimes women resist slavery by hiding, as in the better-known story of Harriet Jacobs, who wrote of spending seven years tucked away in her grandmother's house in order to stay near her children, but who eventually fled to the North. Sometimes they resist as they act out variations on possible identity, as in the literal acting out of Adah Menken, who spent many of the short years of her life traveling around the United States acting in plays as a corollary to her main act of making up stories about her life, writing poems.

I am also drawn to the visual and material emblems remaining from quieter forms of resistance, such as the resistance displayed in the activism of women like Sojourner Truth, who traveled with a *carte de visite* marked "I Sell the Shadow to Support the Substance."[61] I have found inspiration in the artifacts referred to in the private writings of women such as Julia Wilbur. Born in 1815 in New York, she ended up working for the patent office in Washington, DC, the first woman to be hired there. As an activist, during the aftermath of the war, she became close friends with Harriet Jacobs, with whom she plotted to fund and establish schools for those newly freed from slavery. She also, like many souvenir hunters even during the war, began to collect some of the material detritus of slavery.[62] One object that she donated ended up in the vault at Cornell University. Labeled as "Manacles" from "City Jail, Richmond, Virginia, 1865," they served for Wilbur to commemorate the fall of Richmond in the final days of the Civil War and were picked up along with the looting of odd artifacts from a defeated city (figure I.5). While no label remains to explain how these metal circles were used to hold the wrists of humans passing to and from their incarceration in cells, one can speculate concerning their relation to the indignity of exhibition in the marketplace. Whatever the legacy of this heavy set of metal curves, to hold them is to register the fear of the prison from which they came. To hold them is to be haunted. To find them in the archive is to register the weight of a history that has at once been overcome and still persists.

CHAPTER ONE

Visions of Democracy

Reading Culture

Witnessing ghosts in relation to a war that continues to haunt the popular imagination governs the readings in this book. Unlike the solid space of a statue, the space of a poem can move the attention of a reader at once toward and away from the specific call to empathy with a particular cause. Structures of interpretation that focus on the experiments in language by a poet like Walt Whitman, for instance, can use that language to make the foreground (perhaps of touching a wounded man) and the background (why the battle happened) change places. A poem like "The Wound Dresser" might appear intimate and specific in its attention to how men touch each other or, possibly, it can stand in for the thousands of bodies left to turn into skeletons on remote fields during the war. If the poem is understood as an instantiation of wartime encounters, then the letters that Whitman helped transcribe for wounded soldiers, the songs they sang around campfires, the sheet music that copied those songs, all become part of a critical understanding. If the poem addresses the possibility of male intimacy, then the photographs of Whitman with male friends with whom he shared his life become part of a story of sexuality and intimacy in the nineteenth century: a story hidden, so to speak, behind the ghosts of the battlefield.[1] The poem displays recollections of the battlefield as a stage where the speaker wavers between treating wounded men for whom death will bring release ("O beautiful death! / In mercy come quickly") and a place for desiring an experience that brought pleasure ("Many a soldier's kiss dwells on these bearded lips").[2]

The intimacy of Whitman's poem resonates, and yet. If literature is read only to expose such presumed secrets, whether sexual or political, or if reading appears as a lens through which to expose social constructs, the pleasures of nuance, metaphor, or perhaps simple adjectives in all their glory might be seen as diminished. What are the dangers in this attention to ghosts? At the risk of reminding us that stories of haunting can be fun, I propose both pleasure and pain in the recounting. In other words, while haunting has always been attractive as both the inspiration for and as a mode of storytelling, and while the thrill of hearing or seeing a ghost commingles with the desire to know the story, it might be a narrative strategy to remember that both the fear and the story enact a kind of pleasure. So the pleasure mingled with fear and mourning in a continual haunting, I hope to demonstrate, emerges from the skill and the passion that writers and artists bring to the stories they tell about being haunted.[3]

The stories of haunting that permeate the short stories of Charles Chesnutt in *The Conjure Woman* (1899) suggest that the ghosts remaining from conditions of slavery can still retaliate.[4] Inanimate features, such as the wood used to build a schoolhouse on a former plantation in "Po' Sandy," might contain ghosts. When the northern narrator of the stories in *The Conjure Woman* comes to inspect the decayed Southern plantation he considers buying, he is told by "Uncle Julius" that the place is "goophered, conju'd, bewitch'" and that he should beware. Moving there nonetheless, he encounters numerous stories of haunting that are a residue of the practices of slavery on the plantation. In "Po' Sandy," Uncle Julius relates the story of a man turned into a tree by his "conjure woman"; when the tree is cut down the building that supplies the wood used to build the schoolhouse is said to express pain. The narrator's wife cautions him to leave it alone and he does. Through vernacular language and regional dialects, the stories nonetheless convey small victories along with uneasy humor.

At the same time, I do not forget the rage expressed in historical works such as that penned by W.E.B. Du Bois, *Black Reconstruction in America, 1860–1880* (1935). That rage persists as the accusation that this country has not only allowed but even encouraged the sentiments of speeches such as the "Cornerstone Speech" of Alexander Stephens.[5] In that speech, Stephens asserted that the "cornerstone" of the Confederacy was laid in the belief that slavery was a "natural and normal condition," reflecting the "proper status of the negro in our form of civilization." Perhaps the sentiment that Du Bois expressed came too early in the twentieth century: "Never in modern times has a large section of a nation so used its combined energies to the degradation of mankind."[6] Du Bois cites the earlier speech of Frederick Douglass, "What to the Slave Is the Fourth of July?" as he draws out the implications of such degradation as a way to maintain economic domination.[7] In this book, the persistent attention to such literary accusations mingles with attention to visual symbols, invoking a symbolic as well as actual warfare against both words and images. Rage against stone and metal embodiments of nineteenth-century heroes still emerges on both sides. The statue of Douglass in Rochester, New York, was ripped from its foundation as recently as 2020.[8]

Poets in the early republic, recovering from the violence subsequently celebrated as a political revolution, also worked to convey their memories of anger. Such angry writers include Philip Freneau, whose bitterest lines concern his incarceration on a British prison ship during the American Revolution. Freneau's disconcerting rage has a genealogy, although a different target, as it appears in abolitionist poets like John Greenleaf Whittier or in the poems of Frances Harper.[9] In narrative poems like "Then and Now," Harper reflects on the end of slavery while celebrating a hopeful future for national identification. The hopeful narrator says that "slavery, with its crime and shame, / Went down in wrath and blood and flame." Although in this poem the land and sea seem to merge as it "was billowed-o'er with graves," the location has an ambiguous emphasis: "Where men had lived and died as slaves."[10] The denunciation in such poetry deliberately makes readers uncomfortable; such discomfort bears witness to how incarcerated bodies or bodies in chains still haunt. What critical language makes it possible to discriminate between the haunting rendition of scenes of loss (something found later, for instance, in the short stories of Ambrose Bierce) and the polemical accusations that might leave the reader or viewer unmoved? If the language of the poet—or the critic—is too ideological, the reader squirms, whether placed in the position of the dispossessed or that of the heartless murderer. How can a reader continue to inhabit the house, whether of fiction or democracy, that has been compromised by this haunting?[11]

The house of fiction, as a famous novelist once asserted, has many windows.[12] The house of democracy does too, and there are many who stand at those windows looking out. Some windows remain barred and tiny, with limited access to a view. Some look out on the settlement envisioned by John Winthrop in 1630, improbably imagining that to populate the New England coastline with European immigrants represented a "city upon a hill." That very Christian vision involved soldiers who might defend the city, and it also included ghosts, since at least one passenger on the *Mayflower*, viewing the bleak landscape of what we now know as Cape Cod, jumped overboard. The chords of mystic nationalism that have sounded ever since these claims for a Christian nation were first enunciated have sometimes obscured the bodies drowned, let alone the sight of bodies killed by smallpox or those degraded by bondage. Such a call for visibility, whether of soldiers or ghosts, sometimes seems endemic in the language that calls for democracy, an operation that almost always involves death as well as passionate belief, a juxtaposition still traced to John Winthrop's sermon.[13]

Such testaments, such political and religious statements about American identity, persist in the popular imagination. Abraham Lincoln's first inaugural address memorably invoked the "mystic chords of memory." He ended with an allusion to the "better angels of our nature," an optimistic testimony that has been repeatedly cited, without reference, by political candidates who claim to unite a divided country. Seeking to solve the problem of a house divided, Lincoln offered conciliations to Southern states in his first inaugural address. He did not, for example, initially seek to end slavery but rather sought compromise. Lincoln's penultimate paragraph concludes, "You have no oath registered in heaven to destroy the government, while I shall have the most solemn one to "preserve, protect, and defend it."[14] Swearing these oaths presents the overlap of national and literary allusions to a republic constituted over the bodies of the dead.

The act of declaring independence has operated to offer partial freedom since it sparked the American Revolution, a contest that involved both verbal and physical contests between the authority of "the people" and the power associated with owning property. While the originating violence of the revolution continues to be celebrated, however ambivalently, in spectacles like *Hamilton*, declarations about the significance of owning property, whether attached to humans or to land, centrally determined citizenship in the early United States.[15] That itself becomes a form of haunting. Historians of the early republic have aligned the significance of landed property as a political belief with the Federalist party of John Adams; in contrast, the faith in "people," with or without property, appears aligned with the republican idealism of Thomas Jefferson. The contests about how to govern safely given these unequal standards famously generated the long explanations of the Federalist Papers. Relations between property and political identity became increasingly fraught during the nineteenth century, especially because humans were declared as property during the intermittently legalized practice of slavery. On the one hand, before the Civil War, were the consequences of the Fugitive Slave Law, abuses that saw trafficking in human bodies reach extralegal dimensions on both land and sea, well past the ban on shipping humans across the Atlantic.[16] On the other, later in the nineteenth century, the rise of the legal concept that corporations could have personhood often meant the concomitant erasures of the rights of persons who labored for such corporations.[17]

What brings together the concept of corporate personhood—one form of erasure for the category of the human—and the embedded erasure of personhood through legalized slavery is how each invokes the sometimes ghostly and often ghastly relation between humans and property, especially the excruciating erasures caused by considering humans as property and the further legal construction of disembodied personhood. Each (at least temporarily) legal category additionally erases or obfuscates the relation of property to a claim to citizenship by confusing an idea of identity as inhering in the body. Throughout the nineteenth century one's right to citizenship might depend not only on race and gender but also on location in a particular state or nation, a location question that also tests the relation of land ownership to national identity.[18]

That to claim citizenship might be dependent on a relation to land has inspired several critical works. For example, the idea of the commons, a public space understood as both virtual and actual access to a communal identity, has been explored by the scholar Elizabeth Dillon as emerging from two sources. The first concept involves "a demos, the people of a democracy or a republic who wield the power of sovereignty," while the second concerns land as "a shared resource, a material entity possessed . . . by a multitude of people."[19] One source Dillon draws on for such utilitarian enabling appears in the work of the anthropologist Lewis Hyde, who declared that the commons exist as "the land plus the rights, customs, and institutions that organize and preserve its communal uses."[20] But ideas about the community's right to shared land use shift with colonization and the concomitant, usually preemptive, seizure of property. The "theatrics of erasure," counters Dillon, makes the land claims of Native Americans and the labor of "New World Africans" vanish as part of an invisible "expropriative violence."[21] The democratic process thus suppresses differences that later emerge to expose divisions between constituents.

The extraordinary breadth of such constituent parts occupies Lisa Lowe in *The Intimacies of Four Continents*. As she turns to the "project of visualizing, mourning, and thinking 'other humanities' within the received genealogy of 'the human,'" Lowe laments the ways that the "organization of the archives discourages links."[22] These links may also be understood as ruptures in the ability to articulate national identity. To return to the visible relations through which citizens even now interpret the specific territories of the Civil War, bringing together the locations of bodies, land, and death has become a national business: the locations of battlefields have become national parks, further peopled with stone monuments and stone generals atop their horses. That fearsome rendering of blood-soaked earth as a location for improbable picnics as well as mourning has been, almost since the battle ended, a huge attraction in places like Gettysburg, Pennsylvania. But that landscape is also full of ghosts. Ghosts from national conflicts and from genocide appear everywhere in North America, on land and sea. And this haunting emerges in fictional retellings, retellings that make audiences participate in remembrance. The legacy of witnessing and remembering death haunts novels like *Huckleberry Finn*; although it announces an antebellum setting, the postbellum trauma of what to do with "setting a free man free" obsesses the child narrator as he finds himself terrified of the ghosts that live around him.[23]

For more than two centuries, especially during the decades when it fought for, purchased, bartered, or stole its advancement of territorial claims, the United States has existed as a geographical land space bounded by water. Oceans and rivers long provided the only access to interior spaces. The different populations that arrived after crossing the Atlantic Ocean, whether in conditions of bondage or as part of a colonizing mission, arrived to find other concepts of sovereignty in play and other territorial claims. The concept of "manifest destiny" contains a murky fusion of territorial sovereignty with the minute specifics of private land ownership.[24] To posit an Atlantic public sphere in such a location is to bring together the influential discursive maneuver from Jurgen Habermas with the significant reorientation of the space of the Atlantic carried out by Paul Gilroy.[25] An Atlantic public sphere, coordinated with the tumultuous reordering of the territorial claims of the United States in the first half of the nineteenth century, imagines geographical boundaries that describe something other than declarations of national sovereignty bounded by a watery space of transit. To propose any critical rewriting of the past is to negotiate competitions among performances expressed as national identity and the residues of an archive of violence and violations.[26]

Developing this archive merits constant attention. Fresh examples of haunting emerge almost daily in a country that has recently made Juneteenth, the delayed enforcement of the Emancipation Proclamation in Texas, into a national holiday.[27] The wording that declared an "absolute equality of personal rights and rights of property between former masters and slaves" was inevitably to be challenged by the "former masters." The day was long considered as a second Fourth of July although the original Emancipation Proclamation only applied to an assertion that still understood humans as property, as "contraband" in the language of the day, to be potentially converted to soldiers for the Union cause. An acoustic or sonic conversion appears in national songs such as "The Battle Hymn of the Republic," which Julia Ward Howe wrote after witnessing a parade of Union soldiers. Sung to the tune of the earlier campfire song "John Brown's Body," which commemorated yet another symbolic ghost, the song can be understood to take the body "mouldering in the grave" and turn it into a soldier.[28] A paradox appears when finding pleasure in protest songs, yet texts such as these that represent suffering for political reasons can also perversely offer a form of pleasure reading. And to recapture the nineteenth-century embrace of John Brown does not overlook his role as a killer; the account of his activities in Kansas and Missouri can read like a true crime narrative.[29]

Listening to speakers who experience the conflict firsthand means that their passions, large and small, public and private, reflect the distortions of subjective response. What dilemmas face a scholar who wants to follow the thread of participant-observers who lived in a time of war? To visit the archive means to read tiny pages written in pencil in the middle of oppressive camp conditions, many entries that say merely "weather fine" or "was chuck full of ale." It can be distracting to see that amusement includes the reading of dime novels and *Frank Leslie's Illustrated Weekly*. Before going off to drink ale, of course.[30] The difficult task for a scholar reading these notations in the twenty-first century is to remember that the context of pronouncements in the nineteenth century often features ambivalence about the idea of a cause, whether the cause is ending slavery or defending national unity.

A peculiarly outsized set of comments on the issues of the day appears in the autobiography of John Kelso. The handwritten volume presents on its first pages political speeches written in a "fair hand," a large script that seems designed to be read aloud except that the volume is very heavy and 800 pages long. After apocalyptic language that invokes both the Bible and Milton's *Paradise Lost*, the author develops original observations about the effects of slavery. The writing is passionate and convoluted. Kelso recognized that many readers would not be able to follow him through all the ins and outs of the reactions to slavery that he at once catalogues and proposes. His racism is evident, yet he hates slavery and believes in "equal rights." He finds miscegenation horrifying. But he astutely notes that the loudest voices from the South emerge from communities where the procreative effects of slavery include lighter and lighter skin. His idea to "deport" to Mexico everyone who has been held as a slave has a certain terrible novelty. Included in the volume is a speech just after the conclusion of the war where he confines himself to explicitly referencing *Paradise Lost* as a way to evince moral horror about the effrontery of white Southerners who imagine that, after such a terrible rebellion, they should have the right to vote.[31]

The literature of political engagement published in either the North or the South, or, in Kelso's case, Missouri, often moves past clear forms of protest. The desire to speak through words and images, the desire to show beauty as well as pain, affects the move in and out of literary language. Sensation and thought are held in suspension as writers seek to mobilize political action. The dilemmas for a citizen (or possibly a literary critic) interested in witnessing democracy in the United States have appeared in much recent work. For the critic Jonathan Elmer, for instance, "race, sovereignty, and the problem of the individual are all intimately implicated." In *Lingering and Being Last*, Elmer divides his argument between attention to the racialized attitudes of white people in the early United States and the dilemma of the "last" of the original inhabitants.[32] His account appears as part of a series of rich critical attempts that follow literary forms of production and develop interpretations of the figures producing these accounts.[33] Once again, to "linger" in his account is to linger over graves. To ignore the haunting of the ghosts that emerge from these graves involves other abuses. For the sociologist Avery Gordon "haunting is one way in which abusive systems of power make themselves known . . . especially when they are supposedly over and done with. . . . [Haunting] alters the experience of being in time."[34]

Both historical and critical attention to the surface of literary texts reveals an unease with what lies beneath. In turn, both surface and depth are terms that invoke water. The investigations in this book make a watery circuit of rivers, lakes, canals, and oceans. The literary initiatives that make human figures alternately visible and invisible against such mobile landscapes include particular attention to the foreground and background of scenery, landscapes, animals. What inhabits the sky, for example, in the first of James Fenimore Cooper's Leatherstocking novels, a prescient account of ecological disaster, *The Pioneers* (1823)? Clouds of birds that are then shot down almost before a reader realizes these are the same passenger pigeons that have since become extinct.[35]

The waste, the lament, the identification that a reader might still feel with the ecological outrage in such a novel can vanish under the weight of Cooper's unwieldy sentences and a series of plots that revolve around pale characters and scenes of low comedy designed for an audience that expects them from minstrel shows or from the comedic asides of Shakespeare. The challenge becomes how to reconstruct that reader, or how to imagine what that reader has as a gender, as a race, or as ethnicity, within the many embedded quotations of such fiction. The lament for a lost sense of self attached to property, on view in the Federalist Papers, emerges in Cooper's desire for landed gentry while he sends white characters off to wander haplessly, often to die in the wilderness. As these characters make ludicrous speeches in moments of danger, they echo the outrageous world of comedy that buttresses the opposition between Brother John and Brother Jonathan in plays like Royall Tyler's *The Contrast* (1787), which, like Cooper's fiction, mocks the boundaries set between stilted British and buffoonish American habits.[36]

These texts presume white readers. Yet in the best-selling series of James Fenimore Cooper's *Leatherstocking Tales* (1827–1841), as in Henry Wadsworth Longfellow's popular narrative poem *The Song of Hiawatha* (1855), a mythologizing of Indigenous identities appears as a bridge between a landscape still inhabited by humans who have been made to seem part of a nature that recedes into the West and the urban East where the books were printed. The sources for such mythologizing include the appearance of what were then considered Western landscapes through the Hudson River school of painting rivers and trees beheld by tranquil men. They might also be seen in attempts to translate poetry. For instance, the surviving poetry of the Ojibwe writer Jane Johnston Schoolcraft remains as an example of how translation can paradoxically make a culture and a language remote. Her Ojibwe name has been translated as "the sound the stars make rushing through the sky." Whether we understand these translations, not only of her name, but crucially of her poetry, to be her words, depends on our understanding of her own domestic dependence: her husband produced the translation of her words, and his words are distributed in the place that her words might occupy.[37]

The significance of the capacity to circulate text and image alike appeared early in the nineteenth century in the distribution of European concepts as well as American nationalism. For example, access to printed words was often a function of the migrating peddler, such as Mason Locke Weems, who traveled through rural America selling books and then composing stories to sell like the infamous one about George Washington and the cherry tree.[38] The popularity of this mythologizing of childhood appears against the background of death. Weems's *Life of Washington* (1809) provided a best-selling form of a mourning ritual in line with the ceremonial portraits and weeping willow trees and the artifactual display of the hair of the dead that occupied households in the early nineteenth century and provided a way to handle the public death of a national hero in the privacy of home.[39]

Such mourning practices formed different rituals of participation for myriad circles of readers who might have participated in person before the development of more inexpensive printing techniques for newspapers, books, and magazines. After migration to cities became more established, depictions of urban life as a place of opportunity and danger drew new reading communities, often forming themselves around the circulating library.[40] The desire to reproduce, to copy, to circulate, to reach beyond the place of the voice had already influenced the production of newspapers, magazines, pamphlets, broadsides, and books. From the account given by Benjamin Franklin, who repeatedly spoke of his desire to view himself in a new edition, a reader might find the desire to copy with a difference. The typesetting that was Franklin's earliest labor became, in effect, his last allegory, as he wrote his life into history through anecdotal retelling of "errata" that could somehow be mended in retelling. Autobiographical writing, influenced by Franklin, shows the wish to correct, to copy, and to repeat, to replicate the existence of the writer. Even as Franklin often boasted about his extraordinary accomplishments, to speak of other details in his life as "errata" holds out the possibility that the life could have been different.[41]

Spectator and Speculation

The goals of the defining nineteenth-century war keep being revisited by historians while the concepts of "antebellum" and "postbellum" have become obscured by noticing that the battles began decades before the declared outbreak of war and have a startling recurrence. The bodies of Civil War reenactors have merged with twenty-first century violence, notably including that violence of storming the US Capitol building on January 6, 2021. The slogans brandished that day explicitly called attention to the American Revolution—the flags flown included some that proclaimed an affinity with "1776"—but that cannot occlude how horrifying it became to see the Confederate flag brought into the Senate Chamber. That haunting from the nineteenth-century war has meant that to reenact and repeat its violence introduces new deaths. Ghosts appear everywhere.[42] Yet to locate to whom they appear and what testimony they provide becomes as murky as the Mississippi River water that Huckleberry Finn once found merging with the clear waters of the Ohio, the upstream path to freedom.[43]

To propose that the invaders of the US Capitol operated like malevolent ghosts from the nineteenth century does not overlook the twenty-first century deaths that occurred. These deaths, unlike those of the Civil War, have not been converted to symbols. No statues have been erected. Yet the very attention to the symbols of the Civil War, especially in the form of the Confederate flag, enforced the sensation that these were spectral visitors from the past. Haunting suggests a possible remedy in exorcism, but rather than exorcise ghosts, citizens of this country not only participate in battle reenactments, they also ossify battle ghosts in stone or metal and keep looking at their posed bodies. At one end of the National Mall, for instance, Ulysses S. Grant rides his battle horse in perpetuity; at the other, Abraham Lincoln (and his words) continue to haunt national politics.[44] The placing of these statues makes the distance walked from one end of the National Mall to the other into an act of Civil War mourning. We do not want these statues to come alive; we do not want the stone and metal sentinels in town squares to shoulder their muskets and march toward us. We want them to stay rigidly affixed to their plinths. But they keep escaping. Even the empty plinths serve as places of uneasy memory.[45]

The dissemination of both culture and politics in the nineteenth-century United States often relied on images. From the engravings of presidential faces circulated in newspapers to the broadsides of recruiting posters in wartimes, from the circulating *cartes des visite* that carried a simulacrum of identity through the newly developed technology of the photograph to the portrait paintings of Mary Cassatt and Thomas Eakins, from the crowds standing in line to view *The Greek Slave* to the circulation of coins and stamps, the relation between particular representational images and the mass commodification of portraits in common use made some of these, still prevalent, uses of the image recognizable as a commercial trade in visibility. The nineteenth century became accustomed to images in public display in ways that make the relation of imaging technologies and modern identifications of the subject inescapable.[46] At the same time, as the often circulated "spirit photograph" of Mary Todd Lincoln shadowed by the ghost of her dead husband illustrates, images could at once have power and still be manipulated.[47]

Although this book investigates how relations of identity and race might be enhanced by the use of imaging technologies, especially the development of photography, most of its attention to identity follows its emergence in and through language. Throughout, the juxtapositions with literary practice invoke some of the best-known writers, such as Herman Melville and Harriet Beecher Stowe, whose writing spurred tourism (Melville, especially, encouraging visits to the South Seas) and activism (against slavery) as well as the opportunities to engage audiences with music and performance (Stowe's *Uncle Tom's Cabin* appeared in song sheets and broadsides; in dramatic form it was performed for decades in various guises by multiple touring companies). Such engagement overlapped with the emerging nineteenth-century attention to the photograph, which involved new concepts of reality and truth telling.[48] The possibly contradictory sense that photography operates at once as evidence and as an origin point for empathy still dominates its earliest appearance in the United States. The evidence that photographs provide became at once "proof" of an actual event and proof of an event beyond the body, as in the "spirit photographs" that reassured mourners after the war and the abolition torture images such as the infamous photograph of the scarred back of the enslaved man known as "Gordon." I have chosen not to reproduce that image here, preferring to see his face and the eloquence made vivid in the remnants of clothing he wore. This study places such positioning of vision as evidence in relation to the manipulation of other forms of visual and written testimony.[49]

To understand or to resist understanding slavery as a visual category meant that the rather infamous photograph of the formerly enslaved "Gordon" was widely distributed by abolitionists to mobilize Northern sentiment against the scars associated with slavery. Collecting skins from the surface of the visible world, as Oliver Wendell Holmes once characterized the practice of photography, emphasizes what one sees at the surface of the skin. The attention to the literal skin on his back was encouraged and promoted through the activity of looking at the photograph. Memorably reproduced in profile, with little to mark him beyond the scars, this man becomes more vividly present when he faces the camera, with the shreds of what can barely be defined as clothing hanging off his body. Rather than reproduce that familiar image I insert here the figure of a Black Union soldier, standing in for the pride associated with violent resistance (figure 1.1).[50]

To take a different example of these crossing points of visual and literary evidence, I turn to Harriet Beecher Stowe's *Dred* (1856), a novel by one of the most famous antislavery writers that has long been overshadowed by the success of her earlier *Uncle Tom's Cabin*, which became an instant bestseller and a widely performed drama. *Dred* operates as a rejoinder to the often derided "saintly" resignation of Uncle Tom in the more famous novel. Like Uncle Tom, the titular character does not survive the multiple violent actions of the novel. Like Uncle Tom, he works in a household that contains possibly benevolent concepts of enslavement. Unlike in the story of family relations for Uncle Tom, who leaves children behind when he is sold to the South, the white woman of the household is his half-sister.

The novel's many plots include a vision at once alluded to and withheld in a scene that combines the sight of near-white children with the agony of

FIGURE 1.1. Henry F. Steward, African American Union soldier, member of 54th Massachusetts Volunteer Infantry, 1863. Hand-colored ambrotype. 4.1 in. × 3.15 in. (10.5 cm × 8 cm). Photographer unknown. Courtesy of the Library of Congress.

the mother who will kill them to keep them from being sold into slavery. As a novel, *Dred* juxtaposes attention to the law, in this case the law that determined the enslaved status of children, *partus sequitur ventrem*, with scenes infused with sentimental pathos, and yet the effect of the pathos is to distract from the violent cruelty of the moments where women and children are hunted down or starved.[51] These moments often exist off stage or are deliberately mocked in "local color" exegeses of the faintly Shakespearean variety; frequently the use of dialect obscures small acts of heroism carried out by white lower-class characters whose status in the world of the novel remains lower than that of persons escaping from slavery. The set pieces in the novel that involve legal matters of inheritance take a long time to emerge. Nina Gordon seems willfully ignorant that her investment in fancy clothes depletes the resources of the man who knows himself to be her brother. In the opening scene, the suggestive possibility of a man and a woman placed together in the woman's bedroom appears for economic rather than for sexual activity. They are brother and sister, after all, in addition to their legal status as racially different; their activity in the bedroom is to sort the scattered receipts that represent items she deems essential to her fashionable appearance.[52] Such a rendition of the economy of slavery literally embedded into the economy of the family stands behind the explications that this book develops.

The desire to find a connection between seeing the surface and understanding how surface images might create a model of identity appeared very early in the history of responses to photography. Some overlap and confusion between the surface that can be viewed and the eye that views emerges in one of Holmes's evocative examinations of how the development of photography changes the idea of a body. He begins, "Under the action of light, then, a body makes its superficial aspect potentially present at a distance, becoming appreciable as a shadow or as a picture. But remove the cause,—the body itself,—and the effect is removed. The man beholdeth himself in the glass, and goeth his way, and straightway both the mirror and the mirrored forget what manner of man he was."[53] The idea of a "manner of man" that could be reproduced through the development of imaging technologies involved a new kind of remembering and challenged the idea of a subject by fixing the image to the glass. That the man in the mirror remains when the body departs became a nineteenth-century preoccupation.

Describing the daguerreotype as a "mirror with a memory," Holmes expressed fascination with an invention that by his perception changed the nature of the world. Later commentators, such as Susan Sontag and Roland Barthes, find in photography an emotional shift in how subjects encounter the world and themselves. For Sontag, in *Regarding the Pain of Others*, the intimacy with death expressed by the camera in the nineteenth century emerges as an ambiguously manipulative way to fix moments of battlefield horror. In *Camera Lucida*, Barthes presents a photograph of an assassin in terms of his impending death and famously describes the relation between "studium" and "punctum" as a way to discriminate between the effect of photography that lingers or that pierces, fixing spatiality and temporality to the moment of looking at the image.[54] Not incidentally, this assassin, Lewis Hyde, was part of the conspiracy to assassinate Abraham Lincoln; his piercing gaze fixes the viewer and dislodges a temporal relation to the relived assassination.[55]

Celebrating the emergence of image archives, Holmes continues with a prescient account of photography's influence. He asserts that "Men will hunt all curious, beautiful, grand objects, as they hunt the cattle in South America, for their skins, and leave the carcasses as of little worth." As visual archives shift the text on which the world is inscribed, Holmes predicts a time when, wishing "to see any object, natural or artificial," a person "will go to the Imperial, National, or City Stereographic Library and call for its skin or form, as he would for a book at any common library."[56] What I want to notice here for a moment is the sense of both images and books as a kind of taxidermy, as skins in the hunt after knowledge.[57] Further, grief as a condition for both looking and the archive becomes an abstract condition of modern subjectivity.

Frederick Douglass celebrated photography both by the circumstance of being what has been called the most photographed person of the nineteenth century and by his desire to control the photographed image.[58] On December 3, 1861, he gave a talk, "Pictures and Progress," that begins by extolling the invention of Louis Daguerre who, putting his name to the daguerreotype, "by the simple but all abounding sunlight has converted the planet into a picture gallery."[59] In this picture gallery, men "may see themselves as others see them." He notes that the availability of photographs also means an expectation that to open a book is to see the author's face: "the picture must be in the book, or the book be considered incomplete." From Whitman's manipulation of his portraits in editions of *Leaves of Grass* to details of how Douglass controlled his own image, the association of a face with a book became so expected as to be overlooked. And yet, Douglass warns, perhaps joking (and perhaps not) there's a danger in associating the author's image with the book: "On no account whatever . . . can he be allowed any liberties with the style of his coat, the shape of his collar, or the cut of his hair. His position is defined, and his whole *personae* must now conform to, and never contradict the immortal likeness or unlikeness in the Book."

The ways that photographs depict racial identifications—or not—do not seem to preoccupy Douglass. Instead he moves out to consider that moral reform may emerge from these inventions: "Steam and lightening . . . have come up to the help of moral truth as well as physical welfare." War has just broken out and Douglass borrows from Emersonian rhetoric as well as the Bible as he intones: "The cause is deeper down than sections, slaveholders or abolitionists. These are but the hands of the clock. The moving machinery is behind the face. The machinery moves not because of the hands, but the hands because of the machinery. To make the hands go right you must make the machinery go right." He seems to have left photography behind in this incantation, yet the photograph, the telegraph, and the railroad all play a part in his summation: "In every locommotive [sic] a herald of progress—the startling scream of the Engine—and the small ticking sound of the telegraph are a like phrophecies [sic] of hope to the philanthropist, and warnings to the systems of slavery, superstition and oppression to get themselves away to the mirky [sic] shades of barbarism."[60]

As Douglass shows, technological shifts made vision a crucial index of modernity and subjectivity in the nineteenth-century United States. For him, the shifts implicated in the world of vision also meant a possible shift in the "global order." Still, however many photographers went to the battlefield, the changes enacted by photography seemed more intimate than global. Even for Douglass, noting that photographs have emerged on the pages of books, how much does vision become simply the format for establishing an intimacy between reader and viewer? Given the increasingly polemical writing that sought to make political change for lobbyists on both sides of the issues that led to the war, did photographs make a difference? With the development of photography in the United States, political arguments increasingly referred to sight. Yet crucially, the world that might be constituted through questions of photographic visibility was frequently one that privileged whiteness. Here, the surface of the page raises the question of how images reflect readers, as the daguerreotype once reflected the face of the viewer. The tarnish on the surface of the daguerreotype might be a patina that produces what appears to be a physicality of vision. The residue of the story of the object might be understood as inherently present (as an adhesive formation from the looking that has occurred) even as the gaze of the viewer becomes part of that residue.

For the visual theorist Jonathan Crary, interpreting the 1850s as containing a key shift toward the widely accepted use of photography, new relations "between an observing subject and modes of representation" mean that the development of photography "effectively nullifies most of the culturally established meaning of the terms observer and representation." His reaction, much like that of Oliver Wendell Holmes more than a century earlier, includes the problem of the body in an explication of how the observing subject becomes at once embedded in the use of technology and still separate from the way that the camera becomes an extension of the eye. Crary goes on to ask, "how is subjectivity becoming a precarious condition of interface" with technologies?[61] Yet the viewing subject for Crary, as for his nineteenth-century predecessor, remains racially white.

The emphasis that Holmes placed on photographs as producing a philosophical shift in human identity seems well warranted: "form is henceforth to make itself seen through the world of intelligence, just as thought has long made itself heard through the art of printing." The further emphasis on form develops a synesthetic shift in perception as thoughts may be heard on a page that is held by the viewer, and forms that are seen convey the touch of ways that vision lingers on the skin. The delicacy of the lyric voice in Holmes's reactions is still vividly present in his world, while the delicacy of the process of making portraits, a process he describes at length, is embedded in a logic of subjectivity and representation. The relation of language to vision can engage how vision operates in relation to a sense of temporality. Threading through questions of temporality and the question of how to interpret moments there appears an inquiry into how a viewer might ask if this is what happened, this moment is when the photograph was taken. And in that inquiry appears not only the positioning of the subject by photographers, not only the place of the viewer, but also the uneasy position of the text that interprets the sight.

One of the most compelling archives of nineteenth-century photographs in relation to textual evidence that I have examined is a series of albums assembled by and on behalf of the surgeon Reed Bontecou.[62] These photographs of wounded soldiers were produced to illustrate forms of treatment for wounds suffered during the Civil War. In the case of the Bontecou photographs, the text inserted by the surgeon is interspersed with handwritten updates that explain whether the patient had lived, was discharged, or died of "exhaustion." Such photographs, taken during and after surgical treatment for bullet wounds, act out the visuality of evidence. The bodies of the wounded soldiers whose identities have been obscured by faded handwriting on the labels that accompany these photographs have long turned to dust, but we continue to look at their faces. The years of the Civil War saw photographs used for the first time in the United States to illustrate identity as well as treatment, location in addition to event.[63] In each case, the style and texture of the event operates as a matter of or an insistence on recollection, reinhabiting, reliving, perhaps reskinning the surface of the visible world.

Even now, to expose these vulnerable bodies leads to questions about the ethics of such visibility; yet the relation of sight to literary culture is not static, nor, of course, limited to the nineteenth century. Holmes writes poignantly about searching for his son on the battlefield, not knowing if he would find him still alive, while he thinks about how "doings of the sunbeam" (a form of looking that he has been busy promoting as he describes how to develop film) have changed what it is that he might see. Viewing the aftermath of the battle where his son has been wounded, Holmes feels no desire for a photograph. He says, "there was something repulsive about the trodden and stained relics of the stale battlefield. It was like the table of some hideous orgy left uncleared, and one turned away disgusted from its broken fragments and muddy heel-taps." Recalling Antietam through viewing the photographs that had been displayed from Mathew Brady's studio, he comments, it is "so nearly like visiting the battlefield to look over these views, that all the emotions excited by the actual site of the stained and sordid scene, strewed with rags and wrecks, came back to us"; the desire that followed was to bury the images "as we would have buried the mutilated remains of the dead they too vividly represented."[64] The image of burying photographs as though they were the remains of the dead that they display to the viewer suggests a grim relation between the image and the body that persists.

Revisiting images of corpses that have been reproduced for visual consumption raises questions of temporality such that the immediacy of battle becomes something that the viewer wishes to escape. How does the matter of text overlap (or not) with the identification that says: at this moment, the photograph was taken? Through the name of the battle, the viewer can live through its effects even if the subject of the photograph has died. In the case of the Bontecou photographs, exhibiting amputations long past and medical treatments that have been superseded, we might ask for what viewer, and for what purpose, these images are now evidence. Identity, treatment, location, and event have been obscured and we are left facing the trembling bodies of the wounded, sometimes witnessing the traces of blood on the skin. Photographs of Civil War soldiers who had been "contraband" were once used to amplify the action of abolitionist sympathy and to demonstrate the privations of the camps. Such a market for evidence reflects the faith that audiences have that a photograph tells the truth. The sentimental individuation of such photographs assumes a viewer will accept the role of witness. The mourning for injured bodies that these photographs enable allows photography to perform a political act.[65]

War and Sensation

Describing sensation through reactions to images in poetry and photographs is built into responses to the American Civil War. From the best known—the lyrics by Walt Whitman that have come to be indelibly associated with the death of Abraham Lincoln—to the more obscure forms of letters and diaries, responses to war attend to sensation as a legitimate and legitimating strategy. Rather than rehearsing the history of eighteenth-century sources for sensation or revisiting critical trends of more recent centuries, I will take a riveting moment—the assassination of Abraham Lincoln—and trace the rendering of sensation in the antecedents and aftermath. These readings of sensation include grief, regret, and joy, since the attitude of Southern sympathizers and the recently defeated Confederacy featured celebrations of the assassination.

The reactions to war have become conflated with the reaction to Lincoln's assassination. And the commemoration of Lincoln, thanks to the simply unimaginable plethora of books about his words and deeds, can be overwhelming. Attention to the consequences of his assassination for Mary Todd Lincoln as well as for her dressmaker Elizabeth Keckley has unearthed new perspectives. To focus on the emotional resonance of such moments suggests again the saturation of recollection and memory. Historical readings of sensation thus include a sensational reading of history. Whitman's "Song of the Broad Axe," for instance, imagines cultural responses in more than one register—visual and literary, sonic and sighted. As we will see, Whitman's poetry combines politics and sympathy while he promotes poetic concepts of political will.[66]

The political will of either Northern or Southern involvement in the Civil War and the popular response to belletristic engagement have been rewritten as conflicts over race and the practices of enslavement, however contested that interpretation remains. The outbreak of war, however, also emphasized access to markets; economic blockades were understood to be effective military strategy. Recent studies have argued that the capitalism undergirding the successful economic and geographical expansion of the United States was founded on slavery; the remaining trauma from the political and legal engagement with the activities of enslaving or being enslaved has emerged in many different guises.[67] A topsy-turvy effect can appear that makes narratives about war and politics into referential moments of domestic life and labor. Ralph Waldo Emerson, for instance, cannot forgive Daniel Webster for voting for the Fugitive Slave Law. Henry David Thoreau cannot forgive Massachusetts for enforcing it.

Maria Amparo Ruiz de Burton can mock the anxiety about racial identifications presumed to identify those who have been enslaved, an anxiety that suffuses both family and economic relations in *Who Would Have Thought It?* (1872). But she refuses to make it a simple story.[68]

Democratic actions, whether celebrated or mourned (and Ruiz de Burton sometimes does both), often involve violent uprisings, many taking place in cities; they typically invoke an immersion in crowds. The moral economy of the crowd that reacts to stories about slavery or pictures of the slaughter on the battlefield at Antietam evokes the performative authority of the commons embedded in a Lockean social contract. As before, the question arises about what happens in the space of the both the military theatre and the emotional theatre of the poem. Reading appears as a technology of intimacy in works like *Leaves of Grass* with its fantasies of community. "I spring from these pages into your arms," declares Whitman, urging an active embrace of the tactile dimension of his book.[69] Inviting as it might be to imagine an ongoing intimacy with democracy, following Whitman's ideal embrace, this project both maps a territory that has been consistently understood as masculine and works through the assumptions about gender that are overturned by the work of women in the cultural and political space of war.

The book thus seeks to leave a calling card from the present while possibly picking up the card that remains from the past, a *carte de visite* presentation from a visitor who left a mark and also the traces of a ghostly haunting. To leave this card now is to emphasize that the haunting stories of American identity combine narrative and image even as your visitor can be more than one kind of witness. Imperialist expansion and violence appear throughout reproduced images, images that worked as iconography for progressive change as well as for regressive violence. At the same time, cultural productions need an audience; artists and writers need to eat. Personal glimpses emerge of writers who engage with publishers about monetary rewards. Harriet Beecher Stowe wrote letters that fuss about how to have international copyright; Herman Melville frequently wrote to his publisher about royalties. These traces of human hunger in the archives can cause a great deal of excitement for historians and scholars, excitement comparable to recovering works of literary value among the pamphlets of an antislavery collection or the ephemera of something like the scrapbooks left behind.[70] Broadsides and photographs, the visual ephemera of a literary age, might include the production of literature for children with crude woodblock illustrations of an alphabet caught up in abolitionist scenes.

My earlier example of archive excitement involved the underground space of the rare book library at Cornell University, where many artifacts as well as culturally significant literary productions from the American past remain to be unearthed for students and scholars. The librarians who work there thrill to bring out a rare copy of the Gettysburg Address in Lincoln's handwriting. They enjoy the fabrics remaining from "antislavery fairs" in the scrapbooks and the extraordinary histories contained in pamphlets. Yet they now resist showing an item that used to be displayed for students of the nineteenth-century United States, the previously described "manacles." These manacles are heavy, disturbing, and irresistible, at once because of their legacy and their weight (see figure I.5). I have had students refuse to touch them as they have been passed from hand to hand, haunted by the metal heft, with some difficult re-creation of what it might have felt like to wear them. Attached to them is a tag saying that they were donated by Julia Wilbur. However much she might have been forgotten since the nineteenth century, she had quite a history as an abolitionist activist. As a friend of the writer Harriet Jacobs, she moved to Washington, DC, during the Civil War to work with the Freedmen's Bureau before joining the Patent Office. The manacles survive as mementos for the peculiar and surprisingly popular action of bringing home artifacts from the battlefield as souvenirs, a souvenir activity that appears in the accounts of numerous Union visitors to the ruined city of Richmond, the last holdout of the Confederacy.[71]

Increasing resistance has emerged to the act of viewing nineteenth-century photographs such as the controversial portraits still in the possession of Harvard University. Originally produced to illustrate the racist quasi-scientific documentation promoted by Louis Agassiz, these photographs have been claimed as the property of a family descended from the subjects they seem to reveal.[72] Memorably adapted by Carrie Mae Weems in the installation "From Here I Saw What Happened and I Cried," the photographs might be said to contain the residue of tears from viewer and subject alike.[73] They persist as relics of painful acquisitions, of images captured instead of bodies, but at the same time, claimed by the families who could not have been able to claim these bodies, they persist as images that stand in for the bodies that remain as ghosts. That haunting performed by the eyes in the photographs remains as a residue of a refusal to be captured by either the camera or the law.

Political Testimony

Well before the Civil War, congressional as well as judicial debates bore witness to how legislative language policed possibilities for citizenship and national identity in the early republic. Such language frequently asserts a relation between persons and land with residual violence. Declarations of dependence recur; one might assert that declaring property once understood as communal to be now that of "domestic dependent nations" forms a crucial part of understanding humans as property.[74] The vocabulary of witnessing human bondage has a legal component in the legislation that formed and reformed the boundaries understood to belong to the United States. The language of compromise that appears in the political debates of the first half of the nineteenth century operates in conjunction with the language of "forever"—a language reiterated in the Emancipation Proclamation's words, "forever free." Such language finds ambivalent formation in the Declaration of Independence. It may be more fruitfully examined in the legal and juridical language about slavery, possibly authored by Thomas Jefferson, language that appeared in the political declarations about the Louisiana Purchase.[75]

As legislators sought to develop the wording of the extraordinary land transfer known as the Louisiana Purchase, they faced the dilemma of a document that proposes the relationship between the colonial assertions made by France and the "ceding" of an enormous tract of land, for their acquisitive purposes imaged as empty of inhabitants, to the United States. They also created this language concerning the possible extension of legalized slavery: "And be it further enacted. That in all that territory ceded by France to the United States, under the name of Louisiana, . . . contemplated by this act, slavery and involuntary servitude, otherwise than in the punishment of crimes, whereof the parties shall have been duly convicted, shall be, and is hereby, forever prohibited." In other words, the phrase "forever free" was preceded by the phrase "forever prohibited." The territory that was to become American is in this language simply a "contemplated" zone free from the legal practices of slavery.

The language of prohibition repeated here, an apparently unambiguous outlawing of the practices of slavery that involved politicians from the wording of the Declaration of Independence forward, gives way to a proviso that was to haunt the early republic. The modification to the future prohibition of slavery appears in these words: "Provided always, That any person escaping into the same, from whom labour or service is lawfully claimed, in any state or territory of the United States, such fugitive may be lawfully reclaimed and conveyed to the person claiming his or her labour or service as aforesaid."[76] The judicial declaration that legitimized the business of reclamation and the return of humans into conditions of enslavement formed the underpinning for the Fugitive Slave Act that followed almost fifty years later. A dramatic pursuit across the ice floes on a wintry Ohio River into nominally free territory famously adds to

Eliza's heroism in the century's most widely read novel, *Uncle Tom's Cabin*. Dramatizations of that pursuit were awkwardly reenacted on small-town stages well into the twentieth century; searches for remaining traces of the underground railroad that resisted the hunting of humans through the landscape of the eastern United States continue to the present.

Politicians made several attempts to renegotiate the legislation of that provision. The language of the Missouri Compromise, approved March 6, 1820, sought to balance the new admission of the state of Maine against the territory that became the state of Missouri. In so doing, the compromise refers to the Louisiana Purchase as it sought to balance an impossible inequality, pitting freedom against slavery, and declaring that "all that territory ceded by France" north of "thirty-six degrees" latitude should be free, that slavery in that territory "shall be, and is hereby, forever prohibited." All the words in that declaration became suspect after the Kansas–Nebraska Act, introduced by Stephen Douglas to create new states that would be able to determine the legal status of enslaved humans through "popular sovereignty," an act passed over bloody resistance in 1854.[77] The move from "shall be" to "is," language canceled after 1854, holds in suspension a process of becoming free that the language of "forever prohibited" seems to contradict.

These various moves of legislating land and bodies, and the suspension in this language, echo the way that the Declaration of Independence establishes a moment of "becoming" that was built into the declarations of nation and state alike.[78] Repeatedly, such language addresses both land and body as a process of becoming in relation to belonging. Proposals about land claims went along with an uneasy tension about legal assertions that decided that humans could claim the right to own other humans as property. In that way, the legal manipulations that claimed legal dominance over nations such as the Haudenosaunee confederation of six nations and the extension of land claims in order to enforce the Cherokee removals of the 1830s inform the sense that the Missouri Compromise has been overlooked as a space for examining Native American belonging as well.[79]

The Missouri Compromise further abrogated the right of the federal government to make decisions about legalized enslavement within particular territories that might apply within the newly formed states. That language was reinforced by the provisions about runaways at the end of section eight, in which "such fugitive may be lawfully reclaimed and conveyed to the person claiming his or her labour or service." Such provisions continued in the language of the Fugitive Slave Law that established the right for any person calling themselves an enslaver to assert a claim to a person as property in any state of the Union. The Compromise of 1850 refers to acts of legislation passed in 1789 and 1793, referencing the return of escaped servants. It also contains the Fugitive Slave Act.[80]

One of the most frightening aspects of the Fugitive Slave Act was that it overrode the ability of any person, of whatever race, to testify to his or her own right to his or her own body. Once claimed under the provisions of the act, the person claimed not only could not testify, but also could not look to any other legal or judicial protection to establish freedom. The language of the statute reads: "In no trial or hearing under this act shall the testimony of such alleged fugitive be admitted in evidence; and the certificates . . . shall be conclusive of the right of the person or persons in whose favor granted, to remove such fugitive to the State or Territory from which he escaped, and shall prevent all molestation of such person or persons by any process issued by any court judge, magistrate, or other person whomsoever."[81] Certainly, the restriction on the right to speak on behalf of or about one's own freedom troubled abolitionist writers. The Massachusetts towns that set up groups like the Boston Vigilance Committee also had secret "anti-man-hunting" leagues.[82] And the challenge to the ability to claim one's own body once escaped from the system of legalized slavery haunted the words and the lives of writers such as Frederick Douglass and Harriet Jacobs. The "testimony" of the "alleged fugitive" became their eloquent witnessing.[83]

The Kansas–Nebraska Act of 1854, an act whose provisions thread through the debates between Abraham Lincoln and Stephen Douglas, continues such attention to perpetuating restrictions on freedom.[84] In the Kansas–Nebraska Act, a reference to the requirement to return runaways from Nebraska first appears in Section 10.[85] In Section 28, the history of what it will take to control those who might wish to escape is repeated for Kansas: "And be it further enacted, That the provisions of the act entitled 'An act respecting fugitives from justice, and persons escaping from, the service of their masters,' approved February twelfth, seventeen hundred and ninety-three, and the provisions of the act entitled 'An act to amend, and supplementary to, the aforesaid act,' approved September eighteenth, eighteen hundred and fifty, be, and the same are hereby, declared to extend to and be in full force within the limits of the said Territory of Kansas." This apparently quiet language, rooted in sixty years of legislative decisions, was to spark terrible violence along the borders of Missouri and Kansas, including brutal murders carried out by the sons of John Brown.

By contrast, the Emancipation Proclamation, only a few years later, proposes that "all persons held as slaves within any State or designated part of a State, the people whereof shall then be in rebellion against the United States, shall be then, thenceforward, and forever free; and the Executive Government of the United States . . . will recognize and maintain the freedom of such persons, and will do no act or acts to repress such persons . . . in any efforts they may make for their actual freedom."[86] Although it declared "forever free" persons held in a condition of slavery, the Emancipation Proclamation might be understood to encourage revolt more than it established the authority to rescue anyone from a condition of enslavement.

The cultural productions of the nineteenth century often exist outside the understanding of such legal attention to personhood. The ideas of home, of intimacy, of marriage, of children, of nature, can be read in relation to freedom from fear and yet can be inverted with attention to the conditions that keep such fear at bay. The release of language in the most elaborate poetical productions of Walt Whitman or the most nuanced restraint in Emily Dickinson is also about the freedom to speak. In the United States, as it emerged during this fraught century, the legal and the literary attention to personhood developed together. As the inhabitants of the country learned to testify to their own freedom, their testimonies inevitably bore witness to the conditions of unfreedom that bring freedom and mourning together.

The chilling language of Justice Roger B. Taney, writing for the majority in the Supreme Court decision known as *Dred Scott v. Sandford*, handed down on March 6, 1857, has long presented the most disturbing challenge to such an idea of either family or freedom. The story of how Dred Scott came to sue for his freedom is well known. Taken from Missouri, where slavery was legal, to Wisconsin, where it was illegal, and then returned to Missouri, Dred Scott was encouraged to challenge the law.[87] When he was returned to Missouri, he sued in the state court, where he lost, and then pursued the case to the US Supreme Court. The spurious argument that anyone descended from African ancestors was "not intended to be included" as a citizen in the "intent" of the original framers of the Constitution has often been assessed as the tipping point for the outbreak of war. By the end of the war resistance to that framing helped produce the limited claims to citizenship, notably for African American men but not women, with the passage of the Fourteenth and Fifteenth Amendments to the constitution. Justice Taney, writing for the majority in the 7–2 decision of Dred Scott v. Sandford, announced that "The only two clauses in the Constitution which point to this race, treat them as persons whom it was morally lawful to deal in as articles of property and to hold as slaves."[88]

Referring to the announcement about the "unalienable rights" to "life, liberty, and the pursuit of happiness" set forth in the Declaration of Independence, Taney announces that "no one misunderstood" that this declaration was racist in its implications. He states that "it is too clear for dispute, that the enslaved African race were not intended to be included, and formed no part of the people who framed and adopted this declaration; for if the language, as understood in that day, would embrace them, the conduct of the distinguished men who framed the Declaration of Independence would have been utterly and flagrantly inconsistent with the principles they asserted."[89] The extraordinary suggestion that he does not present is that many of those who signed this declaration were enslavers and therefore the language they use must be understood as legally ambiguous. The "indelible marks" to which Taney refers as marking racial distinctions had already been transgressed by reproduction across the color line, while the concept of the "great men" to whom he refers seems suspect. They were, he asserts, "high in literary acquirements" as well as "high in their sense of honor." That "literary acquirements" and honor bolster each other makes the subsequent descriptions of the founding peoples of the United States all the more horrifying.

In his dissent, Justice Benjamin R. Curtis argued that if the defendant were recognized as "capable of contracting a lawful marriage," then his status as well as that of his wife, and his children must be recognized as that of a citizen. By this view, "the contract of marriage and the birth of children" make all the difference. His attention to contract law engaged in the concept of marriage has a sequel in the return to the original purchase of what was then known as the Northwest Territory from France. Suggesting that international treaties might be violated by the careless extension of slavery into land that did not yet exist as a state seems a detour from the contract of marriage, yet keeps the idea of subject and citizen attached to location on land, as well as unstable because of crossing the Mississippi. That a clear claim to either citizenship or freedom can be located anywhere in the convoluted pages of what has become known as the Dred Scott decision was definitively a problematic premise, a premise that sparked the language of war.

CHAPTER TWO

Poetry and War

EMILY DICKINSON, WALT WHITMAN, AND ABRAHAM LINCOLN

Poetry and Perception

Witnessing the war as a central but nearly indescribable rupture in the cultural and political norms of the nineteenth century, poets who addressed it often evaded it at the same time, inviting a sensory response, at once visual and auditory. The most vivid poems invent a sense of touch such that poetry as it emerges during the war invokes crossing points of sound and vision. The poems that this chapter turns to include stellar examples such as Emily Dickinson's "There's a certain slant of light" (Fr320A) and Walt Whitman's "Out of the Cradle Endlessly Rocking." Even the titles, with their invocations to see and to feel the momentum of language, produce an imperative project for poetic language. These poems oscillate between the two senses as part of an inquiry into the nature of human perception. To begin with perception in turning to poems about war will not be a surprising tactic, especially in the poetry of Dickinson and Whitman, long understood as significant innovators in the development of nineteenth-century American poetry. They persist as tent poles for the great canopy of language that emerged as the century progressed. This chapter's attention to poetry ends with Abraham Lincoln, at once the subject of poetry and the wielder of words infused with poetic sensibility.

What an early-nineteenth-century audience found when they encountered poetry often falls into the realm of the ballad or the elegy. That is, on the one hand, such audiences experienced a poetic language that suggests recitation, and that contains a history of past heroic actions or seems to call for future action and, on the other, a poetry of stillness and contemplation. The call for epics that would provide a romance of the nation disappeared during the war. However rousing the language in Whitman might become, both Whitman and Dickinson tended to write lyric contemplations that fit neither model. Both have become identified with forms of introspection that have been exaggerated in their effects but that speak to the iconic way each still tends to be perceived. What an audience learns to identify with in reading these two poets, I will urge, shifts to a relation between perception and contemplation. What linguistic effects happen among images and sound dominates their best poems.

Other poets, such as John Greenleaf Whittier, wrote ballads that spoke for the political cause of abolition. And other nineteenth-century poets produced elegiac contemplation that addressed the politics of land in relation to bodies. To read the first lines of Philip Freneau's "The Indian Burying Ground" and contrast them with the opening lines of William Cullen Bryant's "Thanatopsis" is to be drawn in different directions. On the one hand, in an often-memorized nineteenth-century favorite, Bryant addresses the reader as "him who in the love of Nature holds / Communion with her visible forms, she speaks / A various language."[1] That language, gendered in terms of who might wish communion with a female nature, becomes merged with the voices of those who have died and left some "human trace" to "mix forever with the elements." Such a trace explains itself as consolation for a fear of dying in the poem. The reader of Freneau's poem, asked to behold the "posture, that we give the dead," is presented with a coherent continuous and natural extension from a natural landscape to the dead body that will be swallowed into the trees.[2] But importantly, that reader will walk away thinking about the deaths of others, notably nostalgic about the death of another race, and not about a larger sense of mortality.

In stark contrast, Emily Dickinson writes poems that open with quatrains like this one: "There's a certain Slant of light, / Winter afternoons— / That oppresses like the Heft / Of Cathedral Tunes."[3] The particular changes in light seem at first universal. The careful reader will note that the poem immediately contains a form of synesthesia that implies that light has weight, that to see is also to listen, that sound has the weight, or the "heft," that transfers from the light. The next quatrain condenses this effect into the simple referent "it" and continues: "Heavenly Hurt, it gives us— / We can find no scar, / But internal difference— / Where the Meanings, are—" (Depending on the source, the last two words of the line might appear separated by a comma or a dash.) "We can find no scar," declares the narrator. The image of looking at the inside of the body to distinguish a fleeting change made by the outside change in light suggests looking for what can be written not only about but also inside the body with light, like the inverse of photography.

To be so transparent to the shifts in sight and sound, the poem continues, becomes an overwhelming sensation. An odd temporality appears in the sequencing of "it" as at once a shift in sunlight and a further shift in perception: "When it comes, the Landscape listens— / Shadows—hold their breath— / When it goes, 'tis like the Distance / On the look of Death." Throughout, typical of Dickinson's meter, there appears a persistently hesitating and dash-ridden syntax, a breathlessness with which the poem approaches the idea of synesthesia, of senses that cross and reengage, until the final word "Death" appears to cross out doubts and end the poem in an insistent one-syllable resolution.

The final word of Dickinson's poem recalls the final words, repeated as "death, death, death, death," that Whitman announces in the sound of the sea that he inserts into "Out of the Cradle Endlessly Rocking." That poem develops its own form of synesthesia through the enlarged sense of the call of the bird on the shore, expressed quasi-autobiographically as the idea of the boy's emergence into poetry through loss. For Whitman, in this poem, "the sea whispered me."[4] That sea, personified, at once whispers to "me"—a boy narrator who has been recalled by a particular sensory memory—and whispers the poet into existence. The sibilant sound of the sea in the poem becomes at once a word and a sound beyond words, emphasizing its repetitions as it evades certainty. Listening to the repetitive call of the shorebird, the poet asks, "Is it indeed to your mate that you sing? or is it mostly to me?" For whom, the poem repeats, does the sound of the sea whisper? For whom does the bird call? The language of intimacy mingles with the language of death, becoming a sound of ending and beginning while the lines in "Out of the Cradle Endlessly Rocking" end in death.

Dickinson's poems notoriously reference perception and combine it with the appearance of death, as in often-quoted opening lines such as "I heard a fly buzz when I died" (Fr591A). That perceptual impossibility—a speaker from beyond the grave noting a liminal sound—reappears in allegorical form in lines such as "Because I could not stop for death" (Fr479A) or the short lyric, "I died for beauty" (Fr448A). In Whitman, by contrast, that beauty is the beauty of an ideal democracy combined with the beauty of (sometimes dying) young men. For Dickinson, death is more frequently sensory. She presents an anguished move toward the dropping of a "Plank in Reason," for instance, in the poem "I felt a funeral in my brain" (Fr340A). Yet for literary scholars, a critical challenge to how to read her poems has emerged. The poems that were read for so long as part of a brooding isolation have come to be understood, at least in part, as reflections of the general sorrowing that took place in New England as young men went off to die. That the years of the Civil War were the most productive time for her has reinforced this interpretation. Thus, the marching of the funeral processions in Amherst, Massachusetts, might echo the rhythm of funerals in the poem.

Another way that loss expresses itself in Dickinson's writing has attracted recent critical attention. The grief that sometimes seems to saturate her poems has been traced, especially through letters addressed to her, to a pent up longing for Sue Dickinson, the wife of her brother. Surely, critics note, the longing expressed in poems like "Wild Nights—wild nights" (Fr269) reflects that. The voice that speaks as "I" does speak of how "thee" might appear in "Wild nights"—contravening an interpretation that emphasized the abstract way that desire appears in her poetry. Dickinson's grand sense of privacy becomes almost a loud privacy in its refusal to engage readerly expectations about the end of a poetic line. The very refusals of the line "Pain—has an Element of Blank" in another of her poems engage a reader who has been erased or made "blank" in the monosyllabic end of the line; the line encourages an element of "filling in" the blanks that appear—or the dashes that punctuate—these poems.

The War at Home

Over the many decades that he wrote and revised the poems in *Leaves of Grass*, the Whitman associated with "Song of Myself"—a Whitman of exuberant sensuality and more or less enthusiastic speculations about the identities of American democracy—becomes a Whitman whose desire is more elegiac, whose longings are more mournful. The language of universality—of aggregate being—in his earliest incarnations of the poem mingled hopes for a sense of national belonging with the specificity of type. The conviction that humans are representative or that the poet can choose out of the mix of light and shadow found at once collaboration and refutation when the poet entered the battlefields of the Civil War, at first looking for his brother and then remaining to help with wounded and dying soldiers. As we will see in a moment, the shadows in Whitman's elegiac "A March in the Ranks" line up with the shadows in Herman Melville's poem "Shiloh." When Whitman asks, in the persona of a battlefield visitor, "whoever you are holding me in hand," he moves toward the realization that the men he holds can die.

Whitman's earlier poem, "Out of the Cradle Endlessly Rocking," courts, retrieves, assiduously reiterates the longing of the shorebird, as these poems echo private as well as public loss; yet it has only been in recent years that the question of the relation between private and public loss has emerged. Compare the intimacies of the first edition of *Leaves of Grass* to the poems in *Drum-Taps* that contain Whitman's account of finding men on the battlefield. The love of men and the love of women cross but never encounter each other in these poems. It can be helpful to compare them to the sense of public loss in Dickinson's poetry. For instance, the poem known as "When I was small, a Woman died" (Fr518A), although it sets a stage from the memory of childhood, presents events that occur on the battlefield. She writes, "When I was small, a Woman died— / To-day her Only Boy / Went up from the Potomac— / His face all Victory." The ironic claim of victory recurs in the poem's penultimate stanza: "But, proud in Apparition— / That Woman and her Boy / Pass back and forth, before my Brain / As ever in the sky—."

To take on the writing that Dickinson produced in relation to war is also to recall how she wrote to Thomas Wentworth Higginson, colonel of the First South Carolina Volunteers from 1862 to 1864. He had written "Letter to a Young Contributor" in the *Atlantic* and she responded to him, famously, "Mr Higginson, Are you too deeply occupied to say if my Verse is alive?"[5] That very quality of life in her language, even as its preoccupation is death, invites another form of inquiry into the relation between living words and dead humans, an inquiry that recurs in the next chapter's attention to mourning. Dickinson goes on to ask, "Should you think it breathed—and had you the leisure to tell me, I should feel quick gratitude—." She writes this letter in 1862, in the middle of fervor over the outbreak of war. Higginson had been writing about the war in the same journal where he invited attention to writing. Yet the correspondence concerns poetry and barely touches on the war so that it may be a reading into the attention to death that makes it seem as though the end of the war accompanied, although possibly it did not cause, the great slowing down of her productive streak.

To look at how the Civil War affected such poetry is to look at the relation between intimacy and violence in the poetry of the writers whose language addressed the conflict. Often their words invoked images. To talk about images with this poetry is to invoke ekphrasis; ekphrastic concerns arise as a way to look at how images appear in writing. The structures of interpretation that focus on democracy overlap and infuse that focus on the experiments in language by a poet like Walt Whitman. Whitman uses convoluted language to make foregrounds and backgrounds change places. For Whitman, battlefield intimacy can have the resonance of honoring the dead in the aggregate or entering a particular embrace. A poem like "The Wound Dresser" appears intimate and specific in its attention to how men touch each other or, possibly, it embraces the thousands of bodies abandoned on battlefields. Understood as an instantiation of Whitman's wartime encounters, the poem invokes letters Whitman transcribed for wounded soldiers, songs they sang around campfires, the sheet music that copied those songs. Insofar as the poem addresses male intimacy, then the photographs of Whitman with the male friends with whom he shared his life become part of a story of intimacy that the gathering of men during wartime made possible.

A brief look at Lilly Martin Spencer, a popular nineteenth-century painter who became associated with sentimental domestic images, and especially a glance at her painting *The War Spirit at Home* might allow some contrast (figure 2.1). This popular painting imagines the war as something to be found in the columns of the newspaper read at home, a newspaper that carries columns of names of the men who have died in battle. As the mother reads in the middle distance, her young children march in the foreground in play battle attire. Her baby, sliding toward the ground, seems almost in danger of falling off her lap. The children must be loud, armed as they are with toy trumpet and makeshift drum, but the tense posture of the adults in the room does not seem to be caused by their noise. The curve of the bodies in the foreground leads the eye to the servant, dressed in black, ironing in the background. She watches her mistress with an anxiety that, combined with her black attire, raises the question of whether she has already lost a father, a brother, a son, or a husband. The surprise of the baby who might fall from the mother's lap evokes the falling bodies in William Hogarth's prints—it suggests the disruptive power of the newspaper for interrupting maternal focus, but possibly also points to the poignancy of raising children who might soon die. The potential message of doom for the missing patriarch is belied by the everyday domesticity, the playfulness of the children who have dressed up as small soldiers. The only males in the scene are young boys, marching with paper hats, who carry toy implements of war. However often Spencer's paintings became associated with a picturesque account of domestic scenes, it's somewhat irresistible to read this as a narrative portrait laced with doom.

In contrast, we might look at how the restraint in Melville's poem "Shiloh," published in his short collection *Battle-Pieces and Aspects of the War*

FIGURE 2.1. Lilly Martin Spenser (1822–1902). *The War Spirit at Home (Celebrating the Victory at Vicksburg)*, 1866. Oil on canvas. 30 in. × 32 3/4 in. (76 cm × 82 cm). Courtesy of Newark Art Museum. Provenance: Purchase 1944 Wallace M. Scudder Bequest Fund. 44.177.

(1866), stands in relation to the attention to this domestic scene—or with the battlefield intimacy in Whitman's poems. The stray, spare lines of "Shiloh" connect at once to the sight of the battlefield, emptied of combat, but strewn with the wreckage of warfare, and to the continuation of the natural order. In "Shiloh: A Requiem (April, 1862)," we find "Skimming lightly, wheeling still, / The swallows fly low." Their flight takes the swallows "Over the field where April rain / Solaced the parched ones stretched in pain / Through the pause of night / That followed the Sunday fight." The reference to the battle that has left "parched ones stretched in pain" acts like the line of sight in Whitman's poem "A March in the Ranks Hard Pressed and the Road Unknown" to take the reader in from the sky to the enclosed formation of the church that has been adapted as a field hospital.

The poem continues, "Around the church of Shiloh— / The church so lone, the log-built one, / That echoed to many a parting groan / And natural prayer / Of dying foemen mingled there—." The men who lie in the church are described as "Foemen at morn, but friends at eve— / Fame or country least their care."[6] The identifications with glory or patriotism have been eroded by pain.

With a parenthetical aside, Melville continues his attention to the suffering men in the short poem: "(What like a bullet can undeceive!) / But now they lie low, / While over them the swallows skim, / And all is hushed at Shiloh." The silence that falls over the poem, with the sibilance and internal rhyme that at once focuses and distracts the reader, moves the sight line from the landscape inside the church back out to the pattern of wings against the sky. The slant rhymes accompany the deceptive ways that "What like a bullet can undeceive" creep into the poem in parentheses. The poet asks, in effect, what can act like a bullet, and answers, implicitly, a poem. A poem, like a bullet, can undeceive. The soldiers who confront each other in death find that "Fame or country" are "least their care." The swallows that skim over the fields draw a visual network of relations with the pattern of their wings.

To reach into the darkness that surrounds wounded and dying men concerns Whitman's poems such as "Vigil Strange I Kept on the Field One Night." Trochaic pentameter, the technical term for the poetic language that spells out the first line, helps the reader to understand how deliberately Whitman invites explication of the internal rhymes. In their attention to the sense of touch that the poems evoke, critics quote Whitman, who announced early in his poetic career that "who touches this [poem] touches a man."[7] The tactility of language in Dickinson has received less attention, nor has the withdrawal from touch and the intimacy of metaphor that occurs in Melville—almost as though the poet has removed words. When Whitman published *Drum-Taps* (1865), he introduced the melodrama of battlefield vigilance, while attaching vision to touch in poems such as "Vigil Strange I Kept on the Field One Night," "A March in the Ranks Hard Pressed and the Road Unknown," and particularly in "The Wound Dresser."[8] In "Vigil Strange," the speaker who watches over the man who has died on the battlefield remembers not only "One touch of your hand to mine, O boy, / reach'd up as you lay on the ground," but also "a look I shall never forget." The place of the look in remembering the war recurs in the next section, when the look that the poet exchanged with Abraham Lincoln returns as a motif of remembrance.

Looking at Lincoln

To look at Abraham Lincoln, whether through the poetry of his language, the photographs of his gaunt face, or the poetry about grief at his assassination, is to discover a man so visible he can scarcely be seen. The paradox of that enhanced visibility might be increased by the way that his words are so familiar that we can scarcely hear him. To see Lincoln anew and to hear his words afresh becomes the challenge. This section considers how Lincoln appeared, stiff hair rising as a disheveled crown, top hat silhouetted above the crowd, when he was looked at by artists and writers. It considers how Lincoln looked at himself, mocking his own appearance, and proposing at once rigorous and passionate systems of belief. To carry out attention to the visibility of Lincoln as a writer and politician, I examine his orations while looking at his written statements, attempting throughout to listen to his words.

Abraham Lincoln first rose to regional prominence in rural Illinois as a lawyer whose commonsense rendering of convoluted land claims remains compelling reading. His ability to mock plaintiffs and defendants alike still emerges in the renderings of his speeches before the court. And yet the man who saw brief military service in the so-called Black Hawk War along the Mississippi River, the man who navigated rivers on a raft and saw slavery firsthand, scarcely appears to be the same man who produced the clipped eloquence of the Gettysburg Address.

How Lincoln wrote himself into existence retains a residue in the popular imagination in a register recorded from both oral and written performances. Contemporary anecdotes relate that his speech could be coarse and even vulgar; the classic texts with which he will be forever associated, such as the "Gettysburg Address" and the "Second Inaugural Address," seem to have survived because of the circulation of newspaper accounts. To see Lincoln as a writer is to see someone who draws on biblical cadences as well as the bawdy tall-tales humor of the so-called Southwest—a region he traveled on the Mississippi around the same time that Samuel Clemens was learning to pilot a steamboat. The words that remain show him to be at once meticulous in his phrasing and certain that the lessons of history could enable a coherent strategy and an enduring set of beliefs. What persists, in the middle of such melancholy, urgent reasoning, and tall-tale humor?

The relationships Lincoln had with friends and enemies have received thorough attention, for example in the influential way that Doris Kearns Goodwin set up his crafting of a "team of rivals."[9] The matters of context and cultural expectations have led historians to pore over courtship letters, musing about the homoerotic implications of his bond with his friend Joshua Speed. Produced through text, produced through image, Lincoln's relations preoccupied his contemporaries and continue to draw the rapt inquiries of subsequent scholars. Visual and textual productions contain a form of mythologizing that began long before it was suggested that he grow a beard, by rumor because of the newspaper distribution of the photograph made at Mathew Brady's studio at the time of his Cooper Union address that showed a gaunt clean-shaven face. That the subject cooperated with how his image might be used as a marketing tactic appeared early. If Lincoln is to be identified as a rail splitter, for instance, so shall rails be part of the campaign.

What difference did it make to his words and to his political positions that Lincoln began his rise to prominence as a circuit rider? The difference in how he reads his audience may appear in how he stages his response in the debates with Stephen Douglas—telling the crowd to go eat first, for example, so they can listen more carefully to his rejoinders. Lincoln's words then carried through to the vision for national reconciliation in his second inaugural address, an address that remains all the more unsettling and profound for being so thoroughly ravaged by his assassination.[10] With the years that have passed, the aura around him has continued to be burnished by movies and books. The commentary can be overwhelming. It has been estimated that on average a book a day has been published about him since he was assassinated.

Where does that leave slavery? As a name that could barely be spoken as part of political platforms, abolitionism preoccupied Lincoln while its machinations obsessed political parties and popular culture alike. Hence the excruciating Currier and Ives political cartoon, depicting a political platform made of rails that appears at once to be built on and to hide slavery; it reminds viewers that the president used to engage in rail splitting as well as riffing on clichés about what one might find in a woodpile.[11] Abraham Lincoln with no jacket and rolled up sleeves, in the days before he had a beard, sits in discomfort as though riding a horse as he grasps the top rails of a split rail edifice labeled "Republican Platform." Looking out from the rails, a man drawn with a caricatured and stereotyped grin sits beneath him, echoing his posture. Lincoln says through tight lips: "Little did I think when I split these rails that they would be the means of elevating me to my present position." That position appears at once precarious and uncomfortable. In a letter to Joshua Speed on slavery and the implication of the Fugitive Slave Act of 1850, Lincoln laments that "I confess I hate to see the poor creatures hunted down, and caught, and carried back to their stripes, and unrewarded toils; but I bite my tongue and keep quiet." At once recalling and dismissing this sight, a sight that seems to have been frequently witnessed along the Mississippi River where Lincoln spent his early years as a lawyer, he reminds Speed of a steamboat trip in 1841 when he traveled from Louisville to St. Louis, remembering that the sight of slaves "was a continual torment to me."[12]

These early articulations contain language that can seem suspicious, bolstering Frederick Douglass's later claim that Lincoln became the "white man's president" as he feels "torment," but bites his tongue as he refuses to speak out against what he knew to be a legal determination.[13] Still they help to illuminate the language that led to Lincoln's later and more familiar rhetoric. The debates with Stephen Douglas, for example, contain repetitions that are worth the time it takes to reread them. In these debates, the border territory that was about to be brought into statehood garners much attention because of the possible extension of legalized slavery. For Lincoln, what he calls the "Nebraska-law," was "conceived in violence, passed in violence, is maintained in violence, and is being executed in violence."[14] Here, as elsewhere, the language of conception favors the organic images of birth in the discussion of law. The birth of new states becomes the place for the execution of violence.

During these famed debates with Stephen Douglas, Lincoln speaks in favor of the Missouri Compromise and against the repeal of the Fugitive Slave Law as a safe, middle-ground, Whig position, but he folds support for the law into being both a man and, especially, an American. Shocking as we might still find it today to know that Lincoln upheld the Fugitive Slave Law, it is also the case that, in the same address, he opposes slavery on moral grounds. He describes the embedded necessity of slavery as something that has been inherited, as something that is "hidden away in the constitution just as an inflicted man hides away a wen or a cancer, which he dares not cut out at once, lest he may bleed to death."[15] In spite of the fear of death that he implies confronts the national body, Lincoln promises that the cutting will begin eventually.

Lincoln's position has been understood as ambiguous; it remains painful to read how his addresses work to reconcile his passion for the law with his distaste for legalized slavery. In the politically subtle eulogy he wrote for the statesman Henry Clay, for example, Lincoln recognizes the lack of clarity in Clay's position as an enslaver who presided over the American Colonization Society, the benighted effort to repatriate people perceived as stolen from Africa. Lincoln appears here as someone who recognized in himself the provocation of the position seen as most radical, "immediate emancipation." At that time, and possibly throughout his life, Lincoln did not express a recognition of racial equality, although he promoted political equality. In making that statement, I merely acknowledge that he knew his audience. As an astute political thinker, Lincoln always returned to the holy claims of the law

The emotions that the law aroused in Lincoln show up in his address to the young men's Lyceum in Springfield, Illinois, in 1838. As he often did, Lincoln referred to the American Revolution as a lodestone for political values. Noting that the revolution inspired an ardor for political success, Lincoln warned presciently about the potential for a tyrant or a "genius" who would seek new grounds for ambition. This address contains an almost erotic sense of what ambition looks like. Passion for power, says Lincoln, can give rise to new despotism after the excitement and incentives of the American Revolution have worn off. As he puts it, "towering genius disdains a beaten path" as it "thirsts and burns" for power. He predicts that the nobility of the cause of the American Revolution produced a "state of feeling" that "*must fade, is fading, has faded.*"[16]

That Lincoln invented himself as a political subject through oral performance can be traced to his years riding a "circuit" as a lawyer who had to adapt to uncertain lodging and irregular food in the small towns of western Illinois. In the debates with Stephen Douglas about the historical crises over slavery, Lincoln achieved an eloquence that paved the way to his presidential campaign, although he lost the specific election to the Senate for which the debates were staged. The newspaper accounts are punctuated with responses from the crowd. Lincoln revised and remapped his positions as he spoke over those many months. The debates and the legal decisions to which they responded are still pored over by legal, cultural, and historical scholars; correlating written texts with the accounts in contemporary newspapers makes it possible to hear the roars and hisses of the crowd and to imagine the sight of mud on thrown vegetables.

The debates with Douglas might well be read as a prequel to the Emancipation Proclamation, a declaration that still stands as one of Lincoln's most powerful statements, although its efficacy as a document providing freedom from slavery might have been limited. It has become difficult to reconstruct how much Lincoln might have been engaged in the articulation of this legislation. That he had no speechwriter continues to seem implausible, given the ubiquity of that role in today's presidency. But the revisions that appear in the debates of the 1850s show how Lincoln took ideas and reworded them according to the responses of his audiences as he traveled the length and breadth of Illinois.

The state of Illinois was sandwiched between the western frontier of slavery and the northern routes to freedom. Lincoln's marriage might also seem to have been arranged across the dividing line between North and South. His family had migrated north from Kentucky and he married a Kentucky woman whose slaveholding family was to support, and whose brothers to fight and die for, the Confederacy. The sexual and romantic rivalry that Lincoln engaged in with Stephen Douglas over Mary Todd, it seems incredible to repeat, echoed the political rivalry in which, while they had courted the same Southern woman, each led a crowd to a passionate position about land, slavery, and politics. And as poetic as that might now seem, there is a brutality about it. What voice will emerge to engage the woman's heart? Which voice will control the political direction of the land? In the back and forth of the debates, a reader might find that rivalry over the antislavery positions of the United States barely conceals a potentially erotic tension.

Lincoln understands slavery throughout these debates as a negative blight on the landscape of the United States, but he represents the law, even the law upholding slavery, with a stronger reverence than the Bible. To have an education, by his account, was to have access to history, and to know history was to inhabit the present in a vivid and compelling way. The most provocative instantiation of that historical sense appears in the Gettysburg Address, but it infuses entire speeches on a variety of topics, including the Kansas–Nebraska Act. The correlation of certain moments in the debates shows that some of the lines with which Lincoln has been most vividly associated changed as he practiced their effects on the crowd.

The Missouri Compromise had introduced a skewed and disruptive national balancing act between admitting free and slave states to the union, while the proposals embedded into the so-called Kansas–Nebraska Act left it up to each state to decide. These proposals led to guerrilla warfare along the borders of these states, warfare associated with the killing deeds of John Brown and his sons and the massacre at Lawrence, Kansas. Such violence continued, yet the most controversial moment in Lincoln's debates with Stephen Douglas about the Kansas–Nebraska Act that repealed the Missouri Compromise may have been his declaration that "because I do not want a black woman for a slave, I must want her for a wife." Instead, he famously declared, in a speech delivered on June 26, 1857, "I can just leave her alone."[17] The speeches that lead up to that debate show Lincoln practicing his lines, returning to rephrase the concepts with which he has been so indelibly linked. A house divided cannot stand, he repeats. And, earlier, he follows the comment about the place of the "negro woman" with a comment more appropriate for a working man who once returned part of a fee saying that he had been overpaid. She has the right to work for wages. The right to a fair wage has become a remote point in the attention to Lincoln imagining a "wife," a position that was laid at his door by scurrilous attacks.

Most historians report simply that, on September 18, 1858, Lincoln proposed that "I do not understand that because I do not want a negro woman for a slave I must necessarily want her for a wife." On that occasion Lincoln goes on to say that his "understanding is that I can just let her alone." When he made the comment earlier, in a speech on the Dred Scott decision, in Springfield, Illinois, he was also replying to Stephen Douglas, but Douglas was not in the audience. On this prior occasion, Lincoln stressed that he replies to a "counterfeit logic" and asserts that "in her natural right to eat the bread she earns with her own hands without asking leave of anyone else, she is my equal, and the equal of all others."[18]

In thinking about slavery as the issue that preoccupied political discourse in the years leading up to the Civil War, it matters to remember how political issues surrounding slavery were woven into debates about the expanding geopolitical borders of the country. There were vicious attacks within the Senate during the Missouri Compromise legislation (1820), the Fugitive Slave Law (1850), and the Kansas–Nebraska Act (1854), but starting with the Constitutional Convention there had been a great deal of violence within debates about what property mattered in the North and the South. While slavery dominated some counting of resources within the exchanges between North and South, the violence of debates about resources focused on how goods and people could be moved to markets. These debates included attention to what forms the transportation revolution might take (from canals to steamships to railroads). In thinking about the battles of the Civil War, it can be possible, for example, to overlook the acts of legislation that involve the transcontinental railroad. The violence of the war itself often occurred in the West—for instance, the hanging of Indigenous warriors in Mankato, Minnesota, and the border warfare in Kansas and Missouri must be considered as part of the war's violence. To consider the conflict as one between the North and the South invokes an incoherent landscape that we now think of as belonging to one country. Actions as far flung as the military maneuvers of Andrew Jackson, starting from the Seminole Wars in Florida and moving west, the provocations of Benjamin Butler against the southern women in New Orleans, the early rise of Ulysses S. Grant in skirmishes along the Mississippi River, took place on lands then understood to be western. That Lincoln appeared as a candidate from the west made his geographic appeal more profound.

Crucially, within a network of exchange that emphasized the technological support for military advances during the Civil War, the transportation revolution also included forms of communication such as telegraph wires. The relation between the movement of words along the straight line of the telegraph and the straight line of the railroad, whose beds the telegraphs poles followed, formed a key part of the Industrial Revolution. Drawing on the ideological challenges to national boundaries that had been affected by the revolutions in Europe in 1848, as well as the fervent patriotism that accompanied the boundary crossing of the Mexican–American War, both Union soldiers and Confederate soldiers understood themselves to be part of either a past revolution or a revolution in progress. What preoccupied readers at the time could vary. The terrible violence that took place between proslavery and antislavery factions in Lawrence, Kansas, sometimes faded in the light of the migrations provoked by the Gold Rush in California, while the feminist precepts of the 1848 Seneca Falls Convention can vanish in light of the legislation about slavery that followed so quickly afterward, and, of course, with the outbreak of war. The shifts in political focus that such events encouraged in participants and in those who read about them need to be read as background for Lincoln's position as well as for the cultural contexts into which war intruded.

There remain jarring discontinuities through the popular assumptions that the war was (1) over slavery, (2) fought by men on well-defined battlefields, (3) between North and South. Such assumptions leave out competing claims about national identities between the Union and Confederate states, repeated border skirmishes in contested territory, including Texas, and the battles over the routes to the west, including railroads and rivers, especially the Mississippi. These debated territories included the need for a transcontinental railroad—they invoke the positions in which Lincoln stakes his own ground. The contractual thinking that dominated the war was particularly invested in the question of what it meant to be part of a nation, sometimes formulated as a conflict between states' rights and national dominion. In historical terms, the conflict between the rights of states and the federal government can be traced, as Lincoln so often did, to the American Revolution. During the Civil War, the rhetoric of the American Revolution served to justify rebellion for and in the South. The great challenge to understanding nationalism through the identification of geographical boundaries is that such assertions claim to contain a particular form of belief in a kind of unified field theory of state and nation. Lincoln's beliefs produced possible transcendence.

Images

The standard account of the Civil War is that there's not an "art" of the Civil War. The literary critic Daniel Aaron called it "the unwritten war" and we might also call it "the unseen war" in spite of the simultaneous development of photography that made it one of the first wars to be viewed through photojournalism.[19] Changes in the popularity and form of newspapers reflected changes in lithography and the way that images from the battlefront were reproduced for readers while the proliferation of photographs reflected the shift from daguerreotyping to the wet-plate process. Newly popular magazines such as *Harper's Weekly* and the *Atlantic Monthly* contained literature as well as editorials on the volatile breakdowns in the abolitionist movement that accompanied the transition from the American Colonization Society to the more radical abolitionists such as John Brown.[20]

Throughout these transitions, the face of Abraham Lincoln was disseminated as that of no other president except George Washington.[21] In the years since, the image of Abraham Lincoln has become inextricably tied to his profile on currency and to the statue that anchors one end of the National Mall in Washington, DC. That statue has come to stand in for the presidency and possibly to embody the United States. In front of this statue, for instance, Barack Obama staged his political arrival as president.[22] During the nineteenth century, Lincoln's visibility in the newspapers included political cartoons, engravings in newspapers, statues, and paintings, such as the one by Francis Bicknell Carpenter who spent six months at the White House to paint a portrait of the signing of the Emancipation Proclamation.

Before Daniel Chester French took on the monumental task of sculpting a visible Lincoln for the National Mall in Washington, DC, several sculptors competed for the privilege of sculpting him. Among the competitors were Vinnie Ream, whose position as a young attractive woman made her proposed work as a sculptor of Lincoln highly controversial, and Augustus Saint-Gaudens, who made the memorial to Robert Gould Shaw and the Massachusetts Fifty-Fourth. The competition over the commission for Vinnie Ream made it to the floor of the Senate and has been preserved for an example of an unprecedented rhetorical mixture of how politics addresses artistic competence (figure 2.2). Her statue of Lincoln shows him holding the Emancipation Proclamation as he leans forward toward a

FIGURE 2.2. "Vinnie Ream at Work upon Her Lincoln Bust Which Rests upon the Stand She Used in the White House while President Lincoln Posed for Her," ca. 1865. Photographic print. Sheet: 14 in. × 11 in. (36 cm × 28 cm). Photographer unknown. Courtesy Library of Congress Prints and Photographs Division. 2002712184.

public that used to admire him in the space of the rotunda.[23] The history of how Saint-Gaudens approached his sculpture has much quieter and more elegiac memories. When describing how he sculpted Lincoln, Saint-Gaudens recalled seeing him for the first time in 1860—"Lincoln stood tall in the carriage, his dark uncovered head bent in contemplative acknowledgement of the waiting people."[24] The residue of this first glimpse lingers in the quiet contemplation of his *Standing Lincoln*.

The face and body of Abraham Lincoln only gradually came to stand for the country. The country had previously been identified with an iconic woman referred to as Columbia.[25] The substitution of the male body of the president for the body of Columbia takes place, I argue, because of this resonant crossing of iconographic vulnerability and historical visual presence. Such substitutions might stand (in) for a need to substitute in racial terms, a substitution carried out in ways that the concept of the captive carries over from African American slavery to frontier violence. The shift from Columbia to Lincoln might be understood as accompanying a move from previous images of the nation as a woman to the nation imaged as a tall brooding man. The sexuality that had been attached to white marble women fades away; such thoughts could never reach Lincoln's inviting gaze in Daniel Chester French's rendition in the Lincoln Memorial.

To consider that the visual presence of Lincoln has become folded into iconic portrayals obscures the competitions that artists entered into over how he would be portrayed. The relation between high and low culture appears in tense standoffs in these imaginings of Lincoln's face even as the impact of photography comes to dominate the visual field. As photographed, his face has become so familiar that the faces on the statues have to refer to it. The emphasis on the visual aspect of Lincoln that I want to bring into relation with his writing necessarily includes a look at the enduring language of his Gettysburg Address. In particular, I want to consider not only the way that the words on that occasion concern birth and death, but also the way that they invoke photography.

First, the address invokes birth. We all know the words. This nation was "conceived in liberty and dedicated to the proposition that all men are created equal." I want to add to these familiar words a perhaps unfamiliar question, drawing on my background as a feminist scholar of cultural norms: What kind of conception was this? That is, what figure, other than the founding fathers already invoked by the temporal notation with which Lincoln opens the address, might have conceived? Conception suggests that there might have been a woman somewhere giving birth to the nation whose birth is heralded in the address. Perhaps she is Liberty.

The process that led to the mention of conception in this address—the process that brought Lincoln on the train to Gettysburg immersed in the thoughts that became his short presentation in front of living mourners—emerges from the deaths that so painfully provided the occasion for the cemetery about to be dedicated. To remember the blood that had been spilled on the ground before the crowd is to enact the ache of losing those who were loved—but these deaths also enforce a loss of future possibilities for conception.

The second stressed term in the address is an acknowledgment of death. Lincoln famously and paradoxically, given the occasion, continues: "We

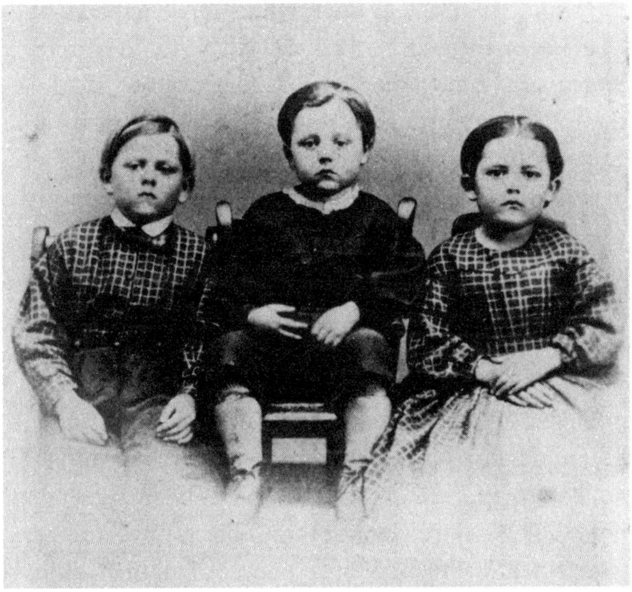

FIGURE 2.3. "Frank. Frederick. Alice,"1863. Photographic print on *carte de visite* mount, albumen. 4 in. × 2.5 in. (10.2 cm × 6.3 cm). Photograph of the children of Amos Huniston. Popularly known as "The Children of the Battlefield." Taylor & Brown Wenderoth. Courtesy of the Library of Congress.

cannot dedicate, we cannot consecrate this ground." The ground before the crowd holds bodies that have been excavated and reinterred, often with uncertain identification. Sometimes these bodies were looted to retrieve photographic images of the family members left behind, and sometimes these images were the only way that the body's identity could be traced. So, third, I want to consider the unmentioned business of identification through photography. Photography became a significant aspect of that battlefield, as with the story of the man whose photograph of three children was found on his body as he lay unremarked on the field of death (figure 2.3). Because newspapers could not then reproduce photographs, it was an engraving of the children that was disseminated; through the image of his children, they discovered his identity. The families that could not be reunited through such displays of visual identifications were those for whom the war was said to have been fought. Their reunifications waited for the newspaper columns that attempted to track dispersed loved ones after the war.[26]

What links these topics is the matter of how bodies and images could be reproduced. Some who were present that day report that the audience at Gettysburg could barely hear the remarks Lincoln made. The dissemination and effect of the address had everything to do with its reproduction in newspapers—newspapers that were consumed at home and that brought the war home through texts and images. The war at home had already happened in the town of Gettysburg: the town was occupied by combatants and then strewn with corpses. The townspeople were angry that they were commandeered to bury bodies. The smell of rotting bodies filled the streets.

Neither causality nor temporality can appear in an even-handed or immaculate way. For example, the operations of Protestant Christianity with respect to concepts of the state surely informs the extent to which Abraham Lincoln's death on Good Friday influenced the sense of him as a transcendent and redemptive president. To return to the impact of statues such as the *Standing Lincoln* is to ask: What is being remembered? Who is being mourned? When you look at these objects now, whether you know it or not, you look at the emotional responses of all the viewers who have come before you.

The Gettysburg Address emphatically asks its audience to think about what nation can be conceived in liberty. When the birth is announced in a site of death, what kind of consecration can be called down? This nation, said Lincoln, shall not perish from the earth. When the earth is saturated with the blood of those who have perished, the concept that you can find a principle "of the people, by the people, for the people," necessarily involves both life and death. As he gave the address, Lincoln stood in the land of the dead. Bodies that lay on Cemetery Ridge, on Little Round Top, and in the Peach Orchard, had just been buried. Bodies had been dug out of rocky soil to be posed for the photographers.

Alexander Gardner and the other members of Mathew Brady's photographic studio have been exposed as manipulating perspective on the images of bodies they produced. Because the same gun appears in more than one picture, it has become clear that they placed a rifle as a prop beside fallen bodies for the collection later published as *The Photographic Sketchbook of the Civil War*.[27] Of special note, since they have been so often reproduced, two key images from that collection show corpses on the field of battle from two different angles. In his commentary for the collection, Gardner writes about the bodies as though they fought on opposite sides. But which bodies are Union soldiers and which are Confederates? The photographer shifts ground and trains his lens on the same bodies from a different direction and calls them enemies of each other when they are instead the same bodies. That may be the point. In the Civil War cemetery in Elmira, New York, for instance, bodies are separated according to their political loyalties. Spectators could not have known, by looking at the bodies, stripped of identification, clothes, and shoes, what side they were on. Such an obsession with images appears in the recent discovery that there is a silhouette within a crowd photograph that has reliably been identified as the outline of Lincoln's head. Why do we care to see this visual evidence? What does it matter that the outline of Lincoln's head appears in the horizontal line of heads bobbing around in Gettysburg?

To stop and remember these elements of language, place, and history forms part of both the visual and the literary accounting for Abraham Lincoln. To tell this story of the Civil War—a story that merges loss, longing, and the formulations of history—the first president of Cornell, Andrew Dickson White, kept a scrapbook of newspaper clippings from the battles, now in the university archives. Such clipping activities, an enlarged version of the history kept by "writing with scissors," keep the war alive and immediate as daily news as well as reminding us of the recruitment posters and everyday domestic items, such as calls to make clothing for soldiers, that surrounded it.[28] To begin by asking about where, in the birth of freedom, were the mothers leads to a further question. What made this a constituent moment, to adapt a phrase from the political scientist Jason Frank?[29] The clarity with which Lincoln produced a sense of rightness for the occasions that drew crowds of people who were mourning or uncertain about the future includes phrases that have been repeated for more than 160 years. Looking at the relation of bodies to land, as these bodies were then lying so recently buried, I want to ask how, through the pain of childbirth, does one bring forth a nation?

Poetry and Memory

To reimagine the figure whose monumentality perversely makes him so difficult to see, it matters to return to the words. Lincoln appears throughout his life as a man who loved poetry. His attachment to poetic renderings was strong enough that he sent three versions of the same poem about his return to his childhood home to correspondents. In the three versions that he sent out, he first inserts a long middle section about a case of madness in his hometown, then cuts the section to make the poem more nostalgic, then adds it again. The insertion, retraction, and reinsertion make the section appear all the more powerful as a jarring presence in the place that he wants to call home. The madness of the figure that Lincoln inserts into the poem includes the detail that he attempts to take the life of his mother.

His explanation does not seem to clarify the need to tell the story as part of a story about home.

To end this chapter with a section on Lincoln's poetry is to encourage a memory of Lincoln as someone attached to poetry as well as to recall once again that Walt Whitman was inspired to write some of the greatest poems of mourning by the assassination of Lincoln. As early as 1838, Lincoln was eloquent about lynch mobs and the terrible violence along the Mississippi River. His comments include a lament about the destruction of printing presses. A poetry appears in his horror about mob violence; he says that dead men hanging from trees have formed a "drapery of the forest." At the same time, he names a man dragged from the streets of St. Louis, chained to a tree, and burned to death. Yes, says Lincoln, the man might have been sentenced to death if the mob had waited for the courts to try him for the murder of which he had been accused, but the "mobocratic spirit" makes it just as likely that innocent people will be killed. That possibility destroys the "attachment of the people" to the law and that is the end of democratic government. Lincoln is prepared to pledge "life, liberty" to protect the government.[30]

These allusions to epic poetry return us to the proclaimed investment in the story of the United States as an emergent nation that should be told in an epic form, a charge frequently made to poets in the early American republic. Interestingly, perhaps, the multitudinous narratives of the Civil War never produced a call for it to be told as an epic poem. Rather, in works like *Battle Pieces* and *Drum-Taps*, writers like Herman Melville and Walt Whitman, who elsewhere found material to engage within the longer genre of epics, found themselves engaged with brevity. The strength of their wartime lyrics may appear in the very formal limitations of short lines.

The poets and novelists who took on the Civil War embedded references to Lincoln at the background of the events they depicted. Only Whitman seems to have more or less obsessively identified Lincoln as the tragic figure at the center—for Whitman, Lincoln stood in for death even before his assassination. The deaths that Whitman observed in the field hospitals and in the gatherings of wounded men around Washington, DC, were punctuated by the sights of Lincoln in his carriage riding out to the Soldier's Home. For Whitman, the natural landscape, the flora and fauna of the United States, evoke the man who had emerged from the natural landscape. Like "Out of the Cradle Endlessly Rocking," the poem "When Lilacs Last in the Dooryard Bloom'd" echoes the song of a bird commemorating death. The residue of the assassination inspired many mourning poems in Walt Whitman, yet I find this one the most moving, as it articulates loss in the context of "battle corpses." Remembering the loss of the president, who is never named in the poem, becomes part of described natural events, such as the song of the thrush, and the unnatural work of mourning carried out by so many others. In the "long panoramas of visions" that Whitman sees, appear "the white skeletons of young men." These skeletons merge with the sights and sounds of the landscape after war.

For the mourning elegy "When Lilacs Last in the Dooryard Bloom'd," Whitman remembers April as the time for lilacs but also the loss of "him who I loved." As he ends the poem, "Lilac and star and bird" become "twined" with the "fragrant pines and the cedars dusk and dim."[31] This memory, this synesthetic version of a sight evoked by a smell, remains. Whitman evokes the hagiography that followed an assassination on Good Friday and the general sense of erasure attending the elision of Lincoln's flaws as he became identified with Christ. The idolatry that the poem's refrain insists on resonated for readers in the north.

But when considered by writers like Nathaniel Hawthorne, the politics of antislavery agitation were distasteful and the sight of the uncouth prairie president proved most distressing. When he traveled to Washington, DC, to view the president, a journey that he recapitulates in the original version of his essay "Chiefly about War Matters," Hawthorne calls him "Uncle Abe" and excoriates the oddity of his physical presence. Called to task by his publisher, James Fields, for his impertinence, Hawthorne retorts that to take out such familiarity is to lose something "very nice."[32]

For the orator and activist Frederick Douglass, to remember Lincoln in the years after his assassination is to remember him racially, as a "white man." When Douglass spoke to commemorate Lincoln at the dedication of the Emancipation Monument on April 14, 1876, he asserted that Lincoln "was preeminently the white man's President, entirely devoted to the welfare of white men. He was ready and willing at any time during the first years of his administration to deny, postpone, and sacrifice the rights of humanity in the colored people to promote the welfare of the white people of this country." Presenting a corrective to the view of Lincoln as the Great Emancipator, Douglass remembers somewhat bitterly that Lincoln "was willing to pursue, recapture, and send back the fugitive slave to his master." Much as it might be appropriate for white people to "sound his praises, to preserve and perpetuate his memory, to multiply his statues, to hang his pictures high upon your walls, and commend his example," it is nonetheless true, says Douglass, recapitulating slightly, that Lincoln "delivered us from a bondage, according to Jefferson, one hour of which was worse than ages of the oppression your fathers rose in rebellion to oppose."[33]

Some of the opposition expressed by Douglass had to do with the appearance of the *Emancipation Monument* statue, a duplicate of which has recently been removed from its pedestal in Boston. Sculpted by Thomas Ball, the statue triggered resentments in Douglass that have been echoed ever since. The drive to raise money for the statue was initiated by Charlotte Scott, formerly enslaved, but the model was a man named Archer Alexander.[34] Because Archer Alexander had emancipated himself, the pose of a kneeling man receiving Lincoln's benediction appeared not only unseemly, but inaccurate.[35]

As he goes on to eulogize him, however, Douglass turns to poetry. Remembering that Lincoln came from a background of hard labor, he continues, quoting from Thomas Hood's "The Lay of the Laborer": "A spade, a rake, a hoe, A pick-axe, or a bill; / A hook to reap, / a scythe to mow, / A flail, or what you will." Echoing the tools of hard labor and the language of poetry at once, Douglass finds that, although he is not the Black man's president, Lincoln was a man of his time.[36] Douglass has at once an astute memory of Lincoln as a white man who enacted the double task of ending slavery and preserving the Union and yet deep resentment for the world still dominated by white perceptions. Like Douglass's most famous address "What to the Slave Is the Fourth of July?" this eulogy contains a residue of bitterness as well as thoughtful appreciation.

In contrast, the woman who made dresses for the first lady of the White House, Elizabeth Keckley, remembered Lincoln with great fondness while she lamented the excessive mourning reactions of Mary Todd Lincoln. For Keckley, the "Moses of my people had fallen in his hour of triumph." Her memory of the speech Lincoln gave at the conclusion of the war evocatively presents the scene as a highly poetic analogy: "The swaying motion of the crowd, in the dim uncertain light, was like the rising and falling of billows—like the ebb and flow of the tide upon the stranded shore of the ocean." The sound from the crowd was "like the subdued sullen roar of an ocean storm, or the wind soughing through the dark lonely forest." Lincoln, like a Byronic hero, stands in the window of the White House, with "pale face and his soul flashing through his eyes."[37]

The sight that Keckley conjures replaces the historic conclusion of the war with a set of natural similes that seek to settle the violence of battle with the sound of the "roar of an ocean storm." To conclude this chapter by remembering Lincoln in relation to poetry is also to remember Lincoln's voice in relation to his poetic language. The man whose repeated references to the Declaration of Independence evoke "our lives, our fortunes, and our sacred honor" voiced words that continue to resonate, continue to evoke, continue to echo. After one hundred and fifty years, readers continue to watch and to listen. Reenacting the battle scenes, finding the widows and orphans, was to preoccupy Americans on either side of the war for many years to come. For Walt Whitman to reenact the war appeared through staging the eulogies he wrote for Abraham Lincoln. As the war recurs for him, the loss of all the young men, and the crisis of nationalism recurs. Looking at the landscape, Whitman sees bodies that have merged with the land; such corpses represent at once the past and the future. As he turned late in life to the rereadings of his own journals that appear in *Democratic Vistas*, Whitman imagines again the troops gathering, and he uses this vision to embrace and to rearticulate the visions of democracy with which he began his poetic career. Meditating on the dispersal of corpses through the landscape, Whitman announces that they have been incorporated with the land and are "Now to be found in every future grain of wheat or ear of corn, and every flower that grows, and every breath we draw."[38] The uneasy suggestion haunts this passage not only that each "ear of corn" set on the table for consumption has absorbed the dust of corpses but also that each intake of breath contains a residue of death.,

CHAPTER THREE

Democratic Mourning

LOUISA MAY ALCOTT, ELIZABETH STUART PHELPS, AND HARRIET BEECHER STOWE

Mourning

To witness the mourning that took place at home preoccupies this chapter as it looks at the work of women writers who consider slavery and war. The repercussions of how much the war becomes a personal matter of families appear, for example, in the witnessing performed by the semi-autobiographical nurse who narrates Louisa May Alcott's stirring story, "The Brothers" (1863). With a short detour into the sororal world of *Little Women* (1868), I also want to ask how the sentimental mourning for "little Eva" in Harriet Beecher Stowe's *Uncle Tom's Cabin* (1852) contrasts with the mourning for lost children in her more brutal novel *Dred* (1856). Wrenching depictions of mourning involving children lost to the brutality of slavery appear in the poetry of Frances Harper. The point to make with this literature, before turning to the stirring passions of Elizabeth Stuart Phelps in *The Gates Ajar* (1868), is that it identifies at once present and proleptic mourning, mourning for the ravages of slavery and the deaths caused by the ravages of slavery in advance of the mourning for the deaths that can be attributed to the war. Such mourning appears in writing across political as well as racial divisions. The sadness in the writing of Augusta Evans, for example, registers a different grief since she so definitely supported a Southern view of slavery. Nonetheless, her defiant writing exposes a passionate grief for the loss of an idealized South, whether she writes about Texas or describes loyalties closer to the Mason–Dixon line. Her work intriguingly mourns lost boundaries from the romanticism of Texas in *Inez* to the rallying cries for the South expressed by the women in *Macaria*.[1]

On the topic of women writers and the war, it is difficult to ignore the possibly apocryphal anecdote that Abraham Lincoln greeted Harriet Beecher Stowe as "the little woman who started this big war." That supposed "start" associates the Civil War with the tears shed over the deaths of *Uncle Tom's Cabin*; the tearful response becomes sometimes condensed to the assertion Stowe makes that readers need to learn to "feel right," a location in feelings that overlooks the difficult relocations that the novel develops. As Martha Schoolman has suggested, *Uncle Tom's Cabin* can be read as a story about geography, the geography of those escaping slavery as well as the landscape of those alternately chasing or protecting them.[2] The physical landscape can appear as a landscape of natural threats, such as the ice on the Ohio River that needs to be crossed.[3]

In Louisa May Alcott's *Little Women*, strong attention to disciplinary order as a formative and crucially Christian matter in the Civil War nation appears in the charitable deeds of the four March sisters. Celebrated for its portraits of sororal affection, with a mother who seeks to model their destiny on John Bunyan's *Pilgrim's Progress*, the novel depicts a resolution to emerge triumphant from the family, whether through writing, art, or marriage. For most of the first half of the book, the sisters are simply waiting, however complicated their activities become, to hear if their father has survived the war. In a novel about the home front, the domestic activities mostly partake in benevolence. Subversion and carnivalesque disruptions nonetheless dominate. Is there a gendered subversion as well? The desire to work, a desire that Alcott later built into her novel *Work: A Story of Experience* (1873), appears interlaced with the masculine soul in the woman's body that Jo March declares she possesses. In contrast, the children photographed in wartime Philadelphia playing around a tent clearly designed to resemble the temporary home of soldiers look somber. They are at play, but they wear the emblems of war (figure 3.1).

Hospital Sketches (1863), about her travel to Washington, DC, to work as a nurse, presents Alcott's account of her own war service. She begins with the fictional Tribulation Periwinkle, who has to struggle simply to leave Boston. Her ideals of independence are shaken since she needs a male protector just to secure a ticket for the free passage to which her proposed volunteer work entitles her. Tribulation's entry into handling the torn bodies of the soldiers who have arrived damaged by the Battle of Fredericksburg becomes her initiation into warfare. Having cleaned the mud and the blood from the bodies and fueled them, she engages with

FIGURE 3.1. Untitled. Photograph. 9 3/8 in. × 7 1/2 in. (24 cm × 19 cm). Attributed to Coonley & Wolfersberger. The playfulness of these children playing at war is undercut by the expressions on their faces. According to a staff member there, Coonley & Wolfersberger was a short-lived partnership between Jacob Frank Coonley and William A. Wolfersberger, who operated a studio together at 920 Chestnut Street in Philadelphia between 1862 and 1863. Courtesy of the Library Company of Philadelphia.

the activities that transfix Whitman in *Specimen Days*. After a slow start, she begins to find heroes. Especially moving is her account of the death of the man she calls John, a man whose body is left in state as a mark of respect when most are moved swiftly to what she calls the "dead house" for dissection.

The activity of caring for wounded soldiers who are likely to die involves both mourning and identification. That activity informs one of Alcott's best-known stories, included in *Hospital Sketches*, but also published separately as a fictionalized version of her nursing activity (1863).[4] Sent to watch over an ill man in a separate wing of the hospital, she finds his brother sitting in a tense vigil. To look at only one side of the face of this wounded man who she does not yet know as a brother is to see beauty; when he turns his head the scars appear. The binary appearance lines up with the way that these Southern brothers appear to act out and to exemplify two sides of the war. Linked now in a hospital room by both love and hatred, they will meet again at the famous doomed charge of the Massachusetts Fifty-Fourth. The nurse who observes them close at hand will only hear from a distance of their final encounter. Her visible empathy when she listens to his story leads the brother with the divided face to take her last name as his own before his fated encounter with his brother on the battlefield. The haunting in "The Brothers" is the haunted look of the face of this man, referred to as "contraband," but it's also the haunting of his wife Lucy, who has been seized by one brother from the other and who appears now as a ghost to stand over the man who has driven her to her death. He cries out, confirming his guilt to the listening brother in the other room: "I swore I'd whip the Devil out of her, and I did; but you know before she cut her throat she said she'd haunt me, and there she is!"[5] The violence of this haunting presages his death, implicitly punishment for the crime of slavery.

Alcott's laboring women, whether doing domestic work or nursing, appear on a class continuum somewhere between the hard physical work of Rebecca Harding Davis's "Life in the Iron Mills" (1861) and the enforced leisure of Charlotte Perkins Gilman's "The Yellow Wallpaper" (1892). Many stories in the postwar nonfiction book titled *Women of the War; Their Heroism and Self-Sacrifice* (1866) treat the work women did to organize nursing and supplies for male soldiers; the women featured in the book often come from the North and travel to the South or the West to provide support. The chapter titled "Loyal Southern Women," by contrast, discusses what it was like for women to live in the South and support the North. Typically, in households decimated by enrollment in one army or the other, there would be no man remaining for either labor or family relations. This chapter discusses the search for plunder, the slaughter of chickens and other livestock, and the resourcefulness of such women, including one who confiscated the guns of inebriated Confederate soldiers and marched them off as prisoners.[6] The book also considers the category of cross-dressing women, in a chapter titled "Women as Soldiers." Some are shown to enlist from loyalty, but the action and the cause are treated with a fair amount of unsurprise. We are told that cross-dressing occurred during "all periods of the war," that such women were "fighting as common soldiers," and that motives were often "unknown." Some, the writer concedes, went from a "pure love of romance and adventure." Others had "a mental hallucination that victory and deliverance would come to the war-burdened land only by the sacrifice of their lives." A particular instance appears of a "destiny" felt by a "young lady of Brooklyn, New York, who was killed at the battle of Chickamauga" because she thought of herself as "an American Joan of Arc."[7]

A more extraordinary account forms the titular subject of *Unsexed; or, The Female Soldier, The Thrilling Adventures, Experiences, and Escapes of a Woman, as Nurse, Spy, and Scout, in Hospitals, Camps, and Battle-fields* (1864). Presented as the true-life adventures of S. Emma E. Edmonds, the account, illustrated with a number of engravings, details disguise as a "female contraband" and an ambivalent white Southern soldier.[8] The author, who had already been passing as a man before the war, delights in fooling Northerners as well as Southerners. Dedicated to the "Sick and Wounded Soldiers of the Army of the Potomac," the volume was published while the war's outcome was still undecided.

Southern women also served as soldiers. One of the best-known remaining accounts is that of Loreta Velazquez, who served as Harry Buford. Unlike the account of Emma Edmonds, who managed to receive a pension for her service and is the only woman listed as a veteran of the Great Army of the Republic, the story of Loreta Velazquez remains controversial. Still, the extraordinary feats that both women recount seem to have a basis in their own physical ability not only to carry out, or at least counterfeit, the deeds of a soldier but also to write movingly about the grim details of war. Probably some skepticism is still in order. For example, Edmonds repeats that a "Southern clergyman" saw "Yankee skulls" for sale and explains that "it is a common thing to see rebel women wear rings and ornaments made of our soldiers' bones."[9] The conversion of bodies into implements appears unnervingly in comments about turning the bones of soldiers into drinking cups. The conversion of bones into stones might be a metaphor rather than a "common thing," but the overlap between domestic duties and the transformation of women into soldiers conveys the unsettling loss of relation between home and battlefield.[10]

In paying such attention to the lighter side of personification, metaphor, and subversion, I do not mean to express indifference to the grim details of battle. Mourning and war go together. Descriptions of and attention to the landscape do not erase the presence of the bodies of men, women, and sometimes children whose lives ended in particular locations, often obscurely and in numbers too large to resonate with the public in the same way as the tragedy of a single loss, such as the death of the young Tad Lincoln. Not only in Whitman's poetry, but also in the recollections of Elizabeth Keckley, who made dresses for Mary Todd Lincoln, and then wrote of the failed attempts to sell them in New York after the assassination, remembrances return to the sense of loss and reclamation of national vision through particular moments of grief. In her memoir, Keckley passes quickly by the death of her own son, but she lingers on the losses suffered by Abraham Lincoln when his sons died. Lincoln's words of mourning and reconciliation fused his own particular sadness with the multitudes of battlefield deaths.

After the war, many writers portrayed it as a terrible atonement for the sin of slavery, itself a nationally sanctioned crime against families. From the time of abolitionist agitation before the war, the Southerner Angelina Grimke, who had grown up with Southern slavery, wrote the passionate "Appeal to the Christian Women of the South." In its attention to Christianity as a rebuttal of the proslavery justification from the Bible, the work begins with Adam, turns from Genesis to later examples, and then asks, "*do the fathers of the South ever sell their daughters?*" (italics in the original). She answers, "my heart beats and my hand trembles, as I write the awful affirmative, Yes!"[11] Turning family members into commercial artifacts in a sexualized system of bondage belies the great attention to family ties that both Northern and Southern writers celebrated.

The task of identifying corpses after battles brought public attention to the combination of grief and family separation. One of the most famous examples was on the field at Gettysburg where, in the melodramatic language of the day, "a Union soldier was found in a secluded spot on the battlefield, where, wounded, he had laid himself down to die. In his hands, tightly clasped, was an ambrotype containing the portraits of three small children . . . and as he silently gazed upon them his soul died. How touching! How solemn! . . . It is earnestly desired that all papers in the country will draw attention to the discovery of this picture . . . so that, if possible, the family of the dead hero may come into possession of it. Of what inestimable value will it be to these children, proving, as it does, that the last thought of their dying father was for them, and them only."[12] The engraving made from the photograph was widely distributed in newspapers and reached the small town where his wife discovered she was a widow by seeing the image (see figure 2.3).

Border Wars

The relation between home fronts and battlefields infused the texture of one of the most beloved postbellum novels. The love that it addresses appears cloaked in the drama of an encounter between two women, one of whom declares, "I will make her so much at home in my house that she shall not remember that it is not her own" (*The Gates Ajar*, 65). Published after the last battles of the Civil War and in the wake of the tragedy of Lincoln's assassination, the best-selling first novel by Elizabeth Stuart Phelps, *The Gates Ajar*, tells a tale remarkable for its stillness. At the beginning of the novel, the narrator, Mary, spends her time as a chronicler of grief. Her brother John has recently been killed on the battlefield and the consolations offered by the members of her small New England town appear to her muted and inadequate. Not until the appearance of her dead mother's sister Winifred, herself a widow, does she find comfort. In her arms, literally and figuratively, Mary can imagine heaven.

That consolation is at once thwarted and confirmed at the novel's close when Winifred also dies, leaving the narrator as a substitute mother for Winifred's orphaned child, not very subtly named Faith. The story that the novel tells, insofar as it is a story rather than simply a meditation on grief and faith, consists mainly of conversations between two women who are the last remaining adults of their family. The popularity of a tale of finding faith in the face of a violently diminished family might stem directly from the similar situation of its audience. In the wake of the war, nearly every family in the newly reconstituted United States had been diminished by violence. It seems not at all surprising that readers sought consolation.

The novel's popularity was such that any subsequent novel published by Phelps that contained the word "gates" was sure to sell.[13] She wrote, among others, *Beyond the Gates* (1883), *The Gates Between* (1887), and *Within the Gates* (1901). While these novels absorbed postbellum tears, her most admired novel today is *The Story of Avis* (1877) a tale loosely based on her mother's marriage.[14] Her mother, named Elizabeth Stuart Phelps, also a writer, had named her Mary. Only a child when her mother died, she renamed herself in her mother's honor, and went on to publish under that name. Such cross-identifications with the name of the author's deceased mother and the name her mother gave her reappear in the novel. The narrator's name is Mary.[15]

This section focuses at once on the underrecognized role of Kansas as a place of tragedy within the novel and on the way that women's affection for each other affects the novel's strong proposal that life after death will provide a sense of home.[16] Far from placing the geographical location of Kansas at the center of the novel's emotional territory, I want to assert that the violence associated with Kansas was a significant enough fact for nineteenth-century progressive readers that Phelps had no need to elaborate on its significance. And, although the novel's action occurs in an unnamed domestic location, mostly confined to the space of one house in a small New England town, the place of Kansas in its events makes the location of loss a place to the west rather than any battlefield in the southern United States.

Directly or indirectly because of losses suffered in the American Civil War, women in this best-selling postbellum sentimental novel confront the boundary between heaven and earth as they cling to each other. Mourning lost loved ones, they live in an emotional border territory. The emotional territory of the novel alludes to and sometimes metaphorically resembles the violent skirmishes and deadly betrayals occurring in border territories between Missouri and Kansas as the newly formed states fought about slavery, a physical boundary crossed by the novel's supporting character and her daughter Grace as they return to the novel's eastern location. Crossing that boundary, the characters in the novel substitute the violence in Kansas for the violence of slavery while they substitute each other's bodies for the bodies they have lost in the Civil War.

This argument follows two chains of substitution. With the first substitution, the novel invokes forms of violence in Kansas connected with the westward expansion of national boundaries to stand in for the violence of slavery—that is, both the violence involved in the practice of slavery and the violence associated with the westward expansion into Kansas. Such violence in the West involved the failed desire for an unbroken antebellum nation. In the second substitution, the narrator's aunt Winifred stands in, via forms of intimacy that seem to allude to incestuous sister–brother desire, for the narrator's never-to-be-arrived-at husband. Having lived through the historical tragedy of Quantrill's raid on Lawrence, Kansas, Winifred forms the link between the two chains. In the novel, Winifred subsumes the narrator's grief as she comes to stand in for any woman who's been affected by the violence of the war. Insofar as her presence in the novel with her daughter Faith performs an allegory, in addition to her religious teachings, Winifred brings peace to the narrator. The narrator's grief over her death suggests a national lesson: Winifred's death from cancer alludes to the cancer of slavery that killed the antebellum body politic, but her child Faith lives.

The question remains: Does that put heteronormativity and the structure of slavery in the antebellum nation in the same position? The new nation, after one more substitution (Faith for Winifred), is structured by a maternal bond and the absence of men. To orient this emotional energy along the east–west axis rather than the north–south axis is to recognize that while the legislative moves connected with westward expansion might be seen as the cause of the war; the extension of slavery westward was the logic of its own undoing. So the novel performs, in a register interwoven with its attention to a vision of the afterlife as a natural mirror of rural happiness, a national mourning connected to westward expansion.

Because it is precipitated by an arrival from Kansas, the novel's primary relationship, the courtship of two women, invokes the violent extension of the nation's boundaries.[17] Implicitly, the extension of national boundaries becomes a crisis about what forms of family can exist on the frontier. The allusions to the violence in Lawrence, Kansas, that precipitated the move back east for the narrator's aunt Winifred involve a violence at the nation's boundary and a proposed extension of that boundary directly related to the novel's core emotional relationship. The arrival in the home of this widow and her daughter escaping the violence in Kansas silently invokes the lingering doubts cast by debates over the Kansas–Nebraska Act.

Violence in Kansas

The Kansas–Nebraska Act has received a great deal of attention from historians as the unraveling of the balance between free and slave states articulated in the earlier Missouri Compromise of 1820, an unraveling that led more or less directly to the Civil War, but it may be considered to be more invisible for literary critics because there exist few performances of its implications in literary terms. The best language associated with the crisis occasioned by admitting both Kansas and Nebraska as states may appear in the debates between Abraham Lincoln and Stephen Douglas as they competed for a seat in the US Senate. For all that Lincoln has been considered as a politician whose resistance to slavery evolved fairly slowly, his statements about the extension of slavery into Kansas resonate today.[18]

The outrage that Lincoln expressed concerned the sense of a broken promise about the boundary between slave and free states that was first enacted by the admission of the state of Maine into the Union; this was a legal arrangement at the federal level that sought a balance between states that legalized or prohibited slavery, resulting in the agreement known as the Missouri Compromise. The broken promise concerned an artificial symmetry between slaveholding and nonslaveholding states; the resistance involved visible bloodshed, to the extent that senators emerged with bloody heads from the floors of the senate.[19] The damaging effects of the Kansas–Nebraska Act, an act proposed by Lincoln's rival Stephen Douglas, included gang violence in reaction to how it marred the concept of a national balance, termed a compromise from the start, and especially to how it legislated boundary expansion and the extension of the practice of slavery into new territories. In the earlier Missouri Compromise, slavery in the new territory "shall be, and is hereby, forever prohibited." All the words in that declaration became suspect after the Kansas–Nebraska Act. The linguistic move from "shall be" to "is" holds in suspension a process of becoming free that the language of "forever prohibited" seems to contradict.[20] For Stephen Douglas, the principle of "popular sovereignty" represented an apparently democratic appeal to "States' rights" that made the issue of determining the extension of slavery a simple matter of arithmetic. Understanding that numbers mattered, and goaded by broadside and newspaper reports, settlers stampeded Kansas to stake out claims that supported either abolition or slavery. Controversial abolitionists like John Brown traveled to Kansas armed to fight what became the skirmishes of guerilla warfare precisely because of the appeal of exerting the rights of a citizen to oppose slavery. The principles were sound; the practices were bloody and fed by the shipping of what were colloquially known as "Beecher's Bibles," guns provided by Christian resistance organizations.[21]

The armed insurrections that fueled the violence in Kansas between 1854 and 1861 led to its being termed "Bleeding Kansas." The literal shedding of blood presaged the bloodshed that would prevail across the eastern half of the United States from 1861 to 1865. Little considered in terms of cultural memory is how much the border warfare in Kansas became sanctioned by the federal government. Not only were the "border ruffians" later commissioned as loosely designated official soldiers by both the Confederate army and the Union army, the acts of retaliation that spilled across the Mississippi were rarely addressed as criminal acts. The criminal acts that took place continued after the war and led to the formation of notorious groups such as that headed by the outlaw Jesse James.[22] Some of these same outlaws, including the James brothers, were present at the massacre to which *The Gates Ajar* alludes, a massacre that took place at Lawrence, Kansas, in 1863.

The guerilla warfare on the western frontier does not usually appear in discussions of Civil War battles, a place more often occupied by Gettysburg, Chancellorsville, or the Wilderness. Nor do we consider, when we consider a nineteenth-century American town, the drama of a group of 450 ruffians riding into town, lining up the men and boys, shooting them, and then burning down their houses, outside of the dusty drama of a spaghetti western (figure 3.2).[23] But these violent threats to home, and especially to women at home, were very much the war experience in Kansas and Missouri. Several pictorial representations, though no photographs, have survived of the violence directed at women. A disturbing version appears in reaction to the violence of the 1850s as *Liberty, the Fair Maid of Kansas in the Hands of the "Border Ruffians"* (1856). In this suggestive cartoon, as Liberty begs for mercy, a "ruffian" laughs. This political cartoon blames the Democratic presidential candidate Franklin Pierce for outrages against women and against democracy. Pierce has been identified as the central figure. On the right, the scalping carried out apparently refers to the historical scalping carried out by white men against each other in an awful imitation of frontier behavior. Within the savage caricature of violence against a female figure who stands for both liberty and America, it matters to remember that the Republican party, from which Lincoln was elected in the next cycle, was what we now think of as the Democratic party and had a moderately abolitionist platform.

In the margin at the top of the frame in this cartoon, essentially too tiny to read, but significant, appear these captions, reading from left to right. First, a bedraggled figure of a woman stands in front of a burning house and says, "Come husband let us go to heaven where our poor children are." An armed man standing beside her says "Ho! ho! She thinks I'm her husband, we scalped the Cus and she like a D__m fool went Crazy on it, and now she wants me to go to heaven with her, ha! ha! ha!" The figure identified as James Buchanan, stealing a pocket watch from a prone dead man, says, "T'was yours once but its mine now, 'Might Makes Right,' dont it." His left hand grips the man's throat while his right holds the watch high. The man identified as Pierce (misspelled here) gloats drunkenly over the kneeling figure of Liberty, complete with Phrygian cap. Responding to the incantation of "might makes right," he slurs his words as he says, "you may bet yer life on that, ole Puddin head. Come Sis . . . sy, you go along wid me, I'le take Good care of you (hic) over the left." His left foot steps on the US flag draped over Liberty's shoulders and his left hand holds a flask. The figure of Liberty cries "O SPARE ME GENTLEMEN, SPARE ME!!" The man labeled as Lewis Cass holds a rifle barrel suggestively over the kneeling figure of Liberty and says, "Poor little Dear, We wouldn't hurt her for the world, would we Frank?" In case viewers miss the point, he concludes in a burst of repetitive laughter: "ha! ha! ha! he! he! he! ho! ho! ho!" Finally, Douglas's words appear just above a silhouette of fleeing covered wagons: "Hurrah for our side! Victory! Victory! 'WE WILL SUBDUE THEM YET.'"[24]

FIGURE 3.2. *Liberty: The Fair Maid of Kansas—in the Hands of the "Border Ruffians,"* 1856. Lithograph on wove paper. 8.3 in. × 15 in. (21 cm × 38 cm). Drawn by John L. Magee. The conflation of the "fair maid of Kansas" with the traditional iconography of Columbia, complete with the Phrygian cap and the cloak of the national flag, make the violent assault into a vivid transgression against the county. To include the detail of scalping farmers along with the implied rape of the symbolic women is to make sure the viewer understands multiple violations. Used by permission of the National Museum of American History.

The story of Quantrill's Raiders changes according to the teller since their exploits were considered simultaneously as heroic for the South and villainous for the North.[25] The attack on families in Lawrence, Kansas, appears as a disturbing aspect of Civil War violence. More significantly, the hidden story of what happened to the women in that town remains underspecified. The Confederate Congress passed a law in 1862, known as the Partisan Ranger Law, that authorized what had been outlaw activities, including murder. Quantrill was a well enough known bandit that he was not authorized to act under it, but he claimed license nonetheless. When engaged with federal troops, Quantrill's Raiders were reported to castrate and even to scalp their male victims. Left untold is the story of their treatment of female victims, but the implications are vividly present in contemporary political cartoons that show women struggling in the arms of bandits.

As they formed a different kind of challenge to what it meant to have a home, I am considering these stories in juxtaposition to the domestic drama of *The Gates Ajar* for the very obvious reason that this violence compels the widow and her child to move into the narrator's eastern home, doubling the impact of emotional displacement caused by battlefields to the south and the west. As a newspaper headline of the time stated: "THE LAWRENCE MASSACRE BY A BAND OF MISSOURI RUFFIANS UNDER QUANTRELL; AUGUST 21, 1863; 150 MEN KILLED EIGHTY WOMEN MADE WIDOWS AND 250 CHILDREN MADE ORPHANS."[26] The emphasis on widows and orphans leads me back to *The Gates Ajar*. I want to raise the question of how the concept of substitution may invoke how the violence, including the sexual violence, of Quantrill's raid, invokes or makes possible the queer desire and the quasi-incestuous longings that the novel expresses.

Within *The Gates Ajar*, the events that have brought Mary's aunt Winifred to her doorstep begin with her presence in Kansas. Winifred has lived through the horrors of "Quantrell's raid" in Lawrence, Kansas.[27] Because of the guerilla nature of this antebellum warfare, it becomes possible to think of Winifred's husband, John, who has been a Christian missionary to Kansas and then died of an unspecified disease, as an early victim of Civil War violence on the western frontier. Not only has his health been affected by the raid on Kansas, but also his death by disease invokes the detail that many casualties of the Civil War died of disease. The death toll from the battlefield includes the movements of populations that introduced disease along with violence. Like the death of young Willie Lincoln of typhoid because of the waters of the Potomac River, many so-called civilians died from tainted waters because they lived near battlefields and massive encampments. The debris of such frontier violence becomes the subtext of these narratives.

Mourning and Substitution

The Gates Ajar does not explain the entire political struggle that led to the violence in Lawrence, Kansas, but it does specifically reference that violence; the main character's loving companion, her aunt Winifred, has gone to Kansas as if to a foreign country to help in a missionary assignment. Her appearance in the household of the mourning narrator, Mary, brings together two women who mourn the loss of men, but it might also be seen to presage a shift in emotional attachment from men to women. The proliferation of death that forms the back story for the novel has taken place away from home, on an unseen battlefield, leaving mourners to remain at home. To mourn is to live on the border between life and death. To see life in the world beyond death, within the world of the novel, relies on a Christian vision of life and death. But I want to propose here that the disrupting violence in Kansas that has precipitated many of the novel's key events permeates the vision of Christian hope with a hidden agenda about the westward expansion of the nation's boundaries as well as an act of occlusion or displacement about the matter of slavery.

Mary spends the first part of the novel in mourning for the loss of her dead soldier brother, Royal, the only remaining member of her immediate family, while declaring her certainty that her future will contain no children. In the closing off of futures, nonfunctional heterosexuality fuses with the loss of future reproductive possibility to make women bond with other women—and with orphans. Remanufactured families obsess the narrator, whose parents died long before her brother was killed in the Civil War. The disruption of her expectations that occurs with Winifred's arrival involves a renaming of her emotional connections and a remapping of familial norms.

The effects of haunting, violence, and redemption in this novel have a precursor in the religious invocations of Susan B. Warner's *The Wide, Wide World* (1850), an earlier best-selling novel about death in the family in which Ellen Montgomery loses her mother and must find new attachments through attention to Christianity. Like *The Gates Ajar* (1868), that novel opens with women waiting in a room and with the domestic scenes of cooking. Attention to lessons from the Bible appear at first significant in the way that conscience works at the edge of consciousness. Ellen Montgomery, the daughter who loses her mother and mourns, must learn lessons from an attractive older woman who seems possessed of an enormous library in terms of citation and reference. Many of these lessons are about patience and about mourning lost objects. Ellen first feels as though her grief will "rend soul and body in twain." As her mother lies dying, she insists that "though we *must* sorrow, we must not rebel." The lessons, drawn from the Bible and from Milton, seem designed to produce more patient women, but perhaps paradoxically also more learned women.[28] As Mary says of Winifred in *The Gates Ajar*, she is a "woman who knows something about fate [and] free-will . . . who is not ignorant of politics, and talks intelligently of Agassiz's latest fossil, who can understand a German quotation, and has heard of Strauss . . ." (67).

In *The Gates Ajar*, the novel's attention to a consciousness that cannot bear its object—specifically the work of mourning—literally describes what lies at the edge of the Civil War. This physical and metaphysical challenge becomes the challenge of how to inhabit simultaneously a place in a heterosexual normative order and the "new normal" of a world of women. The matter of reproduction in heavenly terms is the matter of another life beyond the body. After forming a new domestic unit with her mother's younger sister, who has survived the terrible violence of the raid on Lawrence, Kansas, only to succumb to illness, the narrator is left to perform the role of a mother to her cousin Faith, named by her dying father to bring hope to her now dead mother. The novel links the reforming, or public, identities that Christianity provided in accounts of slavery with the private domestic lives that mourning women could live, producing a postwar combination of mourning and a life lived "doubly" on heaven and on earth.

The substitution that the novel enacts has the dead mother's sister take the place of the dead brother who has previously substituted for dead parents and proleptically taken the place of a never-to-be found husband. The dead mother's sister's child has been named Faith to emphasize her redemptive positioning when her father dies, leaving her mother adrift in the wake of the border warfare in Kansas. Faith becomes the crossing point of the chiasmus of biological ties and erotic connections, substituting her small body for the lost body of her own mother who has been substituting for the body of Mary's lost brother.

To consider the forms of erasure in fiction set in a historical place that draws on a tragedy only seen out of the corner of the eye is not therefore to claim that the search for historical origins is the most important trace, but rather that the search for erasure can lead to gestures of substitution that are themselves significant. Critical commentary on concepts and theories of substitution has relied on Joseph Roach, in *Cities of the Dead,* who talks about substitution in ideas about performance. Roach cites Homi Bhabha on mimicry as "at once resemblance and menace"; performances "raise the possibility of the replacement of the authors of the representations by those whom they imagined into existence as their definitive opposites."[29]

The convolution of prepositional phrases here at once masks and reveals the kind of substitution that intrigues Roach. What agent and what action might be called onto the playing field becomes obscured—and yet the obscurantist action of performing substitution becomes the point. Roach proposes, "That is why the surrogated double so often appears as alien to the culture that reproduces it and that it reproduces. That is why the relentless search for the purity of origins is a voyage not of discovery but of erasure."[30] Adding to the novel's rewriting of domestic happiness, the narrator mourns the loss of her brother who has substituted both for the past loss of their parents and for her unexplained resistance to having a future family. Her desire for him implies incestuous longing, but the presence and the loss of a loved family member are reenacted by the substitutions carried out by her aunt's body.[31]

In thinking about how substitution can work, I am drawing on Rebecca Schneider's work in *Performing Remains: Art and War in Times of Theatrical Reenactment*. Schneider cites Elizabeth Freeman on the compulsions of repetition and queer identification and asserts that "mimesis, theatricality, imitation, simulation, the copy, the double, and the fake cross and confuse each other."[32] That is, in thinking about substitutions, I acknowledge the difficult ways in which religion and war stand in for gestures of desire in this fiction as in others. And in performing a sort of pilgrim's progress, in novels from *The Wide, Wide World* through Louisa May Alcott's *Little Women* and *The Gates Ajar*, women's fiction takes advantage of the teleology of religion to move women toward each other. Unpacking the possibilities that performance might bring onto the stage of this novel, a queer and possibly incestuous doubling appears that accompanies religious instruction.

Within the world of *The Gates Ajar*, for example, Mary sits on the lap of her mother's sister and puts her arms around her neck when she asks her to move into the house. Placing herself in the position of both a child and a lover, she performs a substitution where her body at once takes the place of the daughter Faith and enacts a substitution for the beloved. The discipline that encourages an intimate relation to religion in all three of the novels that focus on grieving and loss in the mid-nineteenth-century United States (*The Wide, Wide World*, *Little Women*, and *The Gates Ajar*) involves a relationship with a spiritual woman who is strongly loved and then lost. The intimacy of the relation is at once nicely enhanced and deflected through death. What has been erased in order to make this double substitution occur are the bodies of the brother and sometimes the husband who might otherwise be positioned in such physical intimacy. What has also been erased in *The Gates Ajar* are allusions to the struggle over slavery long associated with the violence in Kansas.

Scenes of Writing

The opening pages of *The Gates Ajar* appear written as a journal in a house where a woman feels confined; these pages show scenes of a woman writing. The narrator is preoccupied with the question, as in Charlotte Perkins Gilman's iconic short story "The Yellow Wallpaper": where can she find the paper to write on?[33] As the work of women performed in a domestic space, the act of writing is interrupted by a reminder of housekeeping, even as the novel reminds us that she is not doing the housekeeping because her class position enables her to have help. The place of the domestic servant who enters to scold her away from her writing and encourage her to come to dinner recurs in *The Gates Ajar* as it does in other women's fiction, such as Fanny Fern's earlier novel about a woman who encounters many difficulties (especially from the clamor of hungry children) as she begins to write, *Ruth Hall* (1850). In *The Gates Ajar*, the narrator is told to "Put away them papers and come right along!" (5). Her first visitor invites her to come and sew, alluding at once to the wartime contributions of women in the so-called Sanitary Commission and the expectations of separate spheres activities. The intersection of public and private writing appears in the dating of entries as though she were simply writing a journal.

The novel's first section does not provide a date at the top. Instead the narrator indicates that, as of the 21st of February, "The house feels like a prison. I walk up and down and wonder that I ever called it home" (2). Attention to how to name location gives way to the visceral effects of language: "Those two words—'Shot dead'—shut me up and walled me in, as I think people must feel shut up and walled in, in Hell" (4). As the narrator describes the confusion between a confinement at home and the more insubstantial rendering of being sent to hell, the auditory effects imply a different meaning for confinement. The first pages of the novel describe the sensation of spending life alienated in a home in a village where children laugh in the streets. The intrusion of this laughter produces pain, but may proleptically introduce the intrusion of children.

The narrator recalls a winter day where she returns from a walk to the post office; she describes the joy that she feels in reading a letter she found there from her brother Roy who has been away fighting as a soldier for so long that "they" have told her that she should have expected the news that has just come by telegram. The news brought by the telegram cancels the joy of the letter; the telegraphed words have paralyzed her. She speaks of the paralysis as she opens with the scene of writing, finding a notebook in a drawer that she now fills with words. Writing her own words serves to rewrite the words that have confined her.

As the narrator first describes it, she writes to recover from a blow. She explains, "A solid blow has in itself the elements of its rebound; it arouses the antagonisms of the life on which it falls; its relief is the relief of a combat." The writing that she does has a resistance and pressure: "Perhaps I write excitedly and hardly. I feel excited and hard" (6). The hardness and excitation that she feels in this parallel, yet chiasmatic structuring of emotion and writing, makes writing into a container for emotion.

Named Mary Cabot, the narrator calls her brother Roy, short for Royal. As she describes the life that has led to this encounter with her brother's death, an oddity appears, she recognizes, in being so close to her brother that she doesn't think about possibly wanting a husband in the future. Without explaining, she says, "That was settled so long ago. . . . Roy was all there was" (8). She quotes from Elizabeth Barrett Browning: "God keeps a niche / In Heaven to hold our idols" (21). This quotation reinforces the sense that the bond with her brother is that of lovers and that the appearance of her mother's sister will provide a substitute in more than one way.

Winifred Forceythe, her (dead) mother's youngest sister, writes to her from Kansas a letter dated the same day that she begins writing. The strange coincidence encourages the reader to look for parallels in their acts of reading and writing. When they first begin living together, the narrator and her aunt read Charles Lamb's "Elia" (33) and the essay "Dream Children," with its "pathos and symmetry" (35).[34] Charles Lamb and his sister lived together; their closeness persisted in the wake of the tragedy that she had stabbed their mother to death. This detail is never alluded to in *The Gates Ajar*; quite possibly Phelps expected her well-educated readers to know the allusion not only to the work but also to this grim aspect of the biography. In providing the allusion, given the frequent articulation of such references, she might want readers to understand that behind the scenes is an account of another brother and sister who lived together after the death of parents, however ambiguously presented in terms of causality. If I am to consider the semi-outrageous implications that death makes incest possible then I would look at the symmetry where Mary has lost her brother and Winifred has lost her husband, losses that make it possible for them to cling to each other's bodies.

When her aunt arrives, Mary finds that she has brought her daughter, a young girl named Faith (40). Contemplating the change in her household, she says "Take her altogether, I like to look at her" (42). Faith is three years old, a "round, rolling, rollicking little piece of mischief" (42). As the women become acquainted, they talk about "the surrenders and the assassination" (43). With the arrival of this sympathetic auditor, Mary can cry for the first time since her brother's death. The reference to "the surrenders and the assassination," not elaborated on, places the arrival in the summer of 1865, after Appomattox and the Ford's Theatre killing of Abraham Lincoln. Lincoln is not named here, at once because the assassination has happened so recently that readers of the novel will not need reminding and, possibly, as though the naming of the president who was killed on Good Friday is still too close to a sacred invocation. Mary's tears enable her to reflect; she says to her aunt, "It is just as if a great black gate had swung to and barred out the future" (50). The related implication in the title is how to resist this gate, how to have a gate "ajar," or how to open a gate to the future. To write the gate into existence becomes an act of researching spiritual beliefs as well as physically inhabiting a metaphor.

The Sensuous Afterlife

As Mary describes how she first asks her aunt to come and live with her, she explains that she sits in her lap "and I put my arms about her neck" (62). What this new union forms remains unclear since the terms evolve from the situation. She embraces and resists the naming of the relationship: "I am not 'a family,'" protests Mary (63). As she explores "this new promise of home," Mary asserts an odd combination of belonging and amnesia: "I will make her so much at home in my house that she shall not remember that it is not her own" (65). The containing unit of the "house" becomes the boundary for an act of will ("I will make her") that is designed to erase a past home ("she shall not remember that it is not her own"). The inaugural act of sitting in her aunt's lap at once suggests a persistence of maternal attachment from mother to aunt and an erotic performance of desired intimacy.[35]

The further container or boundary for this new intimacy of "home" is the small town in which Mary has her house. The inadequacy of the town and the intrusion of the town's concept of emotional attachments and religious beliefs emerge repeatedly. After her brother's death, Mary notes that she cannot be comforted and explains that various members of the town have come to tell her how to feel. The appropriately named Deacon Quirk, for example, asks why she hasn't been to church and then looks at her as if at a "Mormon or a Hottentot" (16). This very odd pairing, emphasizing an alien identity, prevails in the substitutions and pairings extending to the analogies used between humans and animals. The strangeness applied to domestic objects, or domestic objects made strange, appears in the sermon Mary attends, with its "speculation as to whether Maltese kittens were mulattoes." The racism here at once extends across human and animal lines and indicates confusion about what country is invoked. She is "bewildered and disheartened" by the sermon because it makes heaven out to be an abstract place where one meditates on the goodness of God (44). According to such a creed, members of the town should "subdue . . . earthly affections to God" (45).

Such a subjugation of earthly desires and attachments, for the narrator, is not at all that she wants: "Going hungry, hopeless, blinded, I came back empty, uncomforted, groping" (45–46). Responding to Mary's groping for comfort, Winifred supplies an intimacy in terms at once physical and spiritual, a private form of affiliation for a narrator who needs to feel that the idea of relationship is valued. For Winifred, "wherever the Bible touches the subject, it premises our individuality" (50). That individuality offers a specific attachment that is both physical and spiritual.

The narrator says, "I never supposed before that God would let anyone laugh in heaven" but this supposition is followed immediately, and perhaps oddly, with an allusion to the recent death of someone who was widely known as a practical joker, the president of the United States, when she muses, "I wonder if Roy has seen the President" (52). Her aunt tells her that Roy is "*only out of sight*" and that in the unseen place he inhabits, he must still love her (87). Winifred insists on not only an emotional but also a physical life after death: "To love must mean to think of, to care for, to hope for, to pray for, not less out of a body than in it" (55). Her assurances lead to a long discussion on whether life beyond the grave is embodied or disembodied. "Disembodied?" asks Mary. "I do not think so," replies her aunt. Invoking the Resurrection of Christ, she continues, "All the *tendency* of Revelation is to show that an embodied state is superior to a disembodied one" (113). Her preaching becomes increasingly mystical—and mystifying—until it becomes almost a challenge to established Christian doctrine. Certainly within the world of the novel Winifred's sermons offer a provocative challenge to the preaching of the town minister, Mr. Bland. Speaking of life after death, she asserts, "I suspect that we have some sort of body immediately after passing out of this, but that there is to come a mysterious change, equivalent, perhaps, to a re-embodiment, when our capacities for action will be greatly improved" (114). As she draws further away from the minister's sermon, Winifred's lessons begin to sound like the defiance of Anne Hutchinson.[36] In her view, possibly, the concept of a capacity for action that will be "greatly improved" involves an ambiguous reembodiment.

Developing her explanation of the afterlife, Winifred does not think bodies will be the same on heaven as on earth, for reasons "tedious to specify" (114). Her first example is anything but tedious. Drawing on an exotic combination that serves as a reminder that the New England they inhabit contains missionaries who have returned with tales of other beliefs, Winifred laughs at the option of a "Hottentot" cannibal resurrected within the body of another "Hottentot" who has consumed it. She proposes the concept of the Mohammedan "little bone" that is imperishable (116).[37] In spite of all these strange speculations about the immateriality of the body, there persists a celebration of touch in Aunt Winifred's assertions. "What would be the use of having a body that you can't see and touch? A body is a *body*, not a spirit" (117). And that means that Mary will again be able to kiss and hold her brother, to "feel his kiss on your happy lips" (117). The celebration leaves open the potential for a reembodiment that will be "greatly improved" in its capacity to have physically intimate encounters.

The novel presents the challenge of learning how to inhabit simultaneously a place on earth and a place in heaven, learning to substitute the actual tastes of life on earth with the anticipated tastes of heaven, even to the particular flavor of gingerbread. The speculation continues into appearance. Shall we look the same after death? Why not, replies her aunt in an extended (and footnoted) catechism.[38] The "human form has been borne and dignified forever by Christ" (120). Nonetheless, after death, the "spiritual body is real, is tangible, is visible, is human," but after death is ambiguously "changed" (122). Our "future bodies" will be "vastly convenient," she continues, entering what seems almost the realm of science fiction after reminding her auditor that, after death, Christ could appear and disappear at will (124). The "powers of which there is no dreaming" will, for example, mean that she can time travel to Kansas (124). As she puts it, "I, for instance, sitting here by you, and thinking that I should like to be in Kansas, will be there" (124).[39]

Winifred's vision of Heaven includes "mountains and trees" (137); she describes a relation to the world that involves the pain of human interaction as well as the joy. The need to remember sorrowful memories of humans still attaches itself to the "*ideal* of mountains which we catch in rare glimpses,—as we catch the ideal of everything" (137). Winifred wants a "home of my own" in heaven, with flowers outside the window. Since the narrator seems shocked, she quotes back at her, "in the Father's house are many mansions." As Winifred mentions that her husband John will be waiting for her, the narrator says, "I believe that gave me some thoughts that I ought not to have, and so I made no reply" (139). The potential for jealousy persists in this imagined heaven.

To want a "local habitation and a name" in heaven is to want a location in heaven that will have names (140). Winifred's desire is mimetic: after she dies she wants to be "liv[ing] under the conditions of organized society. . . . Organized society involves homes, not unlike the homes of this world" (140). Many questions emerge from this assertion. They include an uncertainty about what happens with the home of someone who is poor or who has been living under the conditions of slavery in someone else's home. The aspirational quality of this heavenly ideal erases race and involves a middle-class home that can be re-created in heaven. Winifred goes on to say, "I conjecture nothing that the Bible contradicts" (141). The odd placement of subject/verb/object here might implicate Anne Hutchinson again. She continues, "I do not believe as truth indisputable anything that the Bible does not give me. But I reason from analogy about this, as we all do about other matters" (141–142). In her sensuous lists, Winfred continues, "I hope for heavenly types of nature and of art" (144). Her idea is that the material world of pleasure in heaven will be like synonyms: "their pianos and machinery may not be made of literal rosewood and steel" (186). Yet when Winifred thinks of building a home in heaven, she thinks of Kansas (225).

The oddity that she transplants the violent location of Kansas into heaven almost echoes the statement in *Uncle Tom's Cabin* that heaven is "better than Kintuck" (a statement uttered by the dying Uncle Tom).[40] The world of *Uncle Tom's Cabin* can be appropriately referenced here both because it is the "other" bestseller connected with the Civil War in the nineteenth-century United States and because its religious lessons present themselves as explicitly bound up with the physical facts of slavery that *The Gates Ajar* seems to elide. In calling this elision apparent rather than actual, I argue that the significance of Kansas for the novel is about how it relocates the Civil War from the South to the West, and makes its location as a site of violence tied up with the resistance to slavery that the novel never names. The substitutions that the novel enacts, in other words, include the substitution of the violence of Kansas for the violence of slavery while the painful deaths within the novel might still be read as ambiguous sacrifices for the national sins that it does not name.

Possibly tempting a misreading, the tragedy at the novel's close provides moments that might indicate sensual connections, tactile moments that become encounters with the physical precursors of death. Apparently Winifred has breast cancer. She "opened the bosom of her dress . . ."; the ellipses appear in the original (231). The last pages of the novel find Mary immersed in mourning the impending death of Winifred. Her death stands in for and invokes the loss of Mary's brother together with symbolic losses. When she thinks of going to heaven, Winifred thinks of "President Lincoln, or Mrs. Browning" as though they were hanging out there together (238). Her sense of a pantheon includes the promise of intimacy with her heroes. Yet her dying holds other promises of intimacy. As Winifred lies in bed, her physical body gradually loses the ability to use language. The deathbed intimacy between Mary and Winifred involves a scene that would otherwise have been sensual: "I crept up on the bed beside her, for she seemed to wish it. . . . After that I kissed her" (245). The scene of intimacy invites a reading of a possible union in the afterlife, but they are interrupted by Winifred's vision of her husband John, who has preceded her there: "'John!'—she said,—'why, John!'" (246). The turn from the living woman to the dead husband, a husband buried in far off Kansas, interrupts the novel's suggestion of a dying romantic kiss, although it implies that John has appeared in order to interrupt the kiss.

Finally, in the intensely intimate world of Elizabeth Stuart Phelps's *The Gates Ajar*, the matter of reproduction in heavenly terms is the matter of another life beyond the body. The novel links the "other" identities that Christianity provided in accounts of slavery with the lives women could live in the post-war combination of mourning and a life lived "doubly" on heaven and on earth. The double life of mourning and mobility includes the discipline that encourages an intimate relation to religion arrived at through a relationship with a strong spiritual woman who is loved and lost. The intimacy of such a relation is at once enhanced and deflected through death. That the deaths of the novel invoke the absent boundary of Kansas makes the invocation of Kansas into a metonymic instantiation of the national mourning that cannot speak its name, a mourning at once for lost women and for the loss of a nation forever divided by slavery.

CHAPTER FOUR

The Republic of Men at Sea

NATHANIEL HAWTHORNE, HERMAN MELVILLE, AND MARK TWAIN

Men at Sea

Rivers tend to lead out to the sea. Sometimes the sea leads to more rivers. One version of what Mark Twain imagined he would do when, as a young riverboat worker, he traveled down the Mississippi River and reached New Orleans was take a boat into the Atlantic Ocean and head to Brazil. Rather than look for the Amazon River, as he explains it in *Life on the Mississippi,* he was curious about the possibility of a trade in cocaine. That was, of course, legal. As was the trade in human bodies, which might have taken more men to sea than did the hunt for whales that Herman Melville celebrated in *Moby-Dick.* The disturbing aspect of looking for men at sea in order to turn them into goods for sale appears erratically in that novel while it has a more prominent role in his novella *Benito Cereno.*

Contrasting Twain's nostalgia about the Mississippi, and in line with Melville's cynicism, is the polemical piece "The King of Rivers" that first appeared in the proselytizing journal for westward expansion, *The United States Magazine and Democratic Review* in 1849.[1] The Mississippi, according to its pseudonymous author Cora Montgomery, "ensures the harmony of the sovereign sisters of the Union." It acts as "the most persuasive mediator, the most energetic arbiter, and the most vigilant defender of the federal compact." In particular, the operations of the river encourage market mobility. Portraying states as talkative sisters vending wares, the piece continues: "Free-soil Iowa and Illinois may chide the heresies of slave-holding Kentucky and Louisiana, but not the less must wheat-growing and lead-producing Iowa and Illinois vend their wares, and buy their sugar and cotton, in the markets of their southern sisters." Travel along the Mississippi becomes bound up with a racialized landscape. As she describes it, "In ascending the Mississippi," the traveler leaves behind "the darkest and most tenacious shades of African servitude, the tints lighten step by step, and state by state, up to the lofty, health-inspiring shores of genial Kentucky and adventurous Missouri, where slavery visibly relaxes its grasp; and onward, to the romantic and enchanting heights of Iowa and Wisconsin, where it never had a hold." When, two thousand miles later, the traveler reaches Minnesota, these words appear: "Every state must, and every territory ought, decide for itself, and by itself, whether it will admit or exclude slavery" (506).

Continuing to portray states with anthropomorphic reactions to acts of enslavement and genocide, the essay continues by noting that inhabitants of states like "Minnesota, Iowa and Wisconsin, [grieve] over the woes of the African slave a thousand miles off, while, with every art of diplomacy and war, they chase the poor Indian beyond their border." In the meantime, "Louisiana and Mississippi thrill with indignation at the sufferings of the Indian, as he recedes before the march of civilization, or dies in her embrace; but they look calmly on the bondage of the African." The unflattering reflection is that "Those states which have thoroughly exterminated and dispossessed the Indians . . . are tranquil and tender-hearted on Indian matters" (507). The tranquility and "tender-hearted" atmosphere that surrounds the space that has been emptied of the people for whom a reader has been asked to feel compassion will later appear as the space of the river for Herman Melville in *The Confidence-Man*.

Early in "The King of Rivers," noting where benevolence finds its mark, the narrator protests that "Our Indian policy is a blot on the very name of Christianity, yet what Senator or what General proposes any change, except, perhaps, something a little more veiled and indirect in our inexorable system of despoilment and extermination?"[2] The bitterness with which Cora Montgomery portrays the clash of civilizations that the river represents becomes a way to complete the vision of landscapes that the Mississippi divides as it clefts a space between free and slave territories on its journey south. To move against the current and trace the river on a journey to the north is to revisit the source of national landscapes, a place neither to the west nor to the east, neither slave nor free, but nevertheless compromised as the land of dispossession.

When women are portrayed on the river, the scene changes. These women include the imagined granddaughter of Thomas Jefferson in

William Wells Brown's novel *Clotel*, who jumps to her death into the waters by Washington, DC, at once the national capitol and still a place where humans can be bought and sold. For Brown, in a fantasy of the ocean in the seventeenth century, there are two ships heading to what will become America. One, the *Mayflower*, contains the "seed wheat of states and empire." The other, not named, appears as a "low, rakish ship hastening from the tropics, solitary and alone, to the New World." This ship contains a "cargo of slaves on their way to Jamestown, Virginia." For Brown, who views the African slave trade as the "greatest crime ever perpetrated against humanity," these ships are the "representation of good and evil in the New World."[3] The water that conveys them serves as a neutral background, but also as the means through which both good and evil arrive on land.

Turning from the ocean back to the river, I want to ask: Has the Mississippi become an invisible American border, or do we continue to live there, neither on water nor on land? Mark Twain marked twice—and branded forever—the ambiguous flight south on a raft as both freedom and imprisonment. The railroad and the river intersect, mark, and trap humans in spaces designated for enslavement or freedom. Does the river mean that the passengers seek land—or a route to the sea? To read the face of the river is to read the faces of men on the river, to anticipate whether they bring violence. The violence of the river as a border, a violence that Twain tries to contain in the *Adventures of Huckleberry Finn* (1884), resurfaces. The uncertainty of narrative form in that text, as it crosses the river but also crosses from memory to invention, suggests that the internal borders of the United States always invoke race.[4]

Looking at the Water

Recent work on oceans has expanded how often they appear as places of ambiguous identity. Books that feature the Middle Passage as a watery traverse through locations that could contain pirates, whalers, and merchant ships with uncertain futures now look at how the implications of these passages can be reversed.[5] When Frederick Douglass looked at the waters of the Chesapeake Bay, he famously saw the sails of ships as symbolic of freedom. His own route to freedom came when he disguised himself as a sailor and he ended up living in New Bedford, Massachusetts, ironically a place where many ships launched to carry bodies back to the southern United States. His apostrophe to the ships in Chesapeake Bay, repeated in different forms in the three revisions of his autobiography, includes these words: "I will take to the water. This very bay shall yet bear me into freedom . . . when I get to the head of the bay, I will turn my canoe adrift." Alluding to a desire for freedom that resembles the later fictions of Twain, he ventriloquizes his earlier yearning: "Besides, I am but a boy yet, and all boys are bound to someone." The coercion of land yields to the freedom of water. Yet the white sails that draw his eye when resting from the coercions of Mr. Covey also appear as ghosts for a fantasy of freedom: "Those beautiful vessels, robed in purest white, so delightful to the eyes of freemen, were to me so many shrouded ghosts, to terrify and torment me with thoughts of my wretched condition."[6] Douglass retains the metaphors from his time working on ships in speeches like "What to the Slave Is the Fourth of July?" There he calls the existence of the nation into question: "From the round top of your ship of state, dark and threatening clouds may be seen. Heavy billows, like mountains in the distance, disclose to the leeward huge forms of flinty rocks."[7] Such language bolsters the sense that his escape while bearing the papers of a sailor could be verbally established by his "knowledge of ships and sailor talk." He "knew a ship from stem to stern, and from keels on to cross-trees."[8] Knowing ships meant he could escape by sea.

Throughout her life, often to her regret, Harriet Jacobs presented as female. Suffering from the sexual overtures made by the man who claimed control over her, Harriet Jacobs escaped slavery by changing gender in addition to profession, disguising herself as a sailor as part of her route to freedom.[9] Her cross-dressing has not been interrogated as much as her writing has been challenged, and the details of her activism, I would argue, still need celebration. Most striking in recent years has been the attention to the "loophole of retreat" contained in her autobiography as a site for exploring Black women's identity. Inspired by the sculptures of Simone Leigh, several days of celebration at the Guggenheim Museum in New York as well as the site of the Venice Biennial have encouraged forms of inhabiting freedom in performance, dance, spoken word, and drama.[10] For Leigh, the sculpting of women's bodies as vessels enhances the sense that the loophole might be about that set of unseen longings that the woman's body contains in addition to proposing that vessel that can be seen.

As this chapter will show, to change identity on the water involves passengers in a contradictory series of moves: from slavery to freedom, from Confederate sympathizer to anguished "explainer" of the contradictions within slavery, from boy on a whaling vessel to conman on a steamship, from the dreams of a boy to the dreams of a woman. Turning from women in mourning to men in motion, the chapter visits familiar and unfamiliar stories about men on the water as the conditions that led to the war are anticipated or commemorated. What draws these men to the water shifts location and genre with the author. For Nathaniel Hawthorne, whose father was lost at sea, the exercise of ghost-writing *Journal of an African Cruiser*, an account of a ship patrolling the west coast of Africa purportedly to control the traffic in humans, can be juxtaposed with his dislike of the virulent rhetoric of abolition.[11] For Mark Twain, writing a memoir, the Mississippi River becomes a recursive site of memory and loss although he evades the stories of war that traverse it. For Herman Melville, finally, the fictional transformations enabled by a confidence man become at once bitter satire and a ferocious form of rootlessness that engages the violence on the banks of the river.

All three authors went to sea, but the stories told here by Twain and Melville address a famously precarious river that runs to the sea. The sea, or, more precisely, the Gulf of Mexico, waits for that river, and the humans that ride on it, to arrive. That arrival might be anticipated, but does not appear. The Mississippi River threads through this chapter, proposing its own form of crossing from freedom to slavery. Historians such as Walter Johnson have unpacked the sinister aspect of the Mississippi River as a conduit for the "second middle passage."[12] Before the Civil War, ships crossing the Atlantic carried the forced migrations of slavery in addition to economic migrants. The stories and songs on board appear in *Journal of an African Cruiser*, an odd ocean crossing carried out by Hawthorne's friend Horatio Bridge in relation to the policy of the American Colonization Society to return those held in conditions of slavery to begin a new country in West Africa. The mixed feelings that Mark Twain has as he returns on board a steamboat to rehearse his years as a steamboat pilot in *Life on the Mississippi* remain off balance; he remembers and forgets at once that the journey to New Orleans repetitively enacts the trade in human bodies along the river (figure 4.1). The forced displacement, illness, and genocide of the Atlantic crossing appear condensed on board a ship on the Mississippi. In a work such as Melville's *The Confidence-Man*, the oral traditions and trickster narratives that are a cultural survival from West Africa keep all listeners off balance.

While these stories about men on the water might initially seem peripheral to the Civil War, such stories about the water shift attention to how the conditions of war migrate. The attention here to stories set on the river, for instance, must include the detail that rivers that run to the sea, that the sea waits for rivers, and the humans that ride on them, to arrive. Placed and placeless, at once forming a boundary and overflowing that boundary, the

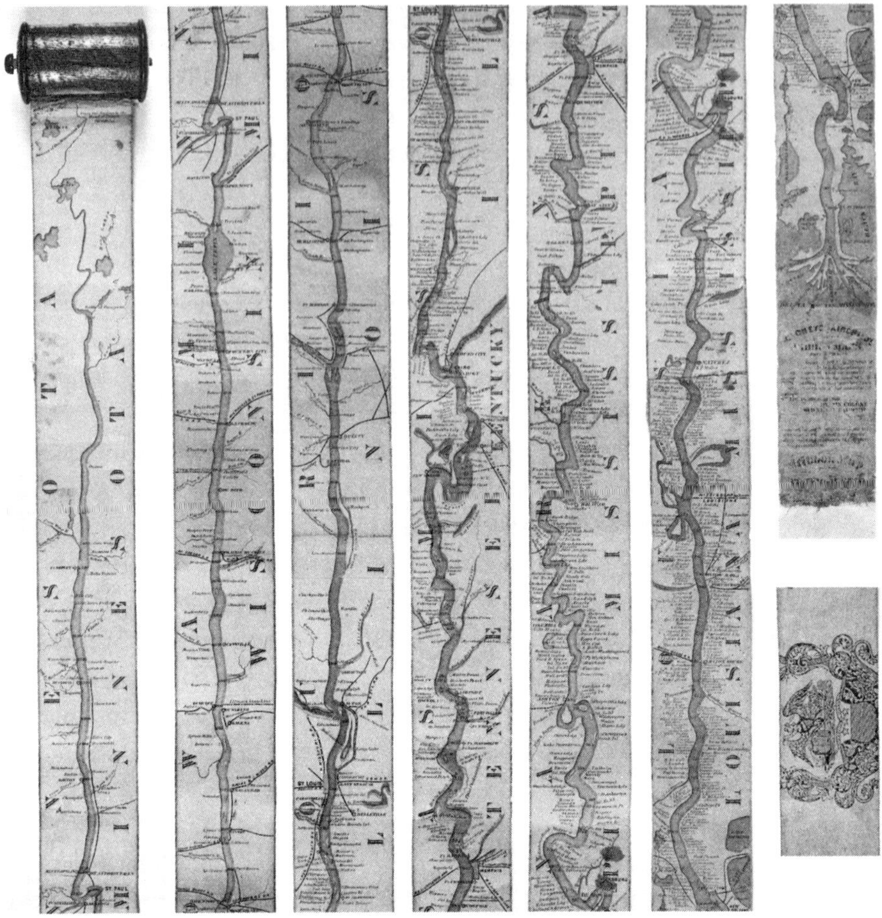

FIGURE 4.1. *Ribbon Map of the Father of Waters*, 1866. Printed on paper as a hand-colored lithograph. The original copy of this scroll is 11 feet long and only 2 inches wide. Coloney & Fairchild. Courtesy of the American Antiquarian Society. BIB ID# 494354 GIGI 494354_0001.

landscapes of both rivers and the sea repeatedly reveal bodies in motion; the forms of migrant labor on board shift with waves of immigrants. That is, the geographical placing in such fiction leads to a placelessness as bodies are moved through watery landscapes.

Both men and women landed on the coasts of the United States after long voyages at sea, but this chapter focuses on how the stories told by male writers about nineteenth-century men on the water turn migration into a destabilizing force. The first part of the chapter looks at ocean voyages and the inadvertent consequences of nineteenth-century attempts to end enforced slavery. The middle part looks at the Mississippi River through the eyes of two writers who viewed it as a place of transformation. The end returns to the ocean. The place of the Atlantic Ocean in mercantile exchange as well as political struggles over land claims and trade routes has been well documented. Many men (and some women) headed to sea looking for profit along complicated ocean routes. Along with the mercantile needs that such shipping routes supplied, accompanying the routes of the movements of goods and people, came ships designed as military transport to protect merchant ships from pirates, to move armies, and, sometimes, to regulate trade in times of war.[13]

Outside of the well-documented militant movement of ships in wartime—from the shipping blockades of the American Revolution to the battles on the Great Lakes during the War of 1812 to smuggling guns during the Civil War—there were less remembered events that involved the US Naval Squadron. One of the least remembered and most ambiguous concerned the requisitioning of naval blockades to safeguard the new settlements—in part promoted by the American Colonization Society—near the coast in Liberia.[14] The new settlements were subject to many threats, including the possible reenslavement of inhabitants, and the US Navy, posted uncomfortably off the coast of West Africa, had a complex task of distinguishing among pirate ships, often flying ambiguous flags, and ships carrying out authorized forms of trade.

During a sea voyage in the 1840s, "one poor fellow" is ill and "his mess mates gently bathe his hot brow, and, watching every movement, nurse him as tenderly as a woman. Strange, that the rude heart of a sailor should be found to possess such tenderness as we seldom ask or find, in those of our own sex, on land! There we leave the gentler humanities of life to woman; here we are compelled to imitate her characteristics."[15] To be at sea for these men is to find tenderness in their hearts. That very tenderness is associated with the women left on land. To imitate the "gentler humanities of life" while at sea still refutes or delays an integration between the man who can "nurse him as tenderly as a woman" and the men who will "leave" women and all they stand for behind on land in order to be together on the water.

These words are not, as a casual reader might expect, from Melville. It seems likely that they were written by Nathaniel Hawthorne as he edited the work of a friend from Bowdoin College. A commodore in the US Navy during the Civil War, Horatio Bridge wrote *Journal of an African Cruiser*, an account of his voyages along the coast of Africa as part of a military monitoring of the experiments in settling Liberia via the American

Colonization Society. Edited by Hawthorne, and first published in 1845, the book was surely read by Melville and contains several scenes with language that resembles Hawthorne's narrators. These are scenes that might lend themselves to a conversation about male vision in other novels Melville wrote such as *Typee* and *Billy Budd*. That is, although they do not reflect Hawthorne's more conservative political bent, the aspects of slavery, violence, and desire that appear in *Journal of an African Cruiser* invite contrast with similar moments in Melville. In short, to think about Melville's sexuality alongside whaling culture takes into account the familiar conundrum of Melville's friendship with Nathaniel Hawthorne and the unfamiliar concept of Hawthorne as someone involved in writing about the ocean.

To return to visuality is to notice forms of the gaze that reach across desire between men on the high seas. For Melville, fraught scenes between men include the transnational stories in his oceanic portraits in *Moby-Dick* and *Billy Budd* as well as the world of overt and implied sexuality in the men who have jumped ship in *Typee*. The invocation of desire between men planning a mutiny in *Billy Budd* seems far removed from the conditions of slavery that surround the ocean voyage of *The Bachelor's Delight* in *Benito Cereno*, but in both cases the confusion about how to interpret visual signals in the absence of verbal clarity leads to violence. The young men who bond in *Typee* begin with an adventurous attention to the inhabitants of the island where they have arrived, but the attention to its colonial setting seems erased by the further adventures of two young men on an island, a *Robinson Crusoe* remake filled with cannibal anxiety and erotic desire. For Hawthorne to suggest to Horatio Bridge that he write a story about his life at sea seems, in contrast, related to the stories he has heard because of his friendship with Franklin Pierce. As the friendship with Melville comes later, it must be assumed that Hawthorne was reading the popular sea stories like *Typee*, *Redburn*, and *White Jacket*—and thinking that there was a market for such stories while he might have also, given his lost seafaring father, enjoyed thinking about men at sea. Desire on the high seas permeates Melville's writing about shipboard life long before *Billy Budd* and the classic exchange with Captain Vere.

The writers whose lives lie behind these texts had intersecting stories. Bridge was appointed to his naval position by Franklin Pierce—his friend from Bowdoin as well as Hawthorne's. Hawthorne wrote a campaign biography for Pierce. Hawthorne dedicated his early collection of stories, *The Snow Image*, to Bridge.[16] Long after Hawthorne's death, Bridge wrote *Personal Recollections of Nathaniel Hawthorne* (1893). Thus, to account for the overlapping stories of men at sea means to think about the familiar aspects of Melville's friendship with Nathaniel Hawthorne and the unfamiliar concept of Hawthorne as someone writing about the ocean.

The ocean sits unquoted in the background of *House of the Seven Gables* and *The Marble Faun*. It performs a key role in *The Scarlet Letter*. (In *The Blithedale Romance* it may just be the water in the river that becomes significant, especially because it turns out to be the fatal resting place of Zenobia.) Readers often frame Hawthorne in terms of the fraught history of New England Puritanism and manage not to remember the father that he lost at sea when he was a child. Like Ahab, perhaps, although long before Melville's story, Hawthorne's father is a captain who has been lost, leaving a young child behind, and that loss leaves a residue of grief. The longing for a man gone to sea who should have returned as a father rather than as a dim memory at once resembles and seems far from the ongoing longing that men at sea sometimes express for each other or the way that men on land, as in the opening of *Moby-Dick*, nostalgically invoke the sea.

Starting as young students at Bowdoin College, Hawthorne and Bridge had a decades-long friendship. The editing of the story told by Horatio Bridge might appear as an unrecognized part of the story. Almost certainly the aspect of the journal that treats Liberia is the most uncomfortable for a reader today. In words that seem likely to have been edited by Hawthorne, words that possibly echo Hawthorne's political bent, Bridge presents himself as "A northern man, but not unacquainted with the slave institutions of our own and other countries—neither an Abolitionist nor a Colonizationist—without prejudice, as without prepossession—he felt himself thus far qualified to examine the great enterprise which he beheld in progress." After all, he explains improbably, "The West Coast of Africa is a fresher field for the scribbling tourist, than most other parts of the world" (vi). The "scribbling tourist" surely describes Hawthorne rather than this active military man. Because of the ambiguity of the voice, my description of the *Journal* uses the term "narrator."

The story of the voyage begins June 5, 1843, with music.[17] The sentimental scene of the ill man who evokes "tenderness" from "the rude heart of a sailor" becomes abruptly terminated when the man dies and is thrown overboard without a name. "Dying, he kept his own counsel and was content to vanish out of life, even as a speck of foam melts back into the ocean" (5). That "speck of foam," white against the dark waves, recalls other bodies abandoned in the water and the barely named mission of the ship, to restrict the slave trade, two words so hard to utter together, as it polices the coast of Liberia.

After describing a conversation with a self-confessed murderer on the crew, the narrator claims, in terms reminiscent of Melville, "The private history of a man-of-war's crew, if truly told, would be full of high romance, varied with stirring incident, and too often darkened with deep and deadly crime. Many go to sea . . . to escape the punishment of guilt, which has left them outlaws of the land" (6). A reader of Melville's fiction will hear echoes as the narrator continues: "An officer sometimes sees his old school-fellow and playmate taken to the gangway and flogged" (6). It can be difficult to separate the tone of the conversations, of which there is no record, between Hawthorne and Bridge from Hawthorne's editing, but occasionally the voice of Bridge seems to enter. After all, says the narrator philosophically, "Many a good seaman has been a slaver and a pirate" (6). As it presents a pragmatic conflation, the account implicitly makes piracy the equivalent of the trade in human bodies.

Upon arriving in Liberia, the narrator estimates half a million people were trafficked each year. Visiting Cuba in 1836, he saw the effects of trafficking. England pretends to recapture those held as slaves, he claims, but then uses them as labor. And the United States also profits, he says, for all the stated goals of a voyage that will help support the colonization effort.[18] The book takes a violent turn when the men leave the ship, with a wrenching scene of murdering civilians and burning down a town in Liberia, the very place the voyage has crossed the Atlantic to protect. The narrator announces the onset of violence abruptly, "The season for palavers and diplomacy being now over" (81). The men go on shore ostensibly to practice diplomacy and then burn several towns, not trying to decide if anyone is guilty. Waxing philosophical and frank at once, the narrator comments, "Man is perhaps never happier than when his native destructiveness can be freely exercised." That is, he continues, "It unites the charms of sin and virtue" (to go around burning down towns, without asking, and after all, he says it makes them very hungry). Freed from the confines of the ship to act out on land, "few of us had ever spent a day of higher enjoyment than this, when we roamed around . . . devastating, what had hitherto been the homes of a people." An ironic commentary appears on "one of the sweetest spots that I have seen in Africa," three homes that are "particularly neat, and giving a pleasant impression of the domestic life of their inhabitants" (83). They burn them down.

Most disconcerting may be the subsequent comment: "Though the burning of villages be a very pretty pastime, yet it leaves us in a moralizing mood" (85). The moralizing of the text is at once ironic and disturbing in its implication of New England mores with transatlantic violence. As the narrator notes, "more vessels come to the coast of Africa from Salem" than from anywhere else (110). Specific elements of trade recur in this chapter and remind us that Bridge was renowned as a supplier of the navy during the Civil War. According to this account, he enjoys his visit to Africa; when he does not engage in such violence, he treats the encounters as a touristic opportunity to acquire souvenirs. For instance, he likes Accra, where he is given an anteater as a pet. And he likes spectacle, as when, in a visit to St. Thomas, in Gabon, he watches a man swallowed by a shark. The account he provides can become disarmingly meditative. After receiving letters eleven months old, he assigns philosophy to the act of writing letters and speaks of an "electric telegraph" for men to send messages when at sea (149).

To turn from this account to more familiar stories about men on the water and to invoke again the image of water as a motif involves the idea of the collection—that is, an assemblage of pieces that treat water—and a form of reorienting the space of memory. To produce order from chronology, from space, from the teleology of political development might find a corollary, for instance, in the work of Susan Stewart, whose attention to narratives of the miniature and the gigantic, overly compressed or overly large instantiations of culture, recognizes that they can be equivalently difficult to see. The large space of the water that carries these men has small details, like the anteater, and large resonance, like bodies tossed overboard. Both can become strangely invisible within the narrative tactics of a "journal," the sequencing of events that seems to leave no room for reflection.

Why does it matter to pay attention to what might be overlooked? Stewart asserts that "the miniature" exists for her "as a metaphor for the interior space and time of the bourgeois subject."[19] The paradoxical abstractness of this claim does not obscure the helpfulness of taking the very size of concepts as an entry point for their effects. Her next sentence continues—and condenses—the point: "Analogously, the gigantic is considered as a metaphor for the authority of the state and the collective, public, life." To clarify, I am not claiming that oceans—or rivers—appear as metaphors, but rather noting that the contested space they both mark and refuse to mark reenacts matters related both to the state and to the souvenirs collected by those who cross these spaces.

Stewart continues, with her investment in "two devices for the objectification of desire, the souvenir and the collection" (xii). In response,

I suggest that these souvenirs about voyages are both objects related to memory and elements in a narrative that evades the very memory it invokes, the terrible struggles over slavery. The relation between the souvenir and the collection might function as an organizing tactic for historical memory in the narratives, but it also becomes what stands in place of memory. The nostalgia or "longing for a place of origin" might translate into the difficult yearning for Union with a lost mother country, a yearning that reached a violent apogee with the War of 1812 when the British marched into Washington, DC, and burned the White House. According to Stewart, the collection is the place where history is transformed into property. The ability of the self at once to incorporate and to control the arbitrary motion of time and space seems to meet its greatest challenge on the water.

Such an appropriation of Stewart's argument to the use of geography and borders might follow her claim that "The souvenir seeks distance (the exotic in time and space), but it does so in order to transform and collapse distance into proximity to, or approximation with, the self" (xii). At the same time, the longing for cohesion seeps into the geographical incoherence of works like James Fenimore Cooper's *Home as Found*, with its retreat from the violence of America back across the Atlantic to Britain, or the profoundly alien rationing of distance of works like Edgar Allan Poe's *Arthur Gordon Pym*. Or, from the inside domestic space out to the estrangement of the city, one might invoke Herman Melville's *Pierre*, with its attention to the relationship between the collection and the chronicle. Remembering how intricate the attention to horological measurements in relation to chronometers appears as a means of measurement in *Pierre* again recalls Stewart: "In allegory, the vision of the reader is larger than the vision of the text" (3). As these narratives assemble archives, they identify points of insertion where what the reader cares about most deeply has an object that sometimes seem to be swept away by water.

Taking Stock

"I don't take no stock in dead people." This sentence, early in *The Adventures of Huckleberry Finn*, could have appeared in its prequel *The Adventures of Tom Sawyer*. For just a moment I want to think about the implications of this familiar but ambiguous statement. As one does, faced with the computer screen, I googled it, looking for its role in pedagogical practice, and was amused, if disheartened, to discover that the top result is part of a multiple-choice exam for ESL students. It seems hard to imagine a more difficult selection.[20] Here are the choices that follow the question:

> *What does Huck mean by his expression that he doesn't "take no stock in dead people"?*

1. *He finds it unpleasant to talk about them.*
2. *He finds them uninteresting, because they're dead and gone.*
3. *He's not sure if they even ever existed.*
4. *He forgets everything about them because he doesn't like history.*

These questions resonate with teaching American history in a number of states right now. The probably unamusing result for me is that, in my opinion, all of the answers are "correct," a reminder of the importance of teaching ambiguity to our students. To "take stock" in dead people is also to figure out how to monetize their existence, something that historians do as a matter of course. In the novels by Mark Twain, to take stock veers in and out of comedy and tragedy. The many dead bodies in *Huckleberry Finn* might be anticipated by the deaths in *Tom Sawyer*, beginning with the grim after effect of digging up a dead body for dissection.

Tom Sawyer speaks, but unlike Huckleberry Finn in the latter novel he does not appear as a narrator. The narrator uses conventional, if spooky, language to describe a key location visited by Huck and Tom. This adventure begins when Tom Sawyer leaves his home in the middle of the night. Setting the tone, we learn that "Huckleberry Finn was there, with his dead cat." The deaths are about to proliferate.

> *It was a graveyard of the old-fashioned Western kind [with] a crazy board fence around it, which leaned inward in places, and outward the rest of the time, but stood upright nowhere. . . . All the old graves were sunken in, there was not a tombstone on the place; round-topped, worm-eaten boards staggered over the graves, leaning for support and finding none.*

The atmosphere established here includes forms of anthropomorphism, as the fence leans and the wooden boards that stand in for tombstones stagger. The very breathlessness of the narrative voice as it stumbles over these details sets the mood.

> *A faint wind moaned through the trees, and Tom feared it might be the spirits of the dead, complaining at being disturbed. The boys talked little, and only under their breath, for the time and the place and*

> *the pervading solemnity and silence oppressed their spirits. They . . . ensconced themselves within the protection of three great elms that grew in a bunch within a few feet of the grave.*
>
> *Then they waited in silence for what seemed a long time. The hooting of a distant owl was all the sound that troubled the dead stillness. Tom's reflections grew oppressive. He must force some talk. So he said in a whisper:*
>
> *"Hucky, do you believe the dead people like it for us to be here?"*
>
> *Huckleberry whispered:*
>
> *"I wisht I knowed."*

What they are about to witness is murder among the graves.[21] You might not remember that the victim of the murder is a doctor seeking to disinter a hanged man for dissection, a fairly common move for doctors in the nineteenth century. The murderer is the so-called Injun Joe, a figure who preoccupies Kerry Driscoll in her wonderfully detailed book *Mark Twain among the Indians and Other Indigenous Peoples*.[22] Later in the novel, this murderer will meet a wretched death, starving after being locked up in a cave that apparently persists as a tourist attraction in the actual Hannibal, Missouri. But before that happens, the two boys head out on the Mississippi.

> *The raft drew beyond the middle of the river; the boys pointed her head right, and then lay on their oars. . . . Now the raft was passing before the distant town. Two or three glimmering lights showed where it lay, peacefully sleeping, beyond the vague vast sweep of star-gemmed water, unconscious of the tremendous event that was happening.* (chapter 13)

The occurrences here are reminiscent of *The Adventures of Huckleberry Finn*, but the adventure is shorter, and that is only part of what makes Tom Sawyer a safer participant on elementary school library shelves. Arguably, as Kerry Driscoll so ably shows, the invisible racism of blaming the Indian continues to make this book seem a neutral exposure of the fear of death for a child along the Mississippi River in the nineteenth century. A contrast about display appears in *The Corpse in the Kitchen*. Adam John Waterman opens this book with a refusal to name the subjects of the blatantly horrifying dissection he describes. A head is severed from a body and the reader doesn't know why. Dr. James Turner, about whom little else is known, was accustomed to unearthing buried bodies for dissection, but with the decapitated head of Black Hawk he sought to have an element to display for money.[23] Since such decapitations of enemy heads appear in works like *Benito Cereno*, as well as in the historical account of the warrior

FIGURE 4.2. George Caleb Bingham (1811–1879). *Raftsmen Playing Cards*, 1847. Oil on canvas. 28 1/16 in. × 38 1/16 in. (71 cm × 96.5 cm). Courtesy of Saint Louis Art Museum. Bequest of Ezra H. Linley by exchange. 50:1934.

Little Crow, the implications are that in battles along the Mississippi River, as well as on the open ocean, the warrior might lose his head.

On the River

I'm going to detour on the journey along the river with a look at the pleasant memory invoked by the work of Caleb Bingham, who produced enormously popular paintings of the Mississippi in the youth of Samuel Clemens, not yet the man called Mark Twain. These mostly familiar paintings, now often used as book covers for Twain's works, show men posing as the workers who would have been on the raft (figure 4.2). That is, in their way, they have been "white-washed" like the fence in Tom Sawyer. The men who labored to sell wood off rafts to steamboats would have been racially ambiguous whether or not they were covered in dirt. Further, even as Twain's novels invoke the phrase "Sold down the river" as a horror, the pastoral ideal of Bingham's paintings, produced when there were still bodies for sale on the river, suggests simply that also sold on the river were the logs of wood to keep the steamboats moving.

Mark Twain began his career finding a name in the measurement of water. His nostalgic account of his career as a pilot, *Life on the Mississippi*, begins with an inscribed "[Trade Mark.]" on the copyright page next to the name of Mark Twain. A typographically complicated enactment of the two names appears, so that the first line reads "BY S. L. CLEMENS." That name stands without explanation over the smaller type (produced in all capital letters): "MARK TWAIN." Both names are enclosed by a large parenthesis and to the left of the parenthetical frame, placed vertically, is the word: "TRADE," while to the right, also placed vertically, is the word "MARK."[24] This enactment of overlapping claims—to a name, to property, and to experiments in typography—reinhabits the claim to the name "Mark" as part of a gesture of property ownership as well as to the classic story of claiming the name because of the announcement by river boat captains on the Mississippi River that they "mark twain," that is, two fathoms of depth, between the boat and the bottom of the river (figure 4.3). The man who marks himself as "Twain" marks himself twice before leaving his mark on the page.

The deception continues further into the text as the preface appears. Inserting other voices alongside his own without always determining the privileges of trademark, Twain cites these words as from the "Editor's Table, Harper's Magazine, February, 1863." The title of the editorial is "The 'Body of the Nation'" and it begins: "BUT *the basin of the Mississippi is the* BODY OF THE NATION." These typographical emphases are in the original, but they also mimic the typographical emphases in the trademark statement on the copyright page. The peculiarity of the emphasis on water as a body is extended as the remarks continue into statistical comparisons with Europe. The excerpt from the testimonial ends with a tribute to the United States and the river alike: "*As a dwelling-place for civilized man it is by far the first upon our globe.*"[25]

One might imagine that these remarks refer to the fertility of the Mississippi River valley, but the ambiguity of the word "it" leads to a superficial reading that understands that humans live upon the watery space of the river. And since the title of Twain's book as well as the biographical details feature his existence as a river pilot, something might be said for imagining the book as a guide for how to live on the water. The first chapter emerges as a series of facts presented almost in the dry tone of a schoolbook. The statistics of the passage from *Harper's* reappear with flourishes. Twelve of the first fifteen chapters of *Life on the Mississippi* first appeared serially in 1875 in *The Atlantic*. That is, they were closer to journalism, the first writing career that Twain pursued. Then the book was, in turn, reviewed in *The*

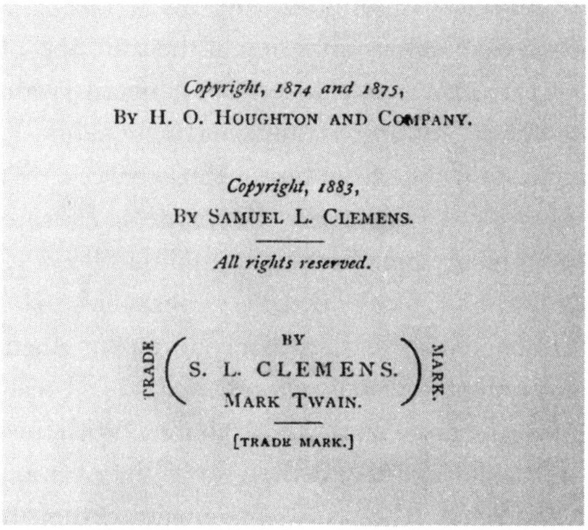

Copyright, 1874 and 1875,
By H. O. Houghton and Company.

Copyright, 1883,
By Samuel L. Clemens.

All rights reserved.

TRADE (BY S. L. CLEMENS. MARK TWAIN.) MARK.

[TRADE MARK.]

FIGURE 4.3. "Trade Mark." Mark Twain, *Life on the Mississippi*, 1883. Division of Rare and Manuscript Collections, Cornell University Library.

Atlantic in September of 1883. This review contains the earliest notice of the character of *Huckleberry Finn*, as yet unnamed, who appears in an excerpt as part of the "rough, hilarious, swaggering, fighting, superstitious ways of the bygone raftsmen."[26]

To change it from the reporting style of *The Atlantic* into a book, Twain inserted three chapters that follow closely the writing of Francis Parkman.[27] For instance, the book turns in the first few pages from providing physical statistics to the history of white people along the river, citing first that De Soto saw it in 1542. To offer perspective, Twain notes that Shakespeare had not yet been born and that this sighting of the river took place a hundred years before Cromwell (6). Twain includes cynical asides about the colonial presence of white Europeans: "in the south the Spaniards were robbing, slaughtering, enslaving, and converting them; higher up, the English were trading beads and blankets to them for a consideration, and throwing in civilization and whiskey" (7). In this section, Twain seems to have gotten his details, if not his language, from Parkman (11). These more flowery phrases have the language Twain quotes from Parkman: "The hazy sunlight, the warm and drowsy air, the tender foliage, the opening flowers, betokened the reviving life of nature" (12).

The earliest days of white people transporting goods and humans on the river involved journeys from St. Louis to New Orleans and back that could take nine months (15). It seems odd to a reader accustomed to other stories of transporting bodies on the river, especially a reader who now might be thinking of the stories that dominate the novels *Huckleberry Finn* and *Pudd'nhead Wilson*, that barely a mention of the transport of people held as slaves appears; the topic does not seem to concern Twain. Instead he says that the boats "changed cargoes there, and were tediously warped and poled back by hand" (15). The humans on those barges are the laborers, described as "hordes of rough and hardy men; rude, uneducated, brave, suffering terrific hardships . . . heavy fighters, reckless fellows . . . prodigal of their money" (15). The journey he describes echoes the one taken by Abraham Lincoln not long before the time he recollects. But when Lincoln was on the river, he noticed the transport of bodies confined because of slavery. For Twain, the bodies he notices are white laborers. With the introduction of the steamboat, the flatboatmen drifted down the river and the steamboats moved up the river: "the keelboatmen selling their boats in New Orleans, and returning home as deck passengers in the steamers" (16).

Nostalgia enters the account early as Twain moves toward the memories that will feed the stories he tells in *The Adventures of Tom Sawyer*. First he says, "I remember the annual processions of mighty rafts that used to glide by Hannibal when I was a boy." Then Twain explains that he will "throw in, in this place, a chapter from a book which I have been working at, by fits and starts, during the past five or six years" (16). He continues: it "is a story which details some passages in the life of an ignorant village boy, Huck Finn, son of the town drunkard of my time out West, there." As the boy runs away, "with him a slave of the widow's has also escaped," "bound for Cairo, whence the negro will seek freedom in the heart of the free States. But in a fog, they pass Cairo without knowing it." Twain next includes these words from *Huckleberry Finn*: "But you know a young person can't wait very well when he is impatient to find a thing out" (17). Ignoring the implications of the missed passage up the Ohio River, and as a divergence from the book that will become *Huckleberry Finn*, Twain inserts a bawdy song to the raft scene and a long version of the "southwest humor" oration. Here he proclaims: "I'm the old original iron-jawed, brass-mounted, copper-bellied corpse-maker from the wilds of Arkansaw!" (18).

This early draft of the crucial wrong turn on the river that drives much of the action for *Huckleberry Finn* contains several changes. The men on the raft "talked about how Ohio water didn't like to mix with Mississippi water" (22). A disturbing difference from the novel appears with a strange tale of being followed by a haunted barrel that contains a dead baby that one of the men has killed (25–26). Such an account of being haunted by a dead baby never appears in *The Adventures of Huckleberry Finn*, but perhaps the ghosts of murdered children pursue Huck down the river, especially since he has staged his own death in order to escape and the reader discovers at the end that his father has been murdered. The traces of morbid terror might lead a reader to think that gestures at humor inadequately cover for how much the entire narrative is haunted by the many bodies that have been discarded in the water along the route of the river. Also omitted from the version that ends up in *Huckleberry Finn* is the suggestiveness of a man discovering Huck's naked body crouched in the darkness on the raft: "I was warm and soft and naked; so he says 'Ouch!' and jumped back" (58). Escaping from the potential consequences of this suggestive discovery, when Twain revisits this episode in developing the plot of the novel, he incorporates a sometimes evasive agency, and Huck becomes the killer.

After this interlude in *Life*, several meandering digressions appear as Twain talks of pilots on steamboats. He describes the sleepy town of Hannibal, Missouri, during his boyhood when the steamboats landed once a day (30–31). Vivid words emerge to show the transformation of the town landscape when the first call is sent that the boat is approaching. Twain's words about the boat make it clear that the desire to live "on" the water involves the desire to be on that boat, a boat that appears "long and sharp and trim and pretty." The boat is a moving house, exhibiting "two tall, fancy-topped chimneys, with a gilded device of some kind swung between them." And cresting it all is a place of glory for a young boy: "a fanciful pilot house, all glass and 'gingerbread,' perched on top of the 'texas' deck behind them." The other accoutrements of the boat seem like a yard afloat: "the boiler deck, the hurricane deck, and the texas deck are fenced and ornamented with clean, white railings" (31). Responding to his desire to work on such a boat, says Twain, "by and by I ran away. I said I would never come home again till I was a pilot" (34). The desire to live on the water takes him to St. Louis, to Cincinnati, and finally to New Orleans with the dream of joining an expedition up the Amazon River. As Twain puts it, inspired by the popular tales of travelers, "I would go and complete the exploration of the Amazon. That was all the thought I gave to the subject. I never was great in matters of detail" (35). That earlier fantasy of leaving the delta to cross the Caribbean and to explore South America gives way to a repetitive cycling up and down the path of the river. The main pleasure of his travel down the Mississippi River as Twain recalls it in the present tense of the book is hearing the language of the men on board, language that he carefully edits, so that an insult becomes "you dash-dash-dash-*dashed* split between a tired mud turtle and a crippled hearse horse" (38).

Wanting to have this language in his mouth enhances his desire to live on the river; the young Twain strikes a bargain with the pilot of the *Paul Jones*, on which he has just arrived in New Orleans, by which he will return upriver to St. Louis and learn how to be a pilot in exchange for the first five hundred dollars he earns. He follows this pilot onto an even larger boat at St. Louis where, "[w]hen I stood in her pilot house I was so far above the water I seemed perched on a mountain." The pilot house is a "sumptuous glass temple" with "showy red and gold window-curtains" (47). Crowding the house are pilots engaged in simply looking at the surface of the water: "the Mississippi changes its channel so constantly that the pilots used to always find it necessary to run down to Cairo to take a fresh look" (49). The tutelage offered by Mr. Bixby, the pilot with whom Twain serves his apprenticeship, is a tutelage in forms of memorizing the river during journeys upstream and downstream. Full of admiration, Twain offers small details about how to look for landmarks on the banks of the river in order to know the river's depth.

For Bixby, in order to understand its shape, the river needs to be more familiar than the interior space of the home: "A clear starlight night throws such heavy shadows that, if you didn't know the shape of a shore perfectly, you would claw away from every bunch of timber, because you would take the black shadow of it for a solid cape."[28] And darkness matters even more: "the river is a very different shape on a pitch-dark night" (58). In frustration, Twain recoils, and Bixby explains that, once you learn the shape of the river, "you learn it with such absolute certainty that you can always steer by the shape that's in *your head*, and never mind the one that's before your eyes" (59). As soon as that reassurance sinks in Twain realizes that every passing storm might change the margins of the river. The transformations between the shadows on the shore and the threat of timber that might sink the boat appear with shifts of light and the rising and falling of the water.

As he studies the shape of the river, Twain learns how to read the surface of the water. "The face of the water, in time," he says, "became a wonderful book" (69). To extend the metaphor, Twain explains that a ripple on the face of the water is "an *italicized* passage" that the pilot must take note of as a "legend of the largest capitals." However often he celebrates the difficulty of the achievement in learning the face of the river, Twain mourns that his knowledge has subtracted poetry. He complains, "I had lost something which could never be restored to me while I lived. All the grace, the beauty, the poetry, had gone out of the majestic river!" (70).[29] To see the river only in terms of diagnoses that invoke safety and danger reminds

Twain of what a doctor must see in the flush on the cheek of the human body, not beauty, but a symptom of disease (72). The desire to memorize the face of the water like a book merges with the desire to have a book feel like the shape of the water—changing the banks of the river, changing the mind of the reader.

Memories of disaster intrude into the humor of his recollections when he recalls that the steamboat his brother is on, the *Pennsylvania*, crashed just ahead of his own journey from New Orleans to St. Louis. The terrible wounds and death that ensue are described at length. The steamboat race in *Huckleberry Finn*, with its ironic commentary, seems affected by this event.[30] There then appears an abbreviated chapter with an extraordinary number of details tossed off in a few sentences. Anticipating the problems of thinking about slavery on the river, both omitted and included, Thomas Buchanan develops a very helpful contrast between Twain's experience of the Mississippi River and that of the formerly enslaved writer William Wells Brown.[31] The disruption to trade on the river becomes practically the only acknowledgment the book indulges. After Twain manages to become a pilot, he tells his readers, "the war came, commerce was suspended, my occupation was gone." The same river that made it possible to travel from North to South has become a war zone. He does not mention that, after losing his occupation as a pilot, he fought, briefly, for a ragtag group loosely affiliated with the Confederate Army in 1861 before he became, over twenty-one years, a "silver miner in Nevada," a reporter, and "finally, I became a scribbler of books" (162).[32]

More than two decades later, past the violence of Reconstruction, Twain returns to the Mississippi under an assumed name, but the pseudonym does not last. The first time he steps into a pilot house, Twain finds himself not only unmasked, but invited to steer the boat: "I had been itching to get my hands on the wheel" (272). Not until late in the book does Twain turn to memories of the unnamed war, a war that would have had a different name in the South, where names such as the "war of northern aggression" linger. The story that he then tells seems influenced by the boat's physical entry into the location of past battles, almost forcing Twain to comment. He says, "Talk began to run upon the war now, for we were getting down into the upper edge of the former battle-stretch by this time" (190). The conversation has been affected because "One of our pilots had his first war experience in the Belmont fight, as a pilot on a boat in the Confederate service" (190). That story appears as an inset piece, as "The Pilot's First Battle." But no trace appears of Twain's war experience, however much the story might be a stand-in for his own brief participation on the Confederate side. The boundary markers between Union and Confederate states seem to exist in the same blur that the river produces on other boundaries between states as it floods farms and state lines alike. On July 4, 1863, as he well knows, the Union army captured Vicksburg and the Mississippi River was controlled by the North. That detail does not appear here. Instead he returns to the other form of pseudonym that dominates the book, that of a tourist.

Because he travels as a tourist, Twain provides context by telling of former tourists on the river, starting with "Captain Basil Hall," who visited in the 1820s, and Frances Trollope. Another visitor, Captain Frederick Marryat, writes in 1837 that "Never, perhaps, in the records of nations, was there an instance of a century of such unvarying and unmitigated crime as is to be collected from the history of the turbulent and blood-stained Mississippi."[33] These recollections are the grimmest that Twain quotes: "There are no pleasing associations connected with the great common sewer of the Western America, which pours out its mud into the Mexican Gulf, polluting the clear blue sea for many miles beyond its mouth" (201). The sordid tales about the human and environmental pollution of the river stand in contrast to much of the language of amazement travelers express.

The war has taken place both on and at the edge of the river, but Twain does not quite seem able to see that there has just been an enormous conflict in the region he traverses. For instance, he briefly mentions a galvanizing event, the Fort Pillow massacre that saw Confederate troops slaughter Union soldiers because of the color of their skin.[34] Then the story turns briefly to the killing of the white outlaw Jesse James. Twain compares James to the marauding white criminal he calls "Murel," which implicitly brings white villainy into conversation with crimes associated with race. The most villainous act, copied into the narrative from a "now forgotten book," is that Murel cruelly swindled people held as slaves (215). They were encouraged to run away and then coldly sold or murdered as the gang fancied (216–219). The stories excerpted are stunningly gruesome. They involve casual slaughter and disemboweling, with corpses dropped into Arkansas streams and swamps.[35]

In a helpful book by Thomas Ruys Smith, *River of Dreams: Imagining the Mississippi before Mark Twain*, the epilogue titled "The Civil War and Mark Twain" quotes the one-time presidential candidate and Union soldier John Fremont saying that, during the war, "whoever controlled the river would 'hold the country by the heart.'"[36] The metaphors offer a contorted eloquence, as though to hold the heart of the nation was also to hold its spine. In seeing the river as a place for commerce, Twain overlooks the division between slave and free states that marks the journeys of *Huckleberry Finn*. That division occupies Smith as he tells the stories first of Jefferson Davis and then of Abraham Lincoln in relation to the Mississippi. In the case of Abraham Lincoln, it seems significant to Smith that he was poling a raft across the Ohio River and then, in 1828, traveling down the Mississippi on a raft to sell goods in New Orleans, returning by steamboat.

On February 22, 1854, the transcontinental railroad first reached the river. Smith notes that the newspapers called it a marriage: "the nuptial feast of the great Atlantic Ocean to the mighty Father of Waters." He comments, "the coming of the railroad oriented the country to two metal tracks running from east to west."[37] That shift from the north–south "spine" of the river to the east–west tracks of the railroad was ideological as well as commercial. The bridge across the Mississippi that was completed in 1856 drew the wrath of the steamboat men, and the fire that burned it down resulted in a legal battle during which Abraham Lincoln was hired. Lincoln's arguments in support of the railroad included the assertion that the railroad's desire to move traffic involved a more absolute fact: "there is a travel from east to west whose demands are not less than those of the river."[38] The equivalence, the spatializing, that Lincoln draws on invokes the competition that the railroad provided. The idea of the river as the spine of the country places the head in the north and the belly in the south. The confusion caused by "crossing" that spine is the writing of a commercial story across the romance of the river.

As he travels down the river, the story that Twain tells of so-called Island 74 appears as a further romance of unsteady belonging: "a freak of the river here has sorely perplexed the laws of men and made them a vanity and a jest" (253). This "freak" is to isolate a location that is claimed by one state as a center and another as a channel. As neither in the channel nor at the center of the river, the island belongs to no jurisdiction. This jurisdictional refusal, an inert land mass notwithstanding, makes the island independent. Such unreliable belonging continues. When he speaks of Vicksburg after the war Twain presents a town where the inhabitants have to hide out for weeks: "The caves did good service during the six weeks' bombardment of the city—May 18 to July 4, 1863" (261). Twain writes sympathetically about life during the siege. Still, obsessed with the river, Twain remains with details about boats: in "the city utterly cut off from the world" there was "hence, also, no running to see steamboats smoking into view in the distance up or down, and plowing toward the town—for none came" (261–262).

At the end of *Life on the Mississippi*, as he heads upriver past St. Louis and past his old home into the territory of Wisconsin, Twain detours into telling the stories of the communities that once claimed the land, including the story of Black Hawk. In the land that the ship passes, the Army of the South had met with spectacularly miserable defeats, but Twain notes, as if casually, "We passed Port Hudson, scene of two of the most terrific episodes of the war" (289). In Baton Rouge, Twain comments on the capitol building that it was inspired by Sir Walter Scott: "The South has not yet recovered from the debilitating influence of his books" (290). The anecdotes that Twain tells in his footnotes are versions of the feud killings that show up in *Huckleberry Finn* (292–294). Twain discusses the dead of New Orleans in a chapter titled "Hygiene and Sentiment" (301). Looking at the vaults, and their resemblance to houses, Twain announces that the phrase "city of the dead" develops "a meaning to him" (301).

In the beginning of his memorable book, *Cities of the Dead*, Joseph Roach comments on a process he calls "surrogation," which combines "memory, performance, and substitution." For Twain, the performances of memory and substitution come naturally after years on the road doing accounts of himself. The surrogation, the almost invisible substitutions of artifactual memory for memories too painful to confront as he travels deeper into the post–Civil War South, can never be completely successful. As Roach expresses it, "The fit cannot be exact. The intended substitute either cannot fulfill expectations, creating a deficit, or actually exceeds them, creating a surplus" (2). The suppression of memory that Twain exhibits when confronted with graves extends to the odd homilies about infectious diseases that they make him engage in. As he puts it, graveyards are "all grotesque, ghastly, horrible" (302). He turns from the grotesque to the economic waste as he continues in the next chapter by proposing that the amount of money spent on funerals has depleted resources that would remain intact if cremation were more widely practiced.

One of the distractions that Twain engages in when he reaches New Orleans is to ask his reader to pay attention to accents, as much a distraction from location as a distraction from the act of reading. A man who keeps Twain company as he walks around "the old French part of New Orleans" is George Washington Cable, "the South's finest literary genius" (310). Twain's ear perks up at Southern speech, and especially at the dropped "r" in "'honah' and 'dinnah,' and 'Gove'-nuh,' and 'befo' the waw,' and so on" (314). The resistance to the interruption of the war in this melody of speech is interesting. A late chapter begins with it: "In the North one hears the war mentioned, in social conversation, once a month; sometimes as often as once a week; but as a distinct subject for talk, it has long ago been relieved of duty." However, he says, this is "very different in the

South. There, every man you meet was in the war. . . . The war is the great chief topic of conversation." Indeed, he continues, "the war is what A.D. is elsewhere: they date from it" (317). For Twain, this provides an insight into "what a vast and comprehensive calamity invasion is," a remark that further exposes his identification as a southerner (318). His search for entertainment in New Orleans includes his brief mention of Mardi Gras (they arrive too late for it) and an only partially humorous dissection of the derangement that the presence of women does to language.

Late in the book, Twain meets Horace Bixby again. He relives his youth by traveling back up the Mississippi with Bixby as a pilot. The journey to the past reaches a kind of culmination when he returns to Hannibal, Missouri, "where my boyhood was spent." The memory of the town as a boy "was still as clear and vivid to me as a photograph" (375). To create a sense of order and limits, as Twain describes it in *Life*, is to find that "this thing has knocked the romance out of piloting" (205). Electric lights at all the landings mean that pilots can literally see in the dark. The "West Point engineers" imagine that they can contain the river: "since they conceive that they can fetter and handcuff that river and boss him, it is but wisdom for the unscientific man to keep still, lie low, and wait till they do it" (207). To give voice to this impossibility, Twain inserts the reflections of "Uncle Mumford," who occupies pages of text and then inserts conflicting opinions, including that "some believed that the higher you build your levee, the higher the river's bottom will rise" (210).

The confusion of references that Twain includes might remind the reader of the unreliable narrator aboard the Mississippi River in *The Confidence-Man*.[39] Both works offer a way to think about the relation between a fantasy of poor boys emerging toward middle-class life and this sequence of adventures carried out by men on the unstable location of water as a foundational element of success as a founding father, however much the crossing of water involves deception.[40] And that time of crossing water, a water crossing that changes affiliation and introduces violence, returns us to Black Hawk as it involves that troubling matter of bodies on the water being carried as property. The autobiography that has become known as the story of Black Hawk contains many crossings of the Mississippi for violent raids or in retreat from violence.[41] To read the face of the river is to read the faces of men on the river, in his account as in others, to anticipate whether they bring violence. To note what effect travel on the river has on the observation of human nature is to note what the stories Herman Melville tells of life on the river might have in common with the nostalgia and the peril on the river visited by Mark Twain.

Confidence Men

The "lightness" of men on the water, a lightness once associated with the world of *Huckleberry Finn*, finds a sinister formulation in Herman Melville's *The Confidence-Man*, one of Melville's most impenetrable novels both because the main character is a chameleon and because the humor is almost invariably grim.[42] Since the action takes place on the Mississippi River, what makes the fluid nature of the space being inhabited a prime territory for the confidence man, or woman? As the central character, a man whose name can never be finally determined, changes disguises, changes races, changes occupation and class standing, it never seems to occur to him to dress as a woman. Each character who appears so elaborately dressed prepares the stage for the appearance of the next character, proposing the credibility of the person to be duped as a matter that relies on belief in the next one to appear, the one who will vouch for the appearance of the first one, or who will have the means to swindle the person whose greed will have been awakened by the assurance that the next man to appear will have the bank stock or the patent medicine that he might invest in or purchase. And yet, of course, these two never appear at the same time, since they are versions of each other.

The narrator assumes and yet does not assume that the reader is in on the secret, since the backstage shenanigans never appear as part of the details that the reader views. The magical transformations take place behind the scenes, out of view of the narrative camera. We do not see the change of clothes, the makeup that must be applied or removed lickety-split. We never know where the "green room" is that this actor must retire to in order to change his character's appearance. Instead, the narrator invites readers to marvel at the multiple ways in which the term "confidence" might be applied, and the sheer absurdity of appeals to "charity" and to forms of insubstantial investment that travelers in transit to and from unknown points along a 1,200-mile stretch of river might be drawn.

The man who appears in the first pages, in a chapter titled "A Mute Goes aboard a Boat on the Mississippi," is pale and dressed in "cream-colors," with "flaxen" hair and a "white fur" hat (1). This pale man, dressed in off-white garb, finds a boat where one peddler sells money belts and another sells pamphlets retailing the stories of bandits such as "Murrel, the pirate of the Mississippi" (a return engagement of the bandit mentioned by Twain). These pirates, the story tells us, have now been "exterminated" and the reader's enthusiasm at hearing such good news might be tempered by the thought that "in new countries, where the wolves are killed off, the foxes increase" (2). Such stories immediately invite a reader to notice that to enter the boat is to enter a place where predators are looking for prey. The stranger who enters the boat holds up a slate and writes on it, in chalk, a series of biblical pronouncements, all beginning with the word "Charity." The word charity, we are told, is not erased from the board even as a tumult of pressing bodies appears. Because the crowd that surrounds him has gathered to read the details of a notice posted on board the ship to watch out for swindlers, they push him out of the way.

As the *Fidele* passes down the river, the slow procession of humans is compared by Melville to Chaucer's Canterbury pilgrims. That the ship's name implies fidelity already contains an irony reminiscent of the naming of the ship, the *Bachelor's Delight*, in *Benito Cereno*. These passengers, we are told, have "no lack of variety"; this description seems designed to encourage the reader at once to look for distinctions and to accept the stereotypes that pervade their very distinctiveness. The narrator finds many men: "men of business and men of pleasure; parlor men and backwoodsmen; farm-hunters and fame-hunters; heiress-hunters; gold-hunters, buffalo-hunters, bee-hunters, happiness-hunters, truth-hunters, and still keener hunters after all these hunters." The last item on this list betrays the invisible hunter on board. The next list mingles men and women with further stereotypes of class, race, and ethnicity: "Fine ladies in slippers and moccasined squaws" mingle with "Japanese-looking Mississippi cotton-planters; Quakers in full drab, and United States soldiers in full regimentals." Mingled in almost without further notice are "slaves, black, mulatto, quadroon; modish young Spanish Creoles and old-fashioned French Jews . . . grinning negroes, and Sioux chiefs solemn as high priests." Melville declares this to be a "piebald parliament, an Anacharsis Cloots congress of all kinds of that multiform pilgrim species, man" (10).[43] The very variety of the crowd invites an interpretation of humans according to their dress although the plot of the book enforces the idea that any such interpretation will be misleading.

The next chapter's title, "In Which a Variety of Characters Appear," shows a kind of transformation where it seems that the former whiteness of the confidence man has been utterly changed into an appearance as a "grotesque negro cripple" who shuffles around the crowd with his "honest black face rubbing against the upper part of people's thighs" (12). That position of course makes a good posture for robbing pockets. What he does, after the narrator compares him to a "Newfoundland Dog" (reminding the astute reader of the duplicitous Babo in *Benito Cereno*) is to lift his head and catch pennies thrown from the crowd in very much the posture of a dog. As he throws back his head, "the cripple's mouth being at once target and purse," he swallows his emotions, but not the pennies (14). The strange suggestiveness of a face that rubs "against the upper part of people's thighs," performing a kind of clothed fellatio, presents the familiarity of the crowd with a man in a position of such subservience. The gesture of the open mouth resembles the posture of the metal jockeys once stationed outside southern homes to hold the reins of horses; the posture of the human assuming such a position removes animation, becoming indistinguishable from such an object.

The commerce on the river that obsessed readers of *The Confidence-Man* try to track is a democratic swindling that mirrors both money and men. Even today, if citizens of the United States are asked the question once posed by a (fictional) visiting Frenchman we have to hesitate: "Does the legislature of your country permit this system of swindling?" This question appears in a little-read satire by James Kirke Paulding, *The History of a Little Frenchman and His Bank Notes*, with the wonderful subtitle *Rags! Rags! Rags!*—a subtitle that might work for Melville's *The Confidence-Man.*[44] Reeling from the effects of fluctuating paper currency values, the French tourist in Paulding's satire asks in a rage: "Does the very concept of democracy depend on a stable currency?"[45] Readers who study both the fiction and the history produced during the uneasy time of the Fugitive Slave Law need to consider what might have counted as currency as well as what counted as a purchase. To follow the money as a strategy for interpretation works more effectively than following disguises in Melville's book. Whenever money appears, the direction that it takes, almost as liquid as water flowing south on the Mississippi River, is the direction of the confidence man. Whatever person the reader sees in pursuit of money has the same identity; the color of green takes over from racial and class distinctions. The ambiguity of place on the river and the ambiguity of the name of the confidence man merge: that person in disguise is always the same—the person who takes money and fakes identifications.

Asking for "confidence" in the opening pages of the book, and met with suspicion, the "negro's appeal" results in one merchant giving him more money (and dropping his "business card" on the deck in the process). The unnamed limping man, whose mouth has been opened for pennies, collects the money, while "unconsciously, his one advanced leather stump covered the card" (24). There will be, of course, nothing "unconscious" in the use he makes of that card, a card that mocks the instability of paper identification. This card having been procured, the next appearance of the confidence man is the "man with the weed," a man in mourning who has earlier been described as a witness, and who now accosts the merchant and pretends to know him, even as he vouches for the character of the now invisible "Black Guinea." The suspicion that this earlier appearance might have been a "white masquerading as a black" is met by the "man in gray" with the question, "if a white, how could he look the negro so?" The exaggerated acting of the cripple is compared to the "negro-minstrels" who are "apt to overdo the ebony." The man in gray, who has previously been in the alternate disguises of white and "negro," is now soliciting donations on behalf of the "Seminole Widow and Orphan Asylum," suggesting a further shift in colors as he makes fraudulent claims on charity. Told "I have not heard of that charity," the man in gray replies that it has been "recently founded" (52). The peculiar business of a "white" masquerading as a "black" on board a boat going downstream on the Mississippi River doesn't seem to suggest someone escaping from slavery mostly because the boat's passage, while essentially ambiguous and apparently endless, appears to be toward the South; the consternation attached to the story about the Indian killer, a story borrowed from James Hall's popular *Legends of the West* (1832) seems designed to cover for the horrors of slavery.

Life on the Mississippi in Melville's last published novel neither names nor builds in resistance to the Fugitive Slave Law as it investigates unstable identities as part of profitable masquerades and identity instability. That topic, perhaps unfairly, returns me to thinking about Abraham Lincoln, who claimed to learn the horrors of slavery on a trip down the Mississippi as a young man and whose political career began along the Mississippi with his brief military service in the Black Hawk War of 1832, reaching what might have been its nadir with the notorious case of the Dakota 38 in the violent executions of 1862. When I think about the Mississippi and the question of unstable identities in a democracy, Lincoln's voyages emerge. Further, as the very name of Mark Twain, on the river at the same time, reminds us, to measure location in water, to sound the depths, is to mark the safety of the boat.

When challenged, and after some disarray in the composition of the crowd, including a one-legged man who limps away, the man who has identified himself as "Black Guinea" asks for "confidence." He sends for specifically described witnesses to his identity. One person says that there's "Something queer about this darkie, depend upon it" (23). What can a person depend on? The "queer" appearance that accompanies his presence might, a reader later realizes, both be that he cannot be seen and that he will never be seen again, swallowed up by the river.

As he explains the concept of the "World's Charity," the elusive disguise artist proposes that a forthcoming transformation in charitable donations will involve "the present system of voluntary and promiscuous contribution to be done away with" as a means of producing the "Wall Street spirit" in benevolence (60, 62). The follow-through would be conversion: "the conversion of the heathen" would be "let out on contract. So much by bid for converting India, so much for Borneo, so much for Africa" (62) The question of scale necessitates that he will be "sending ten thousand missionaries in a body and converting the Chinese en masse" (63). Benevolence as a motif tends to be productive of much danger in Melville. It has recently appeared in the uneasy benevolence in *Pierre*, where, whether to rescue his sister or out of desire for his sister, Pierre seeks to bring her into relation with, possibly substituting for, the woman he had planned to marry. It shows up in the misplaced benevolence of *Benito Cereno*, where Captain Amasa Delano's misreading of the events on board ship actually saves his life. The frustrated desire that the merchant expresses for the exercise of benevolence in "Bartleby the Scrivener" seems rather to encourage its fatal ending.

After finding his way through the male passengers on board, the stranger enters the "ladies saloon" and sits with "an air of melancholy exhaustion and depression" (66). Beginning a conversation with a woman, he asks her if she could have "confidence in me." After all, "No one can befriend me, who has not confidence" (68). The need to read the face of the river that Twain cites as the need to keep a steamboat from crashing into obstacles might be anticipated here by the relentless task of reading the face of a man who keeps shifting identities. The narrator steps forward in the voice of an omniscient author and says, "while to all fiction is allowed some play of invention, yet, fiction based on fact should never be contradictory to it" (103). The possible consistency of characters is rare. And "no writer has produced such inconsistent characters as nature herself has." He cites as evidence the peculiar creature he calls a "duck-billed beaver," known to us now as the duck-billed platypus (104).

In *The Confidence-Man*, the mysterious stranger proposes that a gullible young college student might like to invest in the "New Jerusalem," a "new and thriving city, so called, in northern Minnesota. It was originally founded by certain fugitive Mormons" and "stands on the Mississippi." Notwithstanding the ambiguous status of a city that "stands" on water, the place has a map, a further fraudulent set of marks on paper. The map has "public buildings" and "twenty asterisks" for the "lyceums." The student is suspicious enough to ask if there are "water-lots," and the stranger returns "Water-lots in the city of New Jerusalem? All terra firma . . ." (76–77). This earth is not firm; its relation to water places it, like the boat, on the Mississippi.

The reference invokes the headwaters of the Mississippi River in northern Minnesota, a significant place of contests over what humans can live on what land and location because of the so-called Dakota Wars that were already brewing, although they officially began five years after the publication of the novel. The Dakota Wars erupted around treaties signed in 1837, 1851, and 1858, preceding and surrounding the composition and publication of Melville's novel, which tends to be associated more with the ugly stories borrowed from James T. Hall.[46] Settling in a place that sells "water-lots" might also remind the reader of an earlier publication, Caroline Kirkland's 1839 *A New Home, Who'll Follow?* Kirkland's semi-autobiographical satire about the desire to cash in on swamp lands using fake currency from invented banks on the frontier in Michigan alludes to an insubstantial vision of land when it rests in water and can be washed away.

A new disguise in Melville's novel is that of the "somewhat elderly person, in the Quaker dress," who has passed around pamphlets that are titled "ODE ON THE INTIMATIONS OF DISTRUST IN MAN, UNWILLINGLY INFERRED FROM REPEATED REPULSES IN DISINTERESTED ENDEAVORS TO PROCURE HIS CONFIDENCE" (all caps, 78). The effect of the pamphlet is to encourage investment in his pretended role as an agent of the "Black Rapids Coal Company." This man says to a wary auditor, "if you were other than I have confidence you are, hardly would you challenge distrust that way" (85). Such a challenge raises the stakes for the philosophical intelligence officer that the confidence man seems to become.

Late in the book, a topic arises named as the "metaphysics of Indian hating." In this chapter, the theme of the man in the woods crosses with the man on the river. To hate the Indians is to hate the men who were in the woods before you, but that hatred also performs an annihilation that mirrors what you ascribe to their position. The topic emerges in a chapter titled "Concerning the metaphysics of Indian-hating, according to the views of one evidently not as prepossessed as Rousseau in favor of savages" (224). Here the philosophical intelligence office becomes infused with malevolence. If to hate the Indians is to hate the men who were in the woods before you, thc idea that you might find yourself confronted by an image that you cannot distinguish from your own identity intrudes. Melville is painfully aware of the theme of killing Indians that pervades the popular fiction of the day, such as the lurid but very popular novel by Robert Montgomery

Bird, *Nick of the Woods*, in which the euphoniously named Nick Slaughter masquerades as the very men he will butcher.[47]

To bear witness to how these conflicts about men on the Mississippi River appear is to bring up major clashes along the river, including both the Dakota Wars and the story of Black Hawk. That latter story invokes the brief military career of Abraham Lincoln as an officer in the so-called Black Hawk War of 1832. The multiple evasions that appear in *The Confidence-Man* overlap with refusals to tell these stories except as stories that take place in the woods; hence, that might also expose why and how the explanations of the history of the river told by both Twain and Melville become interrupted by the storytelling that incorporates, on the one hand, "Indian hating" and, on the other, the retellings of Indian legend that Melville relocates from the presentations of Judge James Hall.[48] The multicolored man that next appears, in another evasion of identity specificity, is a man who subsumes racial envy and benevolence at once. When the later chapter shows the "metaphysics of Indian hating," the words are attributed to "my father's friend, Judge Hall" and we are told that "the judge always began with these words" (224). And, after the embedded tale, the next story starts with the matter of misanthropy. The little tricks of swindle and scandal have melted away for several chapters of storytelling that obscure rather than clarifying what the ground is being prepared for. Unlike previous chapters where one character vouched for another no clear victory or succession appears. A reader knows by now to be suspicious when the character's pseudonym is Frank Goodman and he says he has talked to Charles Noble.

Throughout the novel the narrator meditates on the idea of an original character in a work of fiction as a kind of river tourist: "Every great town is a kind of man-show" (373). The occasions of stopping by towns along the river at once allow new characters to appear who can be swindled and interrupt the violence taking place on shore. That violence repeats endlessly through these fictions and through the story of the war that they at once anticipate and relive.

CHAPTER FIVE

Women at Home

CHARLOTTE PERKINS GILMAN, HARRIET JACOBS, LUCY LARCOM, AND FRANCES HARPER

How Feminism Finds "The Yellow Wallpaper"

He stopped short by the door. "What is the matter?" he cried. "For God's sake, what are you doing!"

I kept on creeping just the same, but I looked at him over my shoulder.

"I've got out at last," said I, "in spite of you and Jane. And I've pulled off most of the paper, so you can't put me back!"

Now why should that man have fainted?

But he did, and right across my path by the wall, so that I had to creep over him!

(CHARLOTTE PERKINS GILMAN, "THE YELLOW WALLPAPER")[1]

This ambiguous conclusion appeared in a work that mobilized feminist attention more than a century ago, but that has served to frighten readers ever since. My analysis of feminist motifs in relation to Civil War stories begins with this focus on a short passage from the conclusion of this very famous story by Charlotte Perkins Gilman. At the end of "The Yellow Wallpaper," quite short paragraphs appear from a narrator who seems to have descended into madness. As she crawls around the walls of the room with the eponymous wallpaper, she makes her way over the prone body of her husband. Addressing him, or perhaps the reader, she declares, "I've got out, in spite of you and Jane" (51). The ambiguity of that ending inheres in the question of what it might mean to be "out" of the room, since she has so clearly restricted herself to an orbit entirely within the space of the home.

The further ambiguities of the story have, since the time of its first magazine publication in 1892, marked it as the place to turn for a number of questions about genre. Is it a horror story, a ghost story, or, perhaps, a feminist awakening? The story first appeared around the time of Kate Chopin's ambiguous novel *The Awakening* (1899) and was followed by Gilman's defiantly utopian novel *Herland* (1915). Each work featured women overturning normative expectations. Each was greeted with misgivings at the time of first publication. They have become standard classics in literary classrooms that pay attention to feminism.[2] Further details about Charlotte Perkins Gilman's life, including her significant nonfiction treatise *Women and Economics* (1898) and that she walked away from her marriage to earn her keep as a traveling spokesperson for women's financial independence, have made "The Yellow Wallpaper" subject to intense scrutiny from its first publication.

The publication of *Women and Economics*, subtitled *A Study of the Economic Relation between Men and Women as a Factor in Social Evolution* and first published in 1898, marked Gilman as grappling with the conditions of mostly middle-class white women in turn of the century North America. It can also be interpreted as following on the work of writers like Margaret Fuller who, in *Women in the Nineteenth Century* (1848), presented a more philosophical rendering of the limits on such women's lives. Gilman's work contains literary and philosophical excursions along with its call for women to abjure the economic and social conditions that restricted their activity to the home. The preface to *Women and Economics* calls for an audience made up of "thinking women" who will consider "not only their social responsibility as individuals," but also the "measureless racial importance" they have "as makers of men" (vii).

When Gilman refers to race, she imagines the human race, yet within that last phrase lie some ingredients of the criticisms that have been levied against her work for its elitism and embedded racism, especially in the utopian envisioning of her later novel *Herland* (1915). *Herland* imagines the lives of a group of women who have been isolated in a remote walled-off region positioned oddly in South America; they have learned to reproduce through parthenogenesis. When they are discovered by male explorers, the description indicates an Anglicized community whose racial composition seems to have little to do with the continent where they have been discovered. The work shows the male explorers surprised by the women's ability to carry out all the occupations that their intruders imagine belong solely to the capacities of men.

In *Women and Economics*, Gilman states her premise early on: "We are the only animal species in which the female depends on the male for food, the only animal species in which the sex-relation is also an economic one."[3] The ability of women to make a living, asserts Gilman, depends solely on the social conditions that restrict her to the home and bar her from professions. She acknowledges that "peasant women" work, but notes pointedly that their ability to profit from their labor depends on men. Besides, as she proposes, in an argument at once appropriately controversial and rather blind to race and class, "the women who do the most work get the least money and the women who have the most money do the least work" (13–14). Further, drawing on middle-class morality, it is "held to be their duty as women to do this work" and indeed, Gilman argues, in this view "motherhood is an exchangeable commodity given by women in payment for clothes and food" (15).

The surprising lack of sentimentality about motherhood may affect how "The Yellow Wallpaper" imagines the post-partum existence of a woman who has recently given birth but seems to have little or no relation to the baby heard crying in the house where she has been confined to the "nursery" (27). As the story moves toward its disturbing end, the narrator imagines women crawling everywhere, confined behind the wallpaper, beneath the bushes in the garden; the reader might imagine that they are the ghosts of the economic circumstances Gilman describes in *Women and Economics*. According to the social circumstances Gilman depicts, the condition of motherhood unfits women for other work. But, she asks starkly, does "the human mother, by her motherhood, thereby lose control of brain and body, lose power and skill and desire for any other work?" (19). *Women and Economics* presents an extended comparison of human families to the factors that lead to economic choice and ends by looking to apartment buildings that have communal kitchens and nurseries, an early call for the style of communal living promulgated in some current progressive communities.

Investigating the relation between the crawling woman and the fallen man at the end of the story, I want to ask about the ambiguity of the final sentences. Offering a somewhat different inquiry into the genre of the story, I want to ask especially what might make this a story about the American Civil War. That is, in addition to the resonance of the domestic space as a fraught space of writing, what concepts of mourning and motherhood resonate through its pages in relation to the great agony of the war? Named in the story, and clearly drawing on the experience by its author, is the so-called rest cure developed by the physician and writer S. Weir Mitchell to treat what we now recognize as post-traumatic stress suffered by veterans of the Civil War. Subsequently applied to women, the rest cure was blamed by Charlotte Perkins Gilman for her own descent into terrible depression.

The story displays this author as the genius of neurasthenic imagining as she portrays a character who is never named, so that the name of "Jane" operates as a potential self-naming while it might offer a potential name for a domestic servant.

The anonymity of a narrator who has recently given birth but is herself confined to a "nursery" at the top of a seemingly haunted house displays her as a potential agent as well as subject, as a writer, since she presents the story as containing smuggled writing, and as someone who wants to tear the paper from the walls of the home. This chapter proposes that in addition to the inquiry about domestic space, a relation appears between meanings of paper, including the yellow paper packets used to send home the personal effects of dead soldiers during wartime, and motherhood in the still-potent territory of this suggestive story.[4]

The story refers to the American Civil War through the genealogy of the rest cure, but it takes place at home. The treatment of "nerves" by S. Weir Mitchell invokes wounds that are invisible; in the story, the effect seems caused implicitly by childbirth; it repudiates the form of the family that her act of giving birth might represent because the mother inhabits the nursery. The question of labor invites a reading of labor as multivalent—the labor of writing becomes at once birth and the work associated with inappropriate feminine desires, work that the husband attempts to prevent. The husband becomes an inert obstacle in the narrator's crawling path at the end of the story, but he also substitutes his prone body for the previously prone body of the narrator who has been told to rest in that same room and who has now either disappeared behind the wallpaper or managed to get "out." What has happened within the story might thus make the "rest cure" something portable from the bodies of wounded Civil War soldiers to the post-partum bodies of women. The oddity within the story is that it produces a form of a corpse—the ambiguous casualty of the man's body that she needs to crawl over. What is it for a woman to crawl as she makes that disturbing last inquiry: "Now why should that man have fainted?"[5]

Outside the window, during the story, the lingering question remains about the other bodies that appear at the edge of the garden. An apparent menace clings to them. The narrator first sees a woman "always creeping." She travels the inside of her room to see her: "I often wonder if I could see her out of all the windows at once" (46). A story about a woman alone in a room leads an alert reader of gothic fiction to expect some form of home invasion. The space of the home since the invention of the eighteenth-century gothic novel has invoked violence and mysterious passages behind the walls. What is the configuration that makes the walls of the home still a place that inhabitants leave and return from? As the narrator continues to look out of the window, she sees "so many of those creeping women, and they creep so fast" (50). Their presence seems linked to the woman that she finds inside the wallpaper at the end of the story when she peels the paper away. The woman behind the wallpaper becomes "that poor thing who began to crawl and shake the pattern. I got up and ran to help her." What happens when they peel the paper together is a chiasmic structure of entangled longing: "I pulled and she shook, I shook and she pulled, and before morning we had peeled off yards of that paper" (48).

Throughout "The Yellow Wallpaper," feminist motifs emerge as an aspect of writing, domesticity, and intimacy. The use of paper as both an element for writing and a way to decorate houses overlaps in the story, and the overlap engages an aspect of trust. The narrator asks the reader for trust, but clearly withholds information. For instance, she complains that, having been confined to the nursery, her husband refuses to change the paper: "He said that after the wallpaper was changed it would be the heavy bedstead, and then the barred windows, and then that gate at the head of the stairs, and so on" (28). It does sound like a reasonable sequence of removals. But why do the windows have bars on them? Who has bitten the furniture, or the bedstead that has been "fairly gnawed" (50)? The furniture that was to stay outside the body becomes something that can be ingested. The space that was to be a solid edge to the room becomes permeable.

The narrator resorts to personification: "This paper looks to me as if it knew what a vicious influence it had" (30). Her husband believes there can be no reason for her unease: he "knows there is no *reason* to suffer, and that satisfies him" (28). His dissatisfaction with reason emerges even as he explains, "I am a doctor, dear, and I know" (38). The limits of his knowledge appear in a temporal zone that gives the summer an urgent feel: "If I don't pick up faster he shall send me to Weir Mitchell in the fall" (32).

A certain ambiguity persists about the emergence of other women in the story. Noting the smudges along the wall, the narrator protests, "Most women do not creep by daylight." And yet the narrator quickly informs the reader that "I always lock the door when I creep by daylight." A woman off in the distance catches her eye: "I have watched her sometimes away off in the open country, creeping as fast as a cloud shadow in a high wind" (46). And we are told of the woman behind the wallpaper that "she just takes hold of the bars and shakes them hard" (44). As the narrator confuses the women she views with the actions that she herself performs, both inert ideas and ideas about inertia emerge in the insertion of bodies into domestic spaces—and of domestic spaces into the body. That static position in the home makes for crawling rather than walking, makes the body of an erect human into the body of a crawling woman. The woman crawls, then the husband becomes an obstacle in the path of the crawling woman. Made into a richer aspect of the postscript to the writing of women in the nineteenth century, the question appears: What is it for a woman to write? To escape the position of crawling or to enter into crawling so that the odd emergence of language into the act of crawling seems to make writing into an infantilism.

Interpretations of the story have traditionally drawn on biographical details from Gilman's life. After her father walked out on them, the family relied in part on the resources of his aunts, including the prominent writers Harriet Beecher Stowe and Catharine Beecher. In addition to the fame of her best-selling abolitionist work *Uncle Tom's Cabin*, Stowe had co-authored, with her sister Catharine, an advice manual on domestic concerns, *The American Women's Home* (1869). The introduction to this work addresses the need to train women for their lives at home. Gilman's later authorship of *The Home: Its Work and Influence* (1903) might be traced to the effects of this earlier work. In *The Home*, Gilman might reflect back on "The Yellow Wallpaper" as she answers the question "what is the idea of home?" with the bleak statement: "The man free, the woman confined" (6).[6] In this more sociological work, Gilman proposes the idea of home as a prison for women. In her later reflections in *The Man-Made World, or, Our Androcentric Culture* (1911), Gilman concludes with this last sentence: "an economic democracy must rest upon a free womanhood; and a free womanhood inevitably leads to an economic democracy."[7] The fictional treatment of the home in "The Yellow Wallpaper" presents the nursery as a theatrical space. To adapt the formulation posed by the historian Nancy Cott, what are the bonds of womanhood in this home?[8] In particular, who performs the labor of the home and the garden? In addition to the cryptic and elliptical references to a child crying, the narrator describes moving into a space that seems to have been appropriated for the use of a family after having been an institution. The narrator exists within a hierarchical structure of the family that nonetheless alludes to companionate marriage. Yet not only does the story implode that structure—that is, not only does it erode boundaries—it also inverts structures and empties spaces perceived as solid.

As it is haunted by anonymous crawling women, "The Yellow Wallpaper" asks about what it is for women to be visible. The motif of visibility encouraged by the narrator's attention to what can be seen in the room includes the question of what can be seen from the window. What happens to make a yellow smudge at the height of a shoulder all around the room? When does the narrator start crawling? How does it happen that the woman she sees crawling inside the room becomes a woman to be rescued from a liminal space behind the wallpaper?

Above all, the narrator insistently returns to the form of paper that inhabits the home. Paper to write on is something that she has to hide; the paper to decorate the walls of the home becomes something to attack. At the end of the story, she works hard to peel it off the walls, while the act of writing is ambiguously inserted into her apparent insanity. Paper exists in the boundary between the room and the outside world as well as in the relation between utility and decoration. It leaves a smudge on her body at the same time that she attacks it. No wonder her husband cannot allow this message into his consciousness. The question that the narrator asks seems disingenuous: "Now why should that man have fainted?" Now that she has to crawl over him—and now that he lies there in her path, the man who could once say with such authority, "I am a doctor, dear, and I know"—the narrator produces the final act of unsettling the authority of the medical profession and rearranging the status of the home. In fainting, her husband returns to the status of the enervated casualty of war, in this case a war of the household order and of the separation of the spheres.

How Women Weave

In *Women and Economics*, Gilman analyzes the factors that lead to economic choice for women and ends by looking to apartment buildings that have communal kitchens and nurseries. According to the social circumstances Gilman depicts, the condition of motherhood unfits women for other work. Writing during the postscript to the Industrial Revolution, when the call to "ten hours" as a limit to the laboring day had begun to resonate and the photographs of Lewis Hine had exposed the exhaustion suffered in factory work, Gilman might be said to have idealized laboring women.[9] But, she asks starkly, does "the human mother, by her motherhood, thereby lose control of brain and body, lose power and skill and desire for any other work?" In "The Yellow Wallpaper," Gilman first answered that question with an emphatic "no." Women workers in other occupations who were recent immigrants or who were held under conditions of slavery might have provided different answers.[10]

At the same time, the desire to write found its way into the lives of many women. The labor of the Industrial Revolution in the United States was at first celebrated because it was accompanied by women's voices in print. The way that "The Yellow Wallpaper" has sometimes been treated as a call for women to work, the way that Gilman herself called for access to work for women, begins to appear as a desire for white middle-class women to have access to employment when the work is set in contrast with another voice from the nineteenth century labor force. The factory worker and poet Lucy Larcom ably articulated the ambivalence that such labor might bring to a New England working girl.[11]

Lucy Larcom's poem "Weaving" reminds the reader that, of course, there were women who worked. As the speaker within the poem comments, "I weave, to win my daily food."[12] The labor of the household has been carried out by women who are mostly out of sight and who do not write their thoughts down in "The Yellow Wallpaper," as in other works from the period such as Kate Chopin's *The Awakening*. Whether observed or not, someone in "The Yellow Wallpaper" must be changing that baby's diaper, cooking, shopping, and putting food on the table. The activity in "Weaving," a poem that shifts register and narrative voice several times, opens on the factory floor with a narrator standing in front of a loom. The subject of the poem appears as "she," who, confronted with "flying shuttles," sees instead "the winding river flow," while "fancy's shuttle flieth wide, / And faster than the waters glide." The third person narrator continues in the next stanza with a fantasy that the woman who stands at the loom might be like the "fair-weaver of Shalott."[13] The poem mocks the idea that such a romantic idea is in her head: "Her heart, a mirror sadly true, / Brings gloomier visions into view." At this juncture, after the second stanza, the poem introduces quotation marks and the first-person voice: "I weave," the stanza begins. Repeating the phrase until the final line of the stanza, the speaker, still identified as "she," announces that "The world of women haunteth me."

The poem presents the sense of being haunted very differently from the haunting of women in "The Yellow Wallpaper." The idea that the speaker would have a fantasy of looking at Lancelot, a topic in Tennyson's poem, seems inconsequential to the "gloomier visions" that she has. For Tennyson, elaborating on the legend, the world can only be glimpsed in a mirror as the Lady of Shalott compulsively weaves. For Larcom, the speaker's heart is a mirror that reflects other laboring women. The poem seems at first to move into the standard tropes of romantic poetry, to bring the "Lady of Shalott" into a relationship that will make streams and weaving coterminous, the shuttles imagined as flying on their own. The relation of labor to feminism that Gilman addressed in her writing at first appears to have met a sense of conversion with metaphor. But there next appears an extreme shift from the Lady of Shalott drifting down stream to the woman who stands before her loom so that she can eat. What she sees as she stands there are emphatically not the "flying shuttles," which seem to "come and go" on their own. Instead she sees the "winding river flow" and the movement of "fancy's shuttle . . . faster than the waters." The flying of fancy's shuttle seems driven by water even as the power for the mill must be supplied by the rivers of New England.

Just as the reader begins to settle into the third-person narration of this style of poem, the voice shifts, quotation marks appear, and the first-person voice merges with the prior romantic tendencies to make the poem appear religious. That shift to referencing God as part of a large plan seems consonant with the allusions that Edward Taylor once made in his address to the weaving patient spider.[14] The weaving of a design into human life becomes interrupted when the poem shifts registers again to introduce an identification with the workers who harvest the cotton that has been delivered to New England for making cloth in factories. The philosophical musing about how, "at the loom of life, we weave / Our separate shreds" becomes first a "full pattern wherein man / Works blindly out the eternal plan," and occupies several stanzas. And then, as though the poem shook off such associations, the tone shifts again and the speaker turns to look at how "My sisters toil, with foreheads black; / And water with their blood this root." That inquiry into the condition of other laboring women implicates the speaker: "how much of your wrong is mine / Dark women slaving at the South?"

In "The Yellow Wallpaper," the repetition of strangled heads in the paper, a repetition introduced by the mass reproduction of images in wallpaper, induces a form of madness; "Weaving" introduces a metric repetition based on the mechanical rhythm of the loom. The paper has offered both liberation—the woman behind the bars can escape—and an erasure of the obsessive witness who has been watching for an escape. "Weaving" offers repetition via rhyming patterns and allusions. Metaphors dominate. What is the "work of women" that haunts the speaker of the poem? Early on, the river that "glides along" seems to bring the reference to the Lady of Shalott together with the river that would have powered the mill. The cloth that was white has now become red with blood. The color red recurs on the edges of the poem's set of allusions until it moves onto center stage, as blood. The irresolute feeling that accompanied the poem's shift in style and address seem to reach a form of conclusion when the voice shifts to third person again and the quotation marks end. As the thread of the loom before which the speaker stands appears to turn red with blood, the vision of the poem turns to war, a fateful rendering of costs. "Fathers and brothers falling both / On ghastly, death-sown fields, that lie / Beneath the tearless Southern Sky."

Returning to the idea of the curse that the Lady of Shalott is said to have unleashed, the speaker's words end as the poem's third-person narrator returns to say, "weary weaver, not to you / Alone was war's stern message brought." The last words of the poem are ascribed to war, with this "message": "'Woman!' It knelled from heart to heart, / 'Thy sister's keeper know thou art!'" The "stern message" of war echoes the abolitionist language that resulted in cartoons such as "am I not my brother's keeper?" and "am I not my sister's keeper?" What is it to be "thy sister's keeper"? According to this poem, to be a "sister's keeper" is to know the source of the cotton that will be turned into cloth, to know the labor behind the labor that will feed the mill girls of New England. And to see white cotton turn red before your eyes.

Stories persist about how to understand the abolitionist question "Am I not a woman and a sister?" They tend to be associated with short stories such as the early one by Lydia Maria Child, "Slavery's Pleasant Homes," that is slightly incorporated into the novel by William Wells Brown, *Clotel*, as well as into Louisa May Alcott's "The Brothers."[15] Still to be developed, perhaps, are ways that the labor depicted by scenes in Harriet Jacobs and Frederick Douglass might be understood to begin the relation between labor in the fields and the labor of producing children.

Wartime Labor

The labor that Harriet Jacobs performed as a child claimed as an enslaved person, which included looking after white children, was, she learned through various propositions that she alludes to but does not replicate in her account, expected to overlap with a different labor that her female body was supposed to provide. That is, caring for children not her own was to merge with producing children that she could not claim as her own. The labor already claimed from her body was understood to give way to the expected labor of producing children to feed the machinery of slavery. Critics who read, and who read between the lines, the horror of the propositions she endured from the man who sought to increase his wealth through propagating humans have tended to subsume the question of reproduction under the matters of sexual surveillance that pervade her narrative. Yet the tracking of babies who have been sold away from Dr. Flint's household inserts a numerical reckoning that can cause the reader to remember that Harriet Jacobs was trained from a young age to become very aware of the transactional nature of sexual advances. Repeatedly calculating her own odds for survival as well as calculating the risks that she needs to take for her children's survival, Jacobs has renewed understandings of the labor of watchfulness that she asks of herself and that she asks of the reader. The incomprehensible idea that she spends seven years hiding in what is, in effect, a leaky outdoor closet forms that concept that readers turn to most often in their scrutiny of the "loophole of retreat," but the different forms of labor—writing, reproduction, and watching—make the narrative a complicated venue for understanding her body.[16]

What often disappears from critical considerations of Harriet Jacobs as a writer is her political activism. During and after the war, she engaged in concerted efforts, with her daughter Louisa and with white allies, including Lucy Colman and Julia Wilbur, to turn the tide of Reconstruction toward equal housing and education. The closeness that such women activists shared bears some attention here. A few decades ago, Carroll Smith-Rosenberg provided a boon to many feminist scholars with the publication of "The Female World of Love and Ritual."[17] By illuminating the intimacy that nineteenth-century women had with each other through an extended discussion of their letters, she altered a landscape of suspicion whereby such women were belatedly interrogated about their intentions when they expressed great longing for the times when they held each other's bodies in bed at night. In addition to the relative scarcity of beds, such that travelers often found themselves in bed with strangers, the closeness that such women expressed had a tendency not to compete with the heterosexual marriages into which many of such letter writers entered.

The missing component in the discussion has been the matter of the race of the women affectionately sharing such beds. The fallback assumption that they were white is challenged by several first-person accounts of activist women who traveled to find each other during the antebellum and continuing into the postbellum United States. By her own words, these women include Harriet Jacobs. She expressed affection for women such as Cornelia Willis, who hid her status as a fugitive from her husband, the writer and editor Nathaniel Parker Willis, and then sent her out of state with her own baby to protect her, finally arranging to purchase her from those who pursued her. This account is familiar, as is the ongoing epistolary and sometimes intimate friendship with Amy Post and with Lydia Maria Child.[18]

Less familiar is the friendship she had with Julia Wilbur, a white woman abolitionist from Rochester, New York. A recent biography of Wilbur is based largely on her vivid diary of the years she spent in Washington, DC, working for the patent office and continuing her activism.[19] Wilbur writes that Harriet Jacobs and her daughter Louisa come to call and tells of visiting them and staying the night. That does not, of course, mean anything more than the sort of intimacy that Smith-Rosenberg describes. Yet it changes the story in significant ways. I first learned of Wilbur because I had been curious about the manacles that are held in the archives at Cornell University (see Figure I.5). Bearing a tag that declares them to be "from Richmond, donated by Julia Wilbur," the manacles drew me. They have both drawn and repelled many visitors to the archives, heavy and clunking in the hands that hold them now.

Julia Wilbur writes vividly of traveling to Richmond with Harriet Jacobs to see the ruined city after it had been surrendered. To make their way through even friendly military lines requires much maneuvering. She encounters cross-dressing soldiers such as Maria Lewis, who pass racially as well as changing gender: "A colored woman has been here who has been with the 8th N.Y. Cav. for the last 18 months. . . . She wore a uniform, rode a horse & carried a sword & carbine just like a man. The officers protected her, & she was with them mostly. The regiment did'nt [sic] know that she was a woman. She was called Geo. Harris, but her real name is Maria Lewis. She is from Albermarle Co. Va, & escaped to the Union army. It was not convenient to leave the army at first, & she soon became accustomed to it & began to like the excitement. She rode in the front ranks & scouted, & skirmished, & fought as they did." The excitement of warfare carries over as Julia Wilbur helps her change into the "uniform" of female dress. Fully aware that her presence in history needs recording, she includes the detail of the transition to "womanly ways & occupations" from a wartime career where she helped "the raiders destroy bridges & railroads, & burn houses, mills &c."[20]

The account Wilbur gives of her travel to the newly surrendered city of Richmond, Virginia, just abandoned after the fall of the Confederacy, makes for a disconcerting blend of sadness and the collection of souvenirs, probably including the manacles to which I have recurred in this account. Wilbur notes, like a diligent tourist, that she "went into Hall of Congress, & Hall of House of Delegates, Senate Chamber, & Va. State Senate." Along the way, she "got several relics" and then "on to the Roof" for what she describes as a "Magnificent view." After that "we went to Castle Thunder & were shown all through. A dismal place. A few prisoners are confined there. I brought away some irons that had been used on the limbs of Union soldiers." These various relics and souvenirs have themselves a ghostly presence since they have barely been released from the deaths of both Union and Confederate soldiers. Yet collection seems compulsory, for soldiers as well as activists, as the war came to a close. Wilbur acts as a tourist even as she describes the heavy weight of history.

So does Lucy Colman, who speaks in her autobiography *Reminiscences* of the practices of collecting that followed the war.[21] The account is amusing precisely because she denies the very activity in which she engages: "I have never been a relic-hunter, but had received requests from Northern friends for articles from the 'seat of war,' but I only gathered a few tufts of grass from the home of Jeff Davis. I had already a piece of the whipping-post and a pair of handcuffs, a slave-whip, etc., which I put with a piece of the coffin and the inside lining of the coffin in which President Lincoln's remains were buried, with many other things of like value, but I have given them all away, preserving nothing save a night-shirt of her husband which Mrs. Lincoln gave me; a rather strange article to give one as a keepsake, but Mrs. Lincoln was a very strange woman" (77). The mention of "Mrs. Lincoln" is part of the reputation that Lucy Colman has as the "Zelig" of her time, but Julia Wilbur runs a close second. Shadowing the mentions of the president and first lady are mentions of "Mrs. Kaightly," clearly Elizabeth Keckley, whose stories of access to the president also include relic hunting.

The controversy about Keckley's account resides both in the sense that her attempt to sell the clothing that Mary Todd Lincoln wishes to trade in for her own maintenance is a betrayal by the souvenir hunter of the sacred intimacy that they might be understood to have enjoyed while Keckley made that clothing and a suspicion about how often they might have been sharing a bed as they traveled together. That racial intimacy of women sharing a bed shows up in Colman's humorous retelling. She has been traveling with a niece to Frederick Douglass on an antislavery lecture tour. At "the first place where I presented myself as guest with my new friend" she is met with an anxious welcome. "The lady, who had sent me a pressing invitation to make her house my home, looked at us with consternation on every feature. She at last said: 'Walk in;' and giving my friend a seat near the door, took me into an inner apartment, saying: 'Mrs. Colman, I did not, when you were sent the invitation, know that you had a colored woman with you. I am greatly embarrassed, as I have only one guest-room.'" Mrs. Colman is prepared: "Let me relieve you at once. I consulted my friend's prejudices, as I anticipated such happenings, and she told me she had no prejudice against *white* people, and would be perfectly willing to occupy a room with me. I am sure if you consult her she will not object.'" After giving in to the mild chuckles that the anecdote provokes, the reader still winces at the need to explain that an abolitionist activist, beyond fearing for her life as she alights in railroad stations or enters places of worship, must thread such tiny needles of domestic explanation.

Feminism Falters in the Face of War

Although this section begins with the language of failure, part of the barely concealed optimism of its account is to point out how even in the face of failure, forms of feminist triumph can emerge. An extreme instance, late in the nineteenth century and at the fringe of the time that this book has considered, appears in Frances Harper's novel *Iola Leroy, or, Shadows Uplifted* (1892). This book looks back over the nineteenth century as a place of violence against women and depicts the battle against legalized slavery and racial prejudice as ongoing, yet it asserts plausibly that these accounts can include triumph. What it means to make the home into a place for learning preoccupies the novel, published in 1892 as the failures of Reconstruction meant waves of violent reprisals in Southern states. First published serially in newspapers, the novel saw an initial hardcover appearance after Frances Harper had become known as an activist and educator. The shadows that are to be lifted are the shadows of slavery. The residues of war invoked in the book involve relations among feminism, race, and the aftereffects of slavery on populations both North and South. The labor that the book considers refers at once to the work of women, whether employed in a professional capacity or made to work in forms of sexual servitude, and the question of reproduction, the labor of reproducing humans. Freedom from such labor might only be partial. For example, picturing a strong man with a broken manacle dangling from his wrist, Edmonia Lewis's statue *Forever Free* (1867) nonetheless offers the sense that for women to be free they need to kneel at the feet of a protector (figure 5.1).

Unlike the tradition of emancipation narratives from which it has evolved, the story about the life that Iola Leroy has led when held as a slave has been omitted; the story of sexual subjugation, while alluded to, does not form part of the text. Alluding to her rescue from that life, the novel compares her to "a trembling dove [taken] from the gory vulture's nest and given a place of security." The narrative comment, placed as a form of free indirect discourse into the mind of the Union general who rescues her during the Civil War, takes the form of these questions: "Could it be possible that this young and beautiful girl had been a chattel, with no power to protect herself from the highest insults that lawless brutality could inflict upon innocent and defenseless womanhood? Could he ever again glory in

FIGURE 5.1. Edmonia Lewis (1843/5–ca. 1911). *Forever Free*, 1867. Carrara marble. H. 41 3/4 in. (106 cm), W. 22 1/2 in. (57.2 cm), D. 12 3/8 in. (31.4 cm). The optimism of freedom appears in a sculpture such as this, while it also retains the posture of a woman as a supplicant. Photo: Gregory R. Staley. Courtesy of Howard University Gallery of Art. 67.9.S.

his American citizenship, when any white man, no matter how coarse, cruel, or brutal, could buy or sell her for the basest purposes?"[22] He mourns the engagement of his citizenship status with the practices of slavery, but the language he uses nonetheless collapses humans into property.

The question of citizenship aligns itself with these economic questions. The novel contains a long account of learning to read as a surreptitious (and prohibited) act that occupies the tales of emerging into knowledge. Its early stories all involve reading. We are told that one character, Tom, "can read a little. . . . He got a book of his own, tore it up, greased the pages, and hid them in his hat. Then if his master had ever knocked his hat off he would have thought them greasy papers, and not that Tom was carrying his library on his head" (44). This retelling of the story of how both freedom of thought and physical freedom begin with a journey toward literacy recalls the tales told by Frederick Douglass. The story of "another friend" explains that "One night, when his work was done, his boss came into his cabin and saw him with a book in his hand. He threatened to give him five hundred lashes if he caught him again with a book." The threat encourages resistance, increases his desire: "He said it just harassed him; it set him on fire. He thought there must be something good in that book if the white man didn't want him to learn." That resistance leads to a relation between landscape and language. Whereas Douglass learns to read in an urban environment, using stones on the streets of Baltimore, this character turns to nature, using trees and the sand: "He got the sounds of the letters by heart, then cut off the bark of a tree, carved the letters on the smooth inside, and learned them. He wanted to learn how to write. He had charge of a warehouse where he had a chance to see the size and form of letters. He made the beach of the river his copybook, and thus he learned to write." The natural landscape provides a transition to understanding the violence of the Civil War: "Tom never got very far with his learning, but I used to get the papers and tell him all I knew about the war" (45).

The opportunity to fight in the war, to turn from the struggle to read into appearing as a soldier, could partially explain the resistance to education among Southern enslavers. Turning from reading to the battlefield might appear as the quintessential masculine triumph, a triumph reminiscent of the internal struggles of Henry Fleming in *The Red Badge of Courage* (1895) who begins by invoking stories of past wars. The difference in *Iola Leroy* is that the impulse to freedom accompanies the opportunity to kill former enslavers. There can be something slightly unnerving about the clear direction toward killing in signing up to fight. "Robert waited eagerly and hopefully his chance to join the Union army . . . ready and willing to do anything required of him by which he could earn his freedom and prove his manhood." While he makes his secret plans, a "few faithful and trusted friends stood ready to desert with him when the Union army came within hailing distance." As in the reports from the front, when the Union army arrives, "there was a stampede to its ranks of men ready to serve in any capacity, to labor in the tents, fight on the fields, or act as scouts. It was a strange sight to see these black men rallying around the Stars and Stripes, when white men were trampling them under foot and riddling them with bullets" (36). The language of this passage almost equates the "black men" who rally around the "Stars and Stripes" with the flag for which they fight. To "prove" manhood is to be willing to kill as well as to die. At the same time, the wounded men evoke a tenderness reminiscent of Whitman's war poetry: "when he brought in that wounded scout, he couldn't have been more tender if he had been a woman. How gratefully the poor fellow looked in Tom's face as he laid him down so carefully and staunched the blood which had been spurting out of him. Tom seemed to know it was an artery which had been cut, and he did just the right thing to stop the bleeding" (50–51).

For Iola Leroy, educated in the North and raised to assume herself racially white, the idea that she might have anything in common with the people held in bondage in the South is at first bewildering and strange, even alienating. A friend counsels her about her complacence concerning slavery practices, combining stories that have become familiar, from the dangers besetting Eliza Harris in Harriet Beecher Stowe's *Uncle Tom's Cabin* to the tragedy in William Wells Brown's *Clotel* in the nineteenth century and continuing to the tragedy of Toni Morrison's *Beloved*. Alluding to these stories, she cautions, "I do not think that that slave mother who took her four children, crossed the Ohio River on the ice, killed one of the children and attempted the lives of the other two, was a contented slave. And that other one, who, running away and finding herself pursued, threw herself over the Long Bridge into the Potomac, was evidently not satisfied. I do not think the numbers who are coming North on the Underground Railroad can be very contented. It is not natural for people to run away from happiness, and if they are so happy and contented, why did Congress pass the Fugitive Slave Bill?" (98). As she debates the matter of slavery with her Northern friend, Iola Leroy is being scouted by slave traders who assess her value and comment that she "would bring $2000 any day in a New Orleans market." Knowing that her father has died, and also anticipating her naïveté about the dangers of traveling to the South, they propose to deceive her, telling her that her father has been taken ill; for sentimental reasons, she will come south with them and then they will present her to be "inventoried with the rest of the property" (101).

After escaping from the subsequent horrors of her valuation and sale as a piece of sexual merchandise, when Iola Leroy is courted by a white man who offers an illegal, but vaguely honorable, marriage, he asks her "not [to] judge me by the worst of my race. Surely our country has produced a higher type of manhood than the men by whom you were tried and tempted." Refuting the rather insulting idea that she has been "tempted" as she explains that she has been "sold from State to State as an article of merchandise," Iola explains that she has been "abased, but the men who trampled on me were the degraded ones" (115). Refusing his proposal because she finds that racism remains as an impenetrable flaw beneath the surface of his admiration, a flaw that, perhaps imperceptibly, reveals marriage as another form of bondage, Iola goes on to become an educated and successful woman. Eventually, and in the spirit of heterosexual marriage novels, she will be rewarded. Here her resistance to the idea of passing dominates her refusal.[23] Even as she displays the heroism of soldiers and the deep pain of women who have been bought and sold, Frances Harper enacts at once failure and triumph: she takes up a "weapon of civilization" in using the pen rather than the sword (116).

Final Thoughts

Throughout this book, I look at how nineteenth-century writers and artists witnessed the violent struggles over citizenship as at once political and in need of cultural commentary. Questions about literary visions of democracy emerge repeatedly, from Walt Whitman to Frederick Douglass, but they are also an obsession for women writers from Emily Dickinson to Frances Harper. For the writers of the early republic, shaking off the concept of the sovereign in literature appeared as a corollary to fighting against British rule; anxiety about the production of a cultural heritage meant that they quoted from and yet abjured the legacy of Shakespeare. To make a space for democracy and for culture, to promote a new model of citizenship, underlies much nineteenth-century writing, whether political, sentimental, sensational, or domestic. But however much it might be engaging to notice a commitment to the legacy of democracy shifting in and out of focus in their writing, the legacy of political violence still haunts.

Focusing on war means that *Haunted by the Civil War* in effect bookends its project between the American Revolution and the lengthy aftermath of the Civil War. The questions that I posed at the beginning remain, but I still want to ask new ones. Can we trace the effects that women's writing has on changed landscapes of intimacy and death? Can we generalize reliably from the uncertain and even random collections of material remaining in visual and historical archive, including the uncertain, and uncertainly funded, curation of museums and libraries? How can readers today connect historical violence with shifts in literary genre if the commitment is to a combination of aesthetics and political context? What use can readers make of the specific historical knowledge uncovered by turning the United States upside down so that the mouth of the Mississippi River gapes open at the top or by thinking about some of literature's most famous passages in terms of water?[24]

To return to the earlier discussion of visuality is to recall that this book operates as a frame that emphasizes alternations between figure and ground. Such staging matters. What can be seen depends upon the focal length of the lens. How does a reader know what house you inhabit when you enter the house of fiction? In drawing yourself up short at the threshold, a threshold that seems to separate nature and culture and that can also separate gender and race, you might notice that the liminal space where you have not yet entered the house encourages you to think about these separations. The matter of the archive, or why the archive surrounding literary productions continues to matter, also encourages a reader to think about the elements of choice. What do you choose to notice as you enter the house of fiction? Where is the house of poetry?

Many archives contain handwritten letters that were once the everyday material surrounding epistolary fiction. The letter gives way to the telegraph, the speedy reply tapped out for readers eager for updates as the urgency of war demanded immediate information. Early in the construction of the American republic, the place to read inherited from Europe was the place of retreat, whether to find spiritual solace in reading the Bible, or to find the scandalous or sentimental world of the novel replacing the Bible in intimate domestic spaces. The poets who opened the door to the closet emphasized the chance to enter the landscape, the outside world. Stories about the relation to England imagined as a mother that drew political orators like Thomas Paine encourage readers to look for accounts of families in relation to new ideas about nationalism, while the borders of geographical territory continually shifted the ground about which claims were made. At these borders, white settlers from eastern territories moved to form new ideas of home and acted out national ideas of order that often included the violent removal of people who thought themselves already at home. Borders work at once as metaphors for American identity and as ways to describe a field of inquiry.

Metaphors function successfully on occasions when historical accounts that set out dates and details only partially mobilize thought about historical change. The roots and rhizomes of farming cultures that once formed Thomas Jefferson's visions, the violence directed against bodies held in captivity, the boundaries and borders of a military culture developed partially through deliberate murders of Indigenous people, enable conceptual thresholds. At these thresholds, where a reader might, for instance, look to enter at once the house of fiction and, perhaps even while wincing, the house of national identifications, the concepts of inside and outside function as artifice. And yet there can still be a space in between where, at the moment of entering such a space, a reader stops to notice. Perhaps this book places a mirror at such a threshold. In the middle of naming and translating the cultural artifacts within the house, the reader is invited to think about how they have been produced. To shift to a domestic detail, perhaps in the texture of the cloth in the house, the reader notices the warp and weave, where a thread is followed to its conclusion or pulled out to unravel a scheme.

To engage with the fraught cultures of the United States is to engage with the space still newly understood in terms of geography, politics, and culture, as a place still in flux. The reactions voiced during the nineteenth century affect how readers understand themselves today. Legal constructs that determine what it is be a citizen, to have a form of belonging within the contours of the nation, here appear in juxtaposition with the forms of belonging attached to reading.

Whether at sea or on the river, whether wandering in the woods or in the city, men and women, both free and claimed for labor, both singing and silent, both writing and reading, found themselves reaching for significance in the legacy of future generations. Whether listening to or ignoring the lessons handed down, these generations became the readers and then often the writers of new stories. Sometimes they are in turn lost at sea, left behind in the woods, immersed in the dangers of the city, but sometimes they learn, and pass on, lessons at once of citizenship and of freedom.

A reader thinking about literary history as it threads through this book might have wondered at what point the account would turn to the concept of greatness, as in "the great American novel." That term, improbably coined just after the war by an author who sought to write one, emerges repeatedly in order to prepare the reader for forms of discrimination that were once an ingrained aspect of making choices about reading practices.[25] For decades, I have encouraged students to find pleasure in splendid sentences by propaganda artists such as T. S. Arthur or Susan B. Warner while noting the echoes in the anguished ambiguity of Nathaniel Hawthorne. Fourth of July orations or lyrics from Walt Whitman can perhaps equally convey forms of impassioned patriotism as well as longing for the arousal of fireworks. As they learn that particular narrative tactics are inevitably informed by historical context, students who read carefully can decide for themselves what gives pleasure and value to the body of work from any particular author. To enhance that sense of pleasurable choice—a sometimes remote feeling of aesthetic value in the practice of reading about scenes of dread—this book seeks to provide interpretive strategies for a formative period. The writers and readers of what we, whether citizens of or visitors to the United States, still call American literature understood that just to declare themselves in words created a form of citizenship. As readers, witnesses, and spectators to their declarations, we can choose our form of belonging. But whatever choices we make, we remain haunted by these foundational histories of violence.[26]

For a final example of both archival discovery and the tense anticipatory history of spectator violence, I want to look briefly at a letter written by the poet and actor Adah Isaacs Menken addressed to the theatrical entrepreneur Augustin Daly.[27] The intimacy of address in the letter presents a clear and urgent writing that echoes the urgency of the poetry. An exclamation mark is the favored punctuation. The tendency for biographers to be absorbed into the biographical uncertainties of her life (how many marriages—and did they overlap?) and to become wrecked on the shoals of scandal obscures the vivid remnant of personality available in poems and letters. The oscillation between the forms of performance and portraiture that might be echoed in the later shape-changing of Cindy Sherman and the prurient interest in imagining her naked that obsessed nineteenth-century audiences has made it difficult to view Adah Isaacs Menken in spite of the many images that survive, images that, like Sojourner Truth, she carried with her and sold to maintain a sense of herself as well as to continue earning a living from her performances.

Who Menken was as a creative being, sometimes referred to as "the Menken," overshadows the performance ascribed to her.[28] Yet the way that she re-created her life as an imaginative exercise means that the being and the performance overlap and blur the sense of outline that any reasonable biographer or historian might enjoy. In this letter, she urges Augustin Daly to remember that she can "love my real friends," even as she signs the letter as a multitude of identities. She desires to be called "Dolores," appends the signature "(Infelix)," and signs it as "Menken." The confusion that enters biographical speculations about her race might engage a reader in seeing her as a chameleon since, among other odd options in her political identification, she was once arrested as a Confederate spy.[29] The lyric poem "PRO PATRIA. AMERICA, 1861" shows the influence of both patriotism and Walt Whitman, with whom she became acquainted in New York. In this poem, America is personified as "Columbia" and called "the Queen of the World." "Aloft on the mount of God's liberty," Menken writes, Columbia stood as "mortal" yet with "vigor Immortal unchained in her blood."[30] The poem continues as though paraphrasing the political cartoons that promoted the Northern perspective on the war:

> A bright helm of stars on her white brow was seated,
> And gold were the plumes from its clusters that fell
> To light the gaunt faces of slaves in old kingdoms,
> And show them the way to the hand they loved well.

The celebration of Columbia as "My Country! My Mother!" gives way to grim prognostication. Those who have been "Assassins of Liberty" will meet a dire fate. In a Miltonic climax, the poem predicts that "the spirit of God's Retribution" means that the ocean of blood will "hurl your stained souls, like impurities, from them / Up death's dark slope, to the skull beach of Hell!"[31]

There's nothing remotely ambiguous about this invocation. The haunting curse stands in contrast to the lament of Frances Harper's earlier poem "Ethiopia," first published in *Forest Leaves* in 1843. Here the poet begins by imagining that Ethiopia "yet shall stretch / Her bleeding hands abroad." The sound of her cry will reach "The burning throne of God."[32] But whether they invoke curses or salvation, retribution or understanding, both poets insist that they have grown up in a haunted country.

Afterword

THE HISTORY OF THE PRESENT

THIS AFTERWORD ENGAGES alternative memories from subsequent centuries for a war that still haunts the United States. In so doing, it proposes other forms of haunting. The ghosts that appear here have names and voices that can be difficult to translate: attempts at translation revive the uncertainty of remembering the stories. For example, the 2017 novel *Lincoln in the Bardo*, by George Saunders, develops an amalgamation of Buddhist mourning practices and the combined voices of Lincoln's mourned family members and the Civil War dead.[1] The novel's many voices raise several questions that can serve as a bridge between concluding and continuing my investigations of the nineteenth century. One of them concerns how frequently we still visit the graves of dead presidents—and what we find there. I have in mind the still popular activity of Civil War reenactment, whereby twenty-first-century civilians assume the uniforms and habitations of Civil War soldiers and charge at each other, an activity deftly interpreted by Rebecca Schneider in *Performing Remains* and imagined by the playwright Suzan Lori Parks in *Topdog / Underdog* (2001), which shows a violent struggle between the reenactors and brothers Lincoln and Booth.[2]

Complete with costumes and another kind of reenactment of loss is the more recent play by Parks, *Father Comes Home from the Wars* (2015).[3] In this play the idea of either familial loyalty or loyalty to a particular cause is massively disrupted by both race and romantic attachment. The unfamiliarity of such a hero might attach to the play's use of a loyal dog or the pride shown in a nineteenth-century photograph of a soldier (figure A.1). This play shows that the desire for a hero, a desire attached to both Union and Confederate forces, becomes difficult when a woman waits at home,

FIGURE A.1. *African American Soldier, Half-Length Portrait, with Pistol and Jacket*, 1860–1870. Ambrotype. 4 in. × 3.15 in. (10 cm × 8 cm). Courtesy of the Library of Congress.

in a refracted version of how Ulysses returns to Penelope. Such revisited battlefields appear different when we use the usual language attached to mourning, such as the formal structure of elegy, or the substantial formation of public statues, such as the ongoing removals of what were once considered Confederate heroes in the South. Less frequently do we look at how photographs appear in the mourning marketplace of the Civil War dead.

To think further about memorialization as visual, I will briefly return to images of Lincoln. The title *Standing Lincoln* was attached to a statue sculpted by Augustus Saint-Gaudens, who made several copies of Lincoln with head bent and one foot forward. In providing this title, I want to allude to a statue of Lincoln standing produced earlier by the young Vinnie Ream. Like Lincoln, Vinnie Ream (1847–1914) was born in a log cabin, in her case in Wisconsin. Like Mary Todd Lincoln, she had a brother who fought for the Confederate Army. Like no one except a fictional character you might have heard of, she was a clerk in the dead letter office of the federal government during the Civil War, from 1862 to 1866. Her life thus brings together the back story of Herman Melville's famous short story "Bartleby the Scrivener" with the encounters Walt Whitman remembered having with Lincoln as he walked the streets of Washington, DC, as he took breaks writing letters for wounded and dying soldiers that might be seen as a variant on service in a dead letter office. If you never thought about what it might mean if Bartleby were a woman, it might be time to imagine the possibility that this sorter of dead letters was a woman whose sculpture of Lincoln began with observing him alive.

A vote by Congress, on July 28, 1866, gave Vinnie Ream the commission to create a statue of Abraham Lincoln for the Capitol building.[4] She was only eighteen. This controversial commission led some critics to make false claims that she was chosen because she was not only young and lovely but also someone's mistress. Finished in 1871, when she was twenty-three, the statue displays talent, but it was also the first to show Lincoln standing. Investigating the historical basis of the decision to award her the commission brings together expectations of history and chronicle, architecture and geography, intention and accident that emerge in the photograph of Vinnie Ream standing beside her model of Lincoln's head (see figure 2.2).

I want to weave together these disparate threads of mourning and memorialization in visual culture by examining an event that took place the week before Abraham Lincoln signed the Emancipation Proclamation, a signing that took place on January 1, 1863. The week before that staged signing, on December 26, 1862, in Mankato, Minnesota, a less-celebrated event occurred: the largest mass execution in the history of the United States. Elaborately constructed on an enormous, elevated execution platform that held more than forty standing bodies, most with ropes around their necks, the execution occurred on what was then the western frontier.

While invocations of Abraham Lincoln and the Civil War usually involve an indelible invocation of his profile as a savior of the country, along the path of that war were many executions and, occasionally, pardons, that kept other killings in view. As one of the least discussed of these executions, separated by hundreds of miles from the massacres and executions of the war, this event in Minnesota occurred as part of what was also known as the Dakota War of 1862. The so-called war, an eruption of resistance to land claims and discriminatory treatment, began with violence against white settler towns on August 17, 1862, as a resistance movement among allied Sioux and Dakota peoples who wanted to drive white settlers off their land. They thought they had been unfairly compensated, and they had certainly been insulted by a representative of the government who made an unfortunate comment encouraging them to eat grass. He was one of the first to die, reportedly found with grass stuffed into his mouth.[5] The violence included a somewhat indiscriminate slaughter of women and children and led to the murder of hundreds of white settlers.

Given that the Civil War dominated national consciousness, the publicity was perhaps minimal. Troops that had been training for the war were diverted along the river in Minnesota. They met with violent resistance but eventually captured four hundred warriors, not including one of the leaders of the resistance, Little Crow. The initial outcry was to execute all of them. Lincoln called for trials. After speedy trials, bungled by mistranslations that led to at least one of the Indians who had attempted to protect white settlers being executed, thirty-nine Indians were sentenced to death and an enormous platform was erected in order to hang them all simultaneously. Abraham Lincoln was called upon to endorse the mass execution. He did commute sentences, quite possibly releasing some who deserved to be found guilty of crimes, including one at the last minute. In short, on December 26, 1862, thirty-eight men were executed in Mankato, Minnesota, the largest mass execution in American history.[6] Engravings were circulated in newspapers to commemorate the day. But portraits, such as the one of Little Crow included here, had earlier been made of the men that displayed them in western garb as well as showing the artifacts of a photographic studio (figure A.2).

Preoccupied as I am by the material artifacts that remain to be hefted, while noting that the overlap between image and language becomes interrupted by the three-dimensional acts that involve our bodies lifting or touching these objects, I will stay with photographs a while longer. Mathew Brady's photographic studio made the images of Lincoln with which we are most familiar—after the Cooper Union address, before the assassination. A less known photographic studio, Whitney's Gallery in St. Paul, Minnesota, produced the images of the warriors involved and made them available after the massacres that made these men notorious and before they were killed by the machinery of the state.[7] Given the limitations of photography, the larger events—massacres, mass executions—appear in the reconstructed form of engravings, with inevitable distortions of perspective and scale.

One might reasonably assume that I am following an account proposed by Roland Barthes in *Camera Lucida*, where he notes of the notorious photograph of Lewis Payne, also from Mathew Brady's studio, that he is

FIGURE A.2. Photograph of Little Crow. Cabinet card. 2.3 in. × 3.9 in. (6 cm × 10 cm). Joel E. (Joel Emmons) Whitney (1822–1886), photographer. Note on reverse: “Property of Arthur J. Benjamin, Hutchinson. A copy of the original taken in St. Paul and presented to Dr. John Benjamin by Little Crow. Dressed in civilian clothes and ready to pose for this photograph, Little Crow, thinking he appeared too much like a white man, arose and wrapped his Indian robe about him.” Credited to J. H. Gravenslund, Hutchinson, Minnesota. Courtesy of McLeod County Historical Society. The caption on the image at the Library of Congress reads “Little Crow, a Sioux Chief and Leader of the Indian Massacre of 1862, in Minnesota.” Compare https://www.loc.gov/resource/ppmsca.75533/.

"dead and he is going to die"—and that that forms a part of the fascination of looking at the face looking back at the camera. Barthes elaborates on the relation between "studium" and "punctum" in relation to how an audience looks at such an image. We are pierced with the time for the camera to capture that image in the present time of our looking at it.[8]

To further the conversation about how a statue works to memorialize and a photograph works to stop time, I want to reference the work of Susan Stewart in *Crimes of Writing*. She observes that the nude models who posed for Thomas Eakins, the famous painter of *The Grosz Clinic*, who also photographed extensively, wore blindfolds.[9] That they have a covering over their faces rather than their bodies keeps them from seeing who sees them, stops them from looking as they are looked at. It also enforces the body as separate from the identity of the model, who has no face to establish recognition. Yet, further, in this instance, it resembles the need to hood the face of the man who is about to be hanged. What sight is protected by covering those eyes?

Such allusions raise the question of method. To investigate the material production of styles of looking and being looked at invokes recent works such as the interweaving of photography and poetry in Claudia Rankin's *Citizen*, the racial interrogations presented in Alexander Weheliye's *Habeas Viscus* or Christina Sharpe's *In the Wake*.[10] What adheres? As they provide thoughtful questions about what remains in the wake of historical reflections on violence, these critical works incorporate visual structures as useful placeholders that reflect a search for order in violent chaos. Building on the success of Mathew Brady's studio in Washington, DC, marketing images and portraits of bodies in a time of war, Whitney's gallery in St. Paul, Minnesota appears in a different story of pictures at the front lines. Given the limitations of photography, the larger events—massacres, mass executions—appear in engravings.[11] But why does this moment need so many engravings? An overabundance of the grid appears, perhaps of the way that the grid of the execution platform erected along the river might portend and predict the gridding of the land under the provisions of the Homestead Act into 160-acre-square parcels. Divisible by four, only coherent against the squared off lines of western states, mapped from the undifferentiated mass of the Louisiana Purchase, the land becomes measured.

Inevitably, perhaps, the influential rhetoric of "intersectionality" also appears here.[12] To arrive at intersections of race, gender, class, ethnicity, and sexuality—all the possibilities that arise in the memories and visualization of war—might paradoxically mean that, while in the process of arriving at these intersections, the very moment of arriving at an intersection implies stasis. Whether a reader or a viewer, you need to stop and look, even though the intersection itself seems to be in motion. While I sometimes shift terms to invite the flexibility enabled by conceiving visual and literary modes of remembering (while also invested in a form of geospatial understanding), my attention to the scaffold here marks an arrival at an intersection that forces attention to directions that have been traveled as well as those that could be traveled.

A category of disbelief still attaches to this moment, even though it continues to provoke protests among Indigenous claimants to the territory that was once called the Dakotas. One of the most surprising conversions involved an artist who re-created the physical space of the scaffold on a smaller scale for the Walker Art Center in Minneapolis, Minnesota, in the name of a visual protest against executions. After the fury that the installation aroused, the diminished re-creation had to be publicly dismantled and the boards returned to the Indigenous community for ceremonial disposal. In addition, the artist, Samuel Durant, signed over further rights to his design to the Dakota peoples who had been offended by his work. After ceremonies that included posting the names of the executed and burning sage, the construction was dismantled with chainsaws. The symbolism of visual records from national tragedies, whether representing a dead president or dead warriors, haunts this tale.[13]

In thinking about the relation of looking to empathy, it becomes clear that building a square platform to contain undifferentiated bodies in a mass execution and then making that grid the central figure in engravings resists such a possibility. Writing in *The Civil Contract of Photography*, Ariella Azoulay develops a model of looking that builds off the extended conversations between Carol Pateman's *The Sexual Contract* and Charles Mills's *The Racial Contract*. She explains, "I employ the term 'contract' in order to shed terms such as 'empathy,' 'shame,' 'pity,' or 'compassion' as organizers of the gaze."[14] Azoulay's earliest example overlaps with the matters of slavery and nineteenth-century culture considered here. She displays the photograph from the studio of Southworth and Hawes, "The Branded Hand of Captain Jonathan Walker" (an early daguerreotype, dated 1845, held at the Massachusetts Historical Society). His palm is branded "S S," or rather, since the image has, in effect, been twice reversed, backward images of the two S's in the modeling of what almost looks like infinity. The image of the hand becomes an emblem of the man, a synecdochical marking of a "slave stealer," whose face we cannot see and whose identity has been branded as indelibly as the marks of the whip on the back of the man more frequently displayed for purposes of resistance to slavery. Azoulay describes the brand as the "mark of Cain." In *The Civil Contract of Photography*, she seeks "to develop a concept of citizenship through the study of photographic practices and to analyze photography within the framework of citizenship as a status, an institution, and a set of practices."

The relation of looking and empathy appears obliquely in the account of events leading up to the massacre in *The History of the Sioux Wars* by Isaac Heard, published the year after the executions. Using language that reflects the prejudices of his day, the author says that he "devoted particular attention to obtaining from Indians, half-breeds, traders, white captives, fugitives from massacres, and others, particulars of the various outrages and the causes of the massacre. He has also carefully read the public treaties and other documents connected with Indian affairs, and the various newspaper articles pertinent thereto." To give the book some kind of balance and in the interest of explaining himself as a responsible chronicler, Heard includes an appended unpopular appeal from Bishop Whipple. Titled "For the Red Man," this announces the possibility that there might have been a grievance over land, but presents no voices from the trials or the testimony of the aggrieved. In the space where such testimony might appear, Heard appears instead. Heard explains that "From the information thus derived, he has endeavored to form a connected and reliable history. He regrets that the haste required to place it before the public, while attention is directed to the subject, has militated against the symmetry of arrangement and finish of composition which should accompany such a work. It was his desire that portraits . . . should have a place in the volume, but the publishers were not willing to incur the additional expense" (v).

The portraits would show up in a later edition and their inclusion changes the story by presenting faces for some of the bodies that otherwise appear anonymously as ciphers on the scaffold. As part of his appreciation for the construction of the execution, Heard goes on to commend the staging. As he puts it, "The arrangements for the execution of so many persons at the same instant were most perfect, and great credit is due Colonel Miller for devising, and carrying out so successfully, his well-digested plan." The event had been widely advertised and was much anticipated: "All day and night on Thursday, and on the morning of Friday up to the time of the execution, people were constantly arriving to witness the hanging. Troops were constantly coming in from all points, and the streets were densely crowded. The roofs and windows of all buildings in the vicinity, and all other eligible places were early occupied by anxious spectators, including the sand-bar in the river . . ." (294).[15]

In one final detour about memory, it matters to note that the sandbar became only the temporary destination for many of the hanged bodies. After a hasty burial, many of them were exhumed for the use of medical students craving bodies for dissection. Viewing the ground as the place for the body to reside becomes dramatically challenged by the decision to transfer bodies from the emphatic square of the scaffold to the fluid and excessively soft sand of the riverbank. Competing forces awaited these bodies. On the one hand, the river's currents eroded the banks where they were buried. On the other, the young men who sought bodies for dissection could easily disinter them from the sand. The body of Little Crow, who was shot in 1863 as he tried to return from exile in Canada, was subjected to the further indignity of having his severed head displayed and preserved in St. Paul, where his horrified descendants saw it on display decades later. It was not returned to his family for burial until 1971.

These overlapping accounts of execution and assassination also concern the relation between statues and photographs as emblems of remembering, mourning, and memorializing. Moves between statues and photographs change memory and identification—and there are times when they work together. The photograph of Vinnic Ream with the bust of Lincoln implicitly comments on her beauty in relation to his renowned ugliness, but also challenges the gender and desire invoked by the myth of Prometheus. She stands by the incomplete statue, the bust that would emerge as part of the standing man. The viewer wishes she could bring him back to life.

The peculiar intimacy of her hands on his face, an intimacy remembered but not pictured in the photograph of them together, would remind spectators that she was one of the last to see him alive, drawing in his office as he received constituents. The circulation of this image then becomes a two-dimensional trigger for a three-dimensional "punctum." It also raises the question: can a statue have a "punctum"? Until late in the twentieth century photographs tended to be treated as historical evidence rather than as art. Statues, in contrast, appear as art rather than historical evidence. They cross here: the photograph as historical memory keeps the vanishing Indian in view just before he is to be killed.

Unburied

The idea that the violence of the nineteenth century in the United States attaches to one kind of war, the war historically treated as a temporal and geographical division, omits the contributing and overlapping warfare during the Dakota Wars, the Mexican–American War, the War of 1812, the

Seminole Wars. Each contains the element of displacing invisible populations, or populations made invisible because of the operations of removal sanctioned by the US government in order to claim that land has been made available for "settlement." Especially associated with Andrew Jackson and the so-called Cherokee removal, the legislation passed by the US Congress repeatedly makes land a token of war bounty.

The collective memory of these wars erases violence and bloodshed in the name of safer borders. The so-called Civil War attempted to erase borders that were still shifting, dividing as well as challenging the separation of states in the name of a federal union. The location where the bodies have been placed in the aftermath of these wars becomes the place for the naming of sacred ground. On that ground appear various and competing projects. For a notable example the preserved green spaces of the National Military Park at Gettysburg include tombstones arrayed in spaces near fences that mark the development of statues displayed as representative of sacrifice and honor. Some of the stones merely recount numbers attached to states that have supplied soldiers since the names have been lost. Some of the statues represent the Confederacy. The stories told as oral histories—and then transcribed—have a repeating residue of recognizing no boundaries except the boundaries of the bodies that have decayed into the earth. What is sacred? The place where the bodies are kept.

Twenty years after such violent displays, after the Dakotas had been opened for settlement by the Homestead Act of 1862, with special preference given to returning Union soldiers, my grandmother's grandfather moved to the territory that was not yet a state. Her father was born there, and he used to tease her about selling her to the Indians (he wasn't a nice man). After the Civil War, when he returned to the North after a stint in the Army of the South, this man, my great great grandfather, Seth Thomas Winslow, started working as a mason in the sugar manufacturing enterprise of Havemeyers and Elder in Brooklyn, New York. He married and started a family. The factory where he was a building supervisor burned down in 1882. Instead of sticking around, he followed the lure of the newspaper reports that there was land for the taking in the Dakota Territory. This provision of the Homestead Act had special dispensation for veterans of the Civil War and was widely advertised in New York newspapers. He packed up his family and headed west on the train, building a dugout on the banks of the James River.

The building that replaced the one he had helped to build in New York, the former factory for Domino Sugar, became the location for the 2014 installation by Kara Walker, *The Subtlety, or The Marvelous Sugar Baby*.[16]

FIGURE A.3. Thomas Crawford (1814–1857). *Statue of Freedom*. Cast in bronze by Clark Mills with the assistance of Philip Reid in 1860. H: 19 ft. 6 in. (5.94 m). Courtesy of the Architect of the Capitol.

Notorious during the year that it was installed because of the peculiar behavior of visitors who photographed themselves in close proximity to giant labia, the marvelous sugar baby emphasized the relation of sugar, slavery, and the invisible Southern labor behind the success of the company that had become Domino Sugar. On the frontier of the Dakotas, the aftermath of the so-called Dakota War had meant the incarceration within reservations of both Dakota and Sioux members and the parceling out of land in 160-acre homestead units designed for white settlers. The effects of the distribution of land in combination with removals to reservations controlled by the Bureau of Indian Affairs have been noted by brilliant writers such as Louise Erdrich while continuing political demonstrations call attention to broken treaties.[17]

While scholars ask questions about how the legacies of nineteenth-century history and culture in the United States continue to infiltrate the present, they still work to interpret data. The artifacts of the archive, the papers and photographs that show the effects of silverfish and booklice if not more dramatically chewed by mice, have become resources at once elusively digitized and ephemeral. Whether a scholar has access to the internet or can travel to places where they find original documents, the recorded past can seem at once enormous and dissolving like sugar in the rain, like the deliberate decay of the event of the sugar baby. As a result, sometimes I feel that I am telling a story that cannot end. For example, I have a hunch that no one talks about the statue that stands on top of the US Capitol building, perhaps because it shows an Indian woman turning her back on the gaze of Abraham Lincoln down the length of the National Mall. Her head turns east. Most references to her position on top of the Capitol building simply refer to her as the *Statue of Freedom* (figure A.3). But the original sculptor, who died before the model could be cast in bronze, explained that since the then Secretary of War Jefferson Davis resisted the idea of a liberty cap, a token associated with not only the American but the French Revolution, he had proposed a "bold arrangement of feathers, suggested by the costumes of our Indian tribes."[18] The ambivalent hybridity of her costume as well as the challenge of her look includes an invitation, a legacy, a reminder of broken promises. The spurned woman who holds her head high looks back across the ocean at Europe to face down further invasions while the sword at her side, an emblem of the violent threat behind the promise of freedom, continues to haunt.

ACKNOWLEDGMENTS

I AM ALWAYS GRATEFUL to Ruth and John; they return my thoughts to the present and keep my heart at home.

Academic life has a rich zone of conversation in classrooms; my students have been wonderful interlocutors. I am also thankful for conversations that have taken place over decades with former students, some now employed as educators. While the space for such conversation came under siege during the years of the pandemic, their determination and insights have been remarkable. Particular assistance for this book came from Kimiyo Bremer, Philippa Chun, Susannah Sharpless, Brianna Thompson, and Xine Yao. Colleagues such as Laura Brown, Susan Gillman, Sandra Gustafson, Stephanie Li, Aziz Rana, Philip Richards, Blakey Vermeule, and Candace Waid gave me valuable feedback. I was grateful to be in writing groups funded by the Society for the Humanities with Ben Anderson, Maria Fernandez, Chiara Formichi, Nicole Giannelli, Riche Richardson, Casey Schmidt, and Lenora Warren. Focused writing was aided by various "pomodoro" groups: thank you! My friends have cajoled me into excursions near and far: especially I want to name Lisa Dundon, Donna Eaton, Maria Fernandez, and Zaga Gaeta. Along with my extended family, they keep teaching me to laugh at myself.

The challenge of revision while in conversation with scholars in very different fields was assisted by a welcome stint as the Los Angeles Times fellow at the Huntington Library. I relished the extended opportunity to read primary documents and to have challenges posed by such excellent scholars as Alice Fahs, Dena Goodman, and Steve Hindle. A more isolated, but definitely valuable, research opportunity was afforded by residencies at Quarry Farm in Elmira, New York. Late revisions happened during a short residency at Blue Mountain Lake thanks to the Society for the Humanities at Cornell.

I appreciated the chance to try out earlier versions of these arguments in other locations. These include presentations for the American Literature Association, as well as invited talks at Beijing Foreign Studies University, China Foreign Affairs University, Cornell University, Drew University, Elmira College, the Huntington Library, the Irish Association of American Studies, Keio University, Oxford University, Sussex University, Tsinghua University, UCLA, the University of New York at Albany, and the William

Seward House. I am thankful for those invitations and for the conversations that took place on those occasions. Revision was aided by the anonymous readers of the manuscript, by Alice Fahs, Sandra Gustafson, and Tom Koenigs, who read earlier drafts, and by Susan Bruce, Cole Hutchison, and Timothy Sweet, who offered detailed advice on specific chapters. My editor, Anne Savarese, offered many useful comments.

Earlier drafts of chapters have appeared in the following collections: "Men at Sea: Hawthorne, Twain, Melville," *The Oxford Handbook of Herman Melville*, ed. Jennifer Greiman and Michael Jonik (2025); "Literature and the Civil War," *Companion to American Literature*, ed. Susan Belasco and Linck Johnson (Wiley-Blackwell, 2020); "Mourning and Substitution in *The Gates Ajar*," *Literary Cultures of the American Civil War*, ed. Timothy Sweet (University of Georgia Press, 2016); "How Feminism Finds 'The Yellow Wallpaper,'" *Feminist Moments*, ed. Susan Bruce and Kathy Smits (Bloomsbury Academic, 2016); and "Looking at Lincoln," *A History of American Civil War Literature*, ed. Coleman Hutchison (Cambridge University Press, 2015). In addition, some of the language from my introduction to the collection of essays *Race and Vision in the Nineteenth-Century United States* (Lexington Books, 2019) has made its way into this book.

NOTES

Introduction

1. Walt Whitman, "Death of Abraham Lincoln." This lecture was first delivered in Philadelphia on April 14, 1879. See "Death of Abraham Lincoln," reprinted in the Library of America volume *Walt Whitman: Complete Poetry and Collected Prose* (New York University Press, 1982), 1036–1047. Worth a further look is the handwritten draft and Whitman's corrections for this speech on the website at the Library of Congress: https://www.loc.gov/item/mss454430173.

2. "Death of Abraham Lincoln," *Walt Whitman: Complete Poetry and Collected Prose* (New York University Press, 1982), 1046. Whitman's relation to the Civil War forms a topic in several biographies, but here I am thinking of Cody Marrs in *Not Even Past: The Stories We Keep Telling about the Civil War* (Johns Hopkins University Press, 2020).

3. Evident in my approach is that I provide neither a history of Civil War battles nor, though they repeatedly thread through my analysis, the practices of US enslavement. Both continue to be analyzed by historians, a few of whom I credit in my references. My influences include Michel-Rolph Trouillot, who writes about the history of Haiti in *Silencing the Past: Power and the Production of History* (Beacon Press, 1995). I would also recommend, among others cited in the pages that follow, the collection edited by Ann Laura Stoler, *Haunted by Empire: Geographies of Intimacy in North American History* (Duke University Press, 2006). See also more recent works such as Brigitte Fielder's *Relative Races: Genealogies of Interracial Kinship in Nineteenth-Century America* (Duke University Press, 2020), Koritha Mitchell's *From Slave Cabins to the White House: Homemade Citizenship in African American Culture* (University of Illinois Press, 2021), and Xine Yao's *Disaffected: The Cultural Politics of Unfeeling in Nineteenth-Century America* (Duke University Press: 2021).

4. The ongoing debates over the 1619 Project include both positive reinforcement for using it for lesson plans and criticism for some of its claims. See, for example, https://pulitzercenter.org/lesson-plan-grouping/1619-project-curriculum and https://www.theatlantic.com/ideas/archive/2019/12/historians-clash-1619-project/604093/.

5. See Amy Schrager Lang, *Prophetic Woman: Anne Hutchinson and the Problem of Dissent in New England Literature* (Berkeley: University of California Press, 1987).

6. Writing to his wife from the Dakota territory in 1863, for example, Simeon Folsom said: "I have often wrote you that the war was a big humbug. Their [sic] is not a bit of Patriotism in the whole concern." (June 22nd, 1863. Huntington Library: HM 27798).

7. Recent work on citizenship by such scholars as Christopher Bonner have opened this topic further. See *Remaking the Republic: Black Politics and the Creation of American Citizenship* (University of Pennsylvania Press, 2020). See also Alaina Roberts, *I've Been Here All the While: Black Freedom on Native Land* (University of Pennsylvania Press, 2021).

8. *Democratic Vistas* (1871) is available in a facsimile edition from the University of Iowa Press that relies on the second printing; my page numbers come from this version (2010). Ed Folsom has written a thoughtful introduction. Whitman's attention to the "appalling dangers" of "universal suffrage" does not override his conviction that "America and democracy are convertible terms" (4).

9. "Witnessing" here alludes to both *Democratic Vistas* and *Democracy in America*. A witness who traveled to the United States to view the penitentiary system, Alexis de Tocqueville found himself distracted by the confused jostling of democracy that he described as a "levelling down." To continually assert optimism in the face of violence preoccupies Whitman and appears throughout his collection of war poetry, *Drum-Taps* (1865).

10. The recent book about the Grimké family, *The Grimkes: The Legacy of Slavery in an American Family*, by Kerry K. Greenidge, explores the generations who spread across the United States in relation to the family's history of enslavement and abolitionist activism. See especially the untangling of family relations in the first few pages (Liveright, 2023).

11. Theodore Weld, *American Slavery as It Is: Testimony of a Thousand Witnesses* (American Antislavery Society, 1839), 7. Teresa Goddu says this volume, selling over 100,000 copies, persuaded many readers to become activists. See "'To Thrill the Land with Horror': Antislavery Discourse and the Gothic Imagination," in *Gothic Topographies: Language, Nation Building, and Race*, ed. P. M. Mehtonen and Matti Savolainen (Ashgate, 2013), 74.

12. For an overview focused on the Haudenosaunee, see William N. Fenton, *The Great Law and the Longhouse: A Political History of the Iroquois Confederacy* (University of Oklahoma Press, 2010). The phrase "domestic dependent nations" was delivered by Chief Justice Marshall in *Cherokee Nation v. the State of Georgia*, 1831. Marshall crucially notes that "If courts were permitted to indulge their sympathies, a case better calculated to excite them can scarcely be imagined." But sympathy and the law cannot be united. For a broader perspective on the topic, see Mahmood Mamdani, *Neither Settler nor Native: The Making and Unmaking of Permanent Minorities* (Harvard University Press, 2020).

13. Whitman, *Democratic Vistas*, 4, 17. *Specimen Days* (1882) contains excerpts from his Civil War notebooks as well as ruminations about America. See also "Song of Myself" in *Leaves of Grass*.

14. Alexander Gardner, *Photographic Sketch Book of the War* (Philp & Solomons, 1866), plate 41. Gardner comments that the "trees in the vicinity were splintered, and their branches cut off." By the time his extraordinary volume appeared, however, the appetite for war images had waned. Scholars have noted that the positions of both weapons and corpses were adjusted by Gardner. A paradox of this war is that the advent of photography as an easily reproduced medium and the newly developed machinery of warfare such as the repeating rifle and the Gatling gun meant that the first mechanized attacks on human beings occurred at the same time as the first widespread ability to record their existence. A copy of Gardner's book at the Library of Congress can be viewed here: https://www.loc.gov/resource/ppmsca.12834/?sp=90.

15. *Specimen Days*, 79.

16. Stephen Crane, *The Red Badge of Courage* (D. Appleton and Company, 1895), 3.

17. Ambrose Bierce, *Tales of Soldiers and Civilians* (Lovell, Coryell, and Company, 1891), 53.

18. Reed Bontecou's notebooks, which vary in their collection of wounds and tagged explanations, are kept in archives at Yale, Cornell, and the Library of Congress. Some images appear separately in museums such as the Metropolitan Museum of New York. After the war, Bontecou continued working as a surgeon who developed innovative treatments for war wounds. See the photograph of Stephen Wilbur, an albumen silver print from 1865, at https://www.metmuseum.org/art/collection/search/266769.

19. For a standard account of the transcontinental railroad, see Stephen Ambrose, *Nothing Like It in the World: The Men Who Built the Transcontinental Railroad, 1863–1869* (Simon and Schuster, 2001). An alternative account appears in Gordon Chang, *Ghosts of Gold Mountain: The Epic Story of the Chinese Who Built the Transcontinental Railroad* (Mariner Books, 2020).

20. Famously, "a house divided cannot stand." Abraham Lincoln gave this speech on June 16, 1858, in Illinois just after accepting his party's nomination to run for a Senate seat. See "A House Divided," Springfield, Illinois, June 16, 1858: https://quod.lib.umich.edu/l/lincoln/lincoln2/1:508?rgn=div1;view=fulltext.

21. The dispute over naming the cause of "the war between the states" persists. Seeking to legally enforce slavery emerges in legislative debates from the Declaration of Independence to the Missouri Compromise of 1820 to the Kansas–Nebraska Act. During these compromises, neither the cultural nor the geographical parameters of American identity held still.

22. Inevitably the reference to looking backward alludes to Walter Benjamin's concept of the angel of history. Reprinted in *Illuminations*, the numbered paragraphs in "Theses on the Philosophy of History" include this one, number 11: "Where we perceive a chain of events, he sees but one single catastrophe. . . . The angel would like to stay, awaken the dead, and make whole what has been smashed." But, the paragraph continues, he rides into a "storm which propels him into the future to which his back is turned." In a devastating final sentence, he proclaims "This storm is what we call progress." See *Illuminations*, trans. Harry Zohn, ed. Hannah Arendt (Houghton Mifflin, 2019), 199.

23. As recently as August 28, 2024, the National Federation of Republican Assemblies invoked the 1857 Dred Scott decision refusing citizenship to African Americans as a reason to declare Kamala Harris unfit to be president. See https://www.independent.co.uk/news/world/americas/us-politics/kamala-harris-president-supreme-court-b2601364.html.

24. Immediately after the Civil War, the Oklahoma territory became a federally recognized territory for the so-called Five Civilized Tribes, the Seminole, Choctaw, Cherokee, Creek, and Chickasaw. These groups have recently been shown to have continuing claims on land ownership in Oklahoma due to violated treaties. See Jack Healey and Adam Liptak, "Landmark Supreme Court Ruling Affirms Native American Rights in Oklahoma," *New York Times*, July 11, 2020.

25. Celebrations of Memorial Day officially began in 1868. Then called "Decoration Day," the holiday was explicitly tied to visiting the graves of the Civil War dead. See David Blight, *Race and Reunion: The Civil War in American Culture* (Harvard

University Press, 2002), and Alice Fahs and Joan Waugh, eds., *The Memory of the Civil War in American Culture* (University of North Carolina Press, 2004).

26. For a nineteenth-century account, see Luis Emilio, *History of the Fifty-Fourth Regiment of Massachusetts Volunteer Infantry, 1863–65* (Boston Book Company, 1891), 88.

27. The installation on the Boston Common, commemorating Robert Gould Shaw and the Massachusetts Fifty-Fourth, was unveiled in 1897. One recently removed statue in New Orleans, leaving an empty plinth, previously stood in the entrance route to the New Orleans Art Museum. In North Carolina, the statue that was toppled and kicked in the grass was *Silent Sam*. The fundraising of the Daughters of the Confederacy was to promote historical memory of the "Lost Cause"—but they were not founded until 1894. See Karen Cox, *Dixie's Daughters: The United Daughters of the Confederacy and the Preservation of Confederate Culture* (University Press of Florida, 2019). The formations that commemorate mourning may be seen in the slabs that take the place of counties in the National Memorial for Peace and Justice in Montgomery, Alabama. See also the evocative work by Erin Thompson, *Smashing Statues: The Rise and Fall of America's Public Monuments* (Norton, 2023).

28. Such an assertion might be bolstered by the detail that only in 2022 did West Point begin to remove its symbolic attention to confederate "heroes" such as Robert E. Lee. See Amanda Holpuch, "West Point to Remove Confederate Monument from Its Campus," *New York Times*, December 24, 2022.

29. For an expansion of this concept, see Avery Gordon, *Ghostly Matters: Haunting and the Sociological Imagination* (University of Minnesota Press, 1997). See also Renee Bergland, *The National Uncanny: Indian Ghosts and American Subjects* (University Press of New England, 2000).

30. Toni Morrison, *Beloved* (Knopf, 1987), 122.

31. Here I allude not only to the unease of Toni Morrison's *Beloved* but also to the poignant recounting of a suicide in the first pages of Maxine Hong Kingston's *The Woman Warrior*. In the latter novel the invocation of ghosts is about racial haunting as well as the fear of resurrecting ancestors who have died in ways that make remembering them dangerous. Maxine Hong Kingston, *The Woman Warrior: Memoirs of a Girlhood among Ghosts* (Random House, 1989).

32. For an account of how historical memory tends to be "stuck" on particular events, see Paul Ricouer, *Memory, History, Forgetting*, trans. Kathleen Blamey and David Pellauer (University of Chicago Press, 2007). For a more specifically US-focused set of questions, see Jeffrey Insko, *History, Abolition, and the Ever-Present Now in Antebellum American Writing* (Oxford University Press, 2019). See also W. Caleb McDaniel, *The Problem of Democracy in the Age of Slavery: Garrisonian Abolitionists and Transatlantic Reform* (Louisiana State University Press, 2015).

33. This work has been influenced by essays on the Civil War from my edited *Cambridge Companion to Abraham Lincoln* (Cambridge University Press, 2012).

34. I refer here to several recent works, including Karen Cox, *Dixie's Daughters: The United Daughters of the Confederacy and the Preservation of Confederate Culture* (University Press of Florida, 2019); William Blair, *Cities of the Dead: Contesting the Memory of the Civil War in the South, 1865–1914* (University of North Carolina Press, 2004); Cynthia Mills and Pamela Simpson, eds., *Monuments to the Lost Cause:*

Women, Art, and the Landscapes of Southern Memory (University of Tennessee Press, 2003); and Erika Doss, *Memorial Mania: Public Feeling in America* (University of Chicago Press, 2012). For the UDC statement, see their website at https://hqudc.org/.

35. The essays in *The Culture of Sentiment: Race, Gender and Sentimentality in Nineteenth-Century America* (Oxford University Press, 1992) started me thinking about the overlapping valences of politics and sentiment. It matters to remember the fraught history, to reconstruct the power of a document such as the "Declaration of Sentiments and Rights," first produced in 1848. That very title, so often abbreviated as the "Declaration of Sentiments," alludes to the combined operations of feeling and politics. To "feel right"—as Stowe once articulated the position—is to "feel" rights. A blog from the White House details the search for the originally produced manuscript of the "Declaration of Sentiments," now lost. The last person known to have it in hand was Frederick Douglass, who signed it and then took it to Rochester to publish in his newspaper, *The North Star*.

36. On the Alien and Sedition Acts of 1798, see John C. Miller, *Crisis in Freedom: The Alien and Sedition Acts* (Little Brown and Company 1951). On the raid on Harper's Ferry, see Tony Horwitz, *Midnight Rising: John Brown and the Raid that Sparked the Civil War* (Henry Holt, 2011), and Franny Nudelman, *John Brown's Body: Slavery, Violence, and the Culture of War* (University of North Carolina Press, 2004). On Indian "removal," see Robert Remini, *Andrew Jackson and His Indian Wars* (Viking, 2001), and on events at Little Big Horn, see James Donovan, *A Terrible Glory: Custer and the Little Bighorn* (Little, Brown, 2008). On the Astor Place Riots, see Nigel Cliff, *The Shakespeare Riots: Revenge, Drama, and Death in 19th-Century America* (Random House, 2007). The Astor Place Riots occurred when violent protests broke out over the performances of two actors: the "native" American actor Edwin Forrest, who acted the role of the Indian king Metamora, and British actor William Charles Macready. See the account by Elizabeth Maddock Dillon, *New World Drama: The Performative Commons* (New York University Press, 2014), 17.

37. This image appeared in *Harper's Weekly* on November 15, 1862. There's a copy at the Metropolitan Museum: https://www.metmuseum.org/art/collection/search/349139. On Winslow Homer more generally, see Randall Griffin, *Winslow Homer: An American Vision* (Phaidon Press, 2006).

38. On the "Declaration of Sentiments," usually attributed to Elizabeth Cady Stanton, see this website: http://legacy.fordham.edu/halsall/mod/senecafalls.asp. On Stanton, see her *A History of Woman Suffrage* (Fowler and Wells, 1889). On the "golden spike," see David Haward Bain, *Empire Express: Building the First Transcontinental Railroad* (Penguin, 2000). On the photograph of Lincoln after the battle at Antietam in October 1862, see Alexander Gardner, *Photographic Sketchbook of the War* (Philps & Solomon, 1865–1866), vol. 1, no. 23. The image can be found in the public domain at the Library of Congress. For a copy, visit the Prints and Photographs division: LC-B8171–7951. See also http://www.loc.gov/pictures/resource/ppmsca.12544/.

39. Stuart Hall, "Negotiating Caribbean Identity," *New Left Review* I, 209 (January–February 1995), 6.

40. A copy of this photograph, made by Alexander Gardner on October 2, 1862, is at the Smithsonian. See https://www.civilwar.si.edu/lincoln_mcclellanlincoln.html.

41. Directed by Steven Spielberg and featuring Daniel Day Lewis as Lincoln, the film opened in 2012. The more recent movie, *Civil War*, shows the Lincoln Memorial being demolished in the fighting, but no glimpse of Lincoln's face appears there.

42. On the beating that Preston Brooks gave to Charles Sumner, see this link from the US Senate: https://www.senate.gov/artandhistory/history/minute/The_Caning_of_Senator_Charles_Sumner.htm.

43. Henry David Thoreau's "Civil Disobedience," also known as "On the Duty of Civil Disobedience," was published in 1849 after Thoreau's resistance to paying a poll tax that went to support the war with Mexico led to his overnight stint in the local jail. Frequently reprinted, the essay appeared in book form in Elizabeth Peabody, ed., *Aesthetic Papers* (Putnam, 1849).

44. See the recent book by Matthew Stewart, *An Emancipation of the Mind: Radical Philosophy, the War over Slavery, and the Refounding of America* (Norton, 2023).

45. The transgression of wearing trousers in public shows up in the writing of the popular newspaper columnist Fanny Fern, whose newspaper column contained the piece "A Law More Nice Than Just" in 1858. See *Ruth Hall and Other Writings: Fanny Fern*, ed. Joyce W. Warren (Rutgers University Press, 1986). For accounts of women dressing and fighting as soldiers, see DeAnne Blanton and Lauren M. Cook, *They Fought Like Demons: Women Soldiers in the American Civil War* (Louisiana State University Press, 2002).

46. For an investigation of the Lowell mills and the factory girls who wrote as they worked, see Benita Eisler, *The Lowell Offering: Writings by New England Mill Women (1840–1945)* (Norton, 1997).

47. See Frederick Douglass, *Narrative of the Life of Frederick Douglass* (Anti-Slavery Office, 1845).

48. A helpful visualization of technological changes appears in Trish Loughran's *The Republic in Print: Print Culture in the Age of U.S. Nation Building, 1776–1876* (Columbia University Press, 2007). It's worth noting that the genre switching of propaganda included poetry, songs, journals, pamphlets, envelopes, stationery, cloth, and cartoons. Loughran analyzes a cartoon produced by Currier and Ives in 1876. Titled "The Progress of the Century," the cartoon looks back at the changes made by the steamboat, the railroad, the telegraph, and above all, the steam-driven printing press. For Loughran, print culture is "American nationalism's preferred techno-mythology" (34). See also Teresa Goddu, *Selling Antislavery: Abolition and Mass Media in Antebellum America* (University of Pennsylvania Press, 2020). This image is at the Library of Congress, LC- USZ62–102264. Compare http://www.loc.gov/pictures/item/90716345/.

49. Margaret Fuller wrote *Summer on the Lakes in 1843* (Charles C. Little and James Brown, 1844). Charles Dickens produced *American Notes*, highly critical of the United States, after visiting in 1842 (Chapman and Hall, 1842).

50. John Rollin Ridge published *Life and Adventures of Joaquin Murieta: Celebrated California Bandit* in 1854. Focused on the problems of Mexican ranchers in California after the Treaty of Guadalupe Hidalgo, Maria Amparo Ruiz de Burton published *The Squatter and the Don* in 1885. See also Susan Schulten, *Mapping the Nation: History and Cartography in Nineteenth-Century America* (University of Chicago Press, 2012). The boundaries of the territory in question continued to be

disputed after 1848, but the Treaty of Guadalupe Hidalgo represented an enormous change in the land occupied by the United States. On the text of the treaty, see this link to the Library of Congress site: https://www.loc.gov/resource/llsalvol.llsal_009/?sp=976.

51. Recent overviews tend to be outnumbered by more specific studies of American culture. Two good examples are Carrie Bramen, *American Niceness: A Cultural History* (Harvard University Press, 2017), and Dana Nelson, *Commons Democracy* (Fordham University Press, 2016). Previous studies relevant to this project include Cathy Davidson, *Revolution and the Word: The Rise of the Novel in America* (Oxford University Press, 2004); Nina Baym, *Woman's Fiction: A Guide to Novels by and about Women in America, 1820–1870* (University of Illinois Press, 1993); and Richard Brodhead, *Cultures of Letters: Scenes of Reading and Writing in Nineteenth-Century America* (University of Chicago Press, 1990). See also Lauren Berlant, *The Female Complaint: The Unfinished Business of Sentimentality in American Culture* (Duke University Press, 2008), and Pete Coviello, *Intimacy in America: Dreams of Affiliation in Antebellum Literature* (University of Minnesota Press, 2005). More recently, see Elizabeth Maddock Dillon, *New World Drama: The Performative Commons in the Atlantic World, 1649–1849* (Duke University Press, 2014), and Robin Bernstein's *Racial Innocence* (New York University Press, 2011). The flexibility of the internet has encouraged influential work like that by Bruce Burgett and Glenn Hendler in the keywords project. See *Keywords for American Cultural Studies* (New York University Press, 2014). In addition, edited volumes that offer overviews of American culture as presented by multiple authors continue to appear. See, for instance, my edited book, *A Companion to American Fiction, 1780–1865* (Wiley-Blackwell, 2004).

52. *Democratic Vistas*, 12.

53. Ekphrasis appears as part of the rivalry between painting and poetry in such works as *Museum of Words: The Poetics of Ekphrasis from Homer to Ashberry* by James Heffernan (University of Chicago Press, 1993).

54. The New York City "draft riots" have received increased attention lately, but the history of the treatment of children has only begun to be visible. See the portrayal by the nineteenth-century cartoonist Thomas Nast at https://blackhistory.harpweek.com/7illustrations/civilwar/ColoredOrphanAsylum.htm.

55. See, for instance, the work on Lewis and Clark in Duncan Faherty, *Remodeling the Nation: The Architecture of American Identity, 1776–1858* (University Press of New England, 2009).

56. In "A True Story, Repeated Word for Word as I Heard It," Twain tells the story of the family cook, whose children have been sold away from her. The story first appeared in *The Atlantic* (November 1874), 591–594. It's somewhat chilling that the story is followed by an installment of "A Rebel's Recollections."

57. Quarry Farm is not open to the public. The home of John W. Jones, adjacent to Woodlawn national cemetery, is now a museum. See https://www.johnwjonesmuseum.org/.

58. Compare Cody Marrs, *Not Even Past: The Stories We Keep Telling about the Civil War* (Johns Hopkins University Press, 2020). See also Elizabeth Young, *Disarming the Nation: Women's Writing and the American Civil War* (University of Chicago Press, 1999).

59. Such conflicts include the controversy over the statue known as *Silent Sam* in Chapel Hill, North Carolina, and the violence in Charlottesville, Virginia, initially spurred by the proposed removal of a statue of Robert E. Lee. The former statue, created by John Wilson, was commissioned by the UDC and erected in 1913. See https://museum.unc.edu/exhibits/show/civilwar/silent-sam.

60. See https://www.cnn.com/2020/06/19/us/portland-george-washington-statue-toppled-trnd/index.html.

61. See the copy held by the Metropolitan Museum here: https://www.metmuseum.org/art/collection/search/301989.

62. See also Paula Whitacre, *A Civil Life in an Uncivil Time: Julia Wilbur's Struggle for Purpose* (Potomac Books, 2020).

Chapter 1. Visions of Democracy

1. Many books consider images of Whitman in relation to his writing. For a starting point, see F. O. Mathiessen, *The American Renaissance: Art and Expression in the Age of Emerson and Whitman* (Oxford University Press, 1941). Mathiessen's introduction notes, paradoxically, that the best photograph for his purposes is an early daguerreotype of the shipbuilder Donald McKay from the Boston studio of Southworth and Hawes. See a copy at http://www.metmuseum.org/collection/the-collection- online/search/268306. Among other fine works, see also Michael Moon, *Disseminating Whitman: Revision and Corporeality in Leaves of Grass* (Harvard University Press, 1993).

2. "The Dresser." https://whitmanarchive.org/published/LG/1867/poems/170.

3. See, for example, Dana Luciano's helpful exploration *Arranging Grief: Sacred Time and the Body in Nineteenth-Century America* (New York University Press, 2007). See also Drew Gilpin Faust, *This Republic of Suffering: Death and the American Civil War* (Vintage, 2009). For an account of haunting that considers the genre of the gothic, see Teresa Goddu, "The African American Slave Narrative and the Gothic," in *A Companion to American Gothic*, ed. Charles L. Crow (John Wiley and Sons, 2014).

4. I'm thinking especially of "Po' Sandy," first published in *The Atlantic Monthly* in 1888 and later collected in Chesnutt's *The Conjure Woman* (Houghton Mifflin, 1899).

5. This speech was delivered extemporaneously by Alexander Stephens on March 21, 1861, reported in a Southern newspaper, and subsequently referred to by a number of Southern politicians. As the vice president of the Confederacy, Stephens later argued that he had been misquoted, but he approved the transcripts made by reporters. See https://www.owleyes.org/text/the-cornerstone-speech/read/text-of-stephenss-speech#root-46. Also see *Southern Confederacy* (Monday, March 25, 1861), 1. https://www.newspapers.com/article/southern-confederacy-cornerstone-speech/84885277/.

6. W.E.B. Du Bois, *Black Reconstruction in America, 1860–1880* (Harcourt, Brace, 1935), 13.

7. Du Bois, p. 239. Douglass first gave the speech "What to the Slave Is the Fourth of July?" on July 5, 1852 in Rochester, New York. It was first published as a pamphlet titled "Oration Delivered in Corinthian Hall Rochester" in 1852 and included

in several subsequent collections. Du Bois proposed it as simple logic that the "sexual chaos" of slavery "arose from economic motives . . ." (44).

8. The act of dismantling the statue on the anniversary of the famous address from Frederick Douglass drew global attention. See, for example, the article in *The Guardian* newspaper on July 6, 2020: "Frederick Douglass statue torn down on anniversary of famous speech."

9. Philip Freneau, "The British Prison Ship," is an unusually bloodthirsty poem in which Freneau wants to "glut revenge on this detested foe." See https://poets.org/poem/british-prison-ship. For a good example of Freneau's rage with Caribbean slavery, see his poem "To Sir Toby" here: https://poets.org/poem/sir-toby. John Greenleaf Whittier wrote out his abolitionist position in poems such as "The Hunters of Men." See https://www.bartleby.com/lit-hub/poetical-works-in-four-volumes/the-hunters-of-men/. Frances Harper's "The Slave Auction" represents one of many poems of protest. See https://www.poetryfoundation.org/poems/47686/the-slave-auction.

10. Harper's late poem, "Then and Now," can be found here: https://scalar.lehigh.edu/african-american-poetry-a-digital-anthology/frances-ew-harper-poems-full-text-1895.

11. Such a model of haunting is informed by the ideas of trauma in Cathy Caruth, *Unclaimed Experience: Trauma, Narrative, and History* (Johns Hopkins University Press, 1996). Drawing on psychoanalysis for her account, Caruth notes that "If Freud turns to literature to describe traumatic experience, that is because literature, like psychoanalysis, is interested in the complex relation between knowing and not knowing" (3). See also her *Literature in the Ashes of History* (Johns Hopkins University Press, 2013), which begins with an account of Freud encountering traumatized veterans of World War I. The business of Civil War reenactment that has spread across the United States might be seen to participate both in ideas about trauma and in site-specific reclamation of memory.

12. Henry James used this image in his preface to *Portrait of a Lady* (1882). See also *The Art of Fiction: Essays on the Novel* (Oxford University Press, 1948). James proposes that "The house of fiction has in short not one window, but a million, a number of possible windows not to be reckoned . . . every one of which has been pierced . . . by the need of the individual vision" (8).

13. For the text of the original sermon, "A Model of Christian Charity," by John Winthrop, see http://history.hanover.edu/texts/winthmod.html.

14. Abraham Lincoln, "Inaugural Address." See https://avalon.law.yale.edu/19th_century/lincoln1.asp.

15. The stage production of Lin Manuel Miranda's *Hamilton* continues to draw crowds; the "book" for the show is Jeremy McCarter and Lin Manuel Miranda, *Hamilton: The Revolution* (Grand Central Publishing, 2016).

16. Britain outlawed the trafficking of humans across the Atlantic in 1807, but did not abolish the practice of slavery in the Caribbean until 1834. The US Constitution (Article One, Section 9) allowed the importation of people held as slaves until 1808. The domestic traffic in humans was not affected by the criminalization of trafficking, nor indeed did such traffic end completely until the end of the Civil War made the practice of slavery illegal, an act not passed until December of 1865. See https://www.archives.gov/education/lessons/slave-trade.html.

17. See Eric Cheyfitz, "Disinformation: The Limits of Capitalism's Imagination and the End of Ideology," in *Boundary 2* vol. 41, no. 3 (fall 2014), 55–91. Citing James Madison in Federalist 10, Cheyfitz announces that the tension between economic privilege and public good has haunted the United States since the constitutional convention and the debates known as the Federalist Papers. See also Leonard Richards, *Shays's Rebellion: The American Revolution's Final Battle* (University of Pennsylvania Press, 2002). The idea of the commons also strongly informs Dana Nelson's *Commons Democracy: Reading the Politics of Participation in the United States* (Fordham University Press, 2015).

18. See Susan J. Stanfield, *Rewriting Citizenship: Women, Race, and Nineteenth-Century Print Culture* (University of Georgia Press, 2022). Much violence against humans living in cities in the nineteenth century reflected anxiety about property, an issue graphically and painfully described by Ida B. Wells in such works as *The Red Record: Tabulated Statistics and Alleged Causes of Lynching in the United States* (1895). Wells attests that the late nineteenth century saw "more than ten thousand Negroes killed in cold blood" while the government "which had made the Negro a citizen found itself unable to protect him" (4).

19. Elizabeth Dillon, *New World Drama: The Performative Commons in the Atlantic World, 1649–1840* (Duke University Press, 2014), 3, 15–16. Dillon terms the resulting unevenness of a sense of belonging in these spaces "intimate distance" (16).

20. Lewis Hyde, *The Gift: Imagination and the Erotic Life of Property* (Vintage, 1983), quoted by Dillon, 4. Dillon focuses on communal resistance including public action in riots (such as the Draft Riots in New York in 1863) and public action as theater (riots sometimes emerged from the permeable space of the theater, as in the Astor Place Riots of 1849). Her account challenges that proposed by Michael Hardt and Antonio Negri. See Michael Hardt and Antonio Negri, *Empire* (Harvard University Press, 2001). For Dillon, a "performative commons" posits an "Atlantic world" as a space of performance, thus conceiving of a space beyond the "nation-state" (7).

21. Dillon, 8.

22. Lisa Lowe, *The Intimacies of Four Continents* (Duke University Press, 2015).

23. See Laurence Holland, "A 'Raft of Trouble': Word and Deed in *Huckleberry Finn*," in *American Realism: New Essays*, ed. Eric Sundquist (Johns Hopkins University Press, 1982), 66–67.

24. See David Kazanjian, *The Colonizing Trick: National Culture and Imperial Citizenship in Early America* (University of Minnesota Press, 2003).

25. See Jurgen Habermas, *The Structural Transformation of the Public Sphere: An Inquiry into a Category of Bourgeois Society*, trans. Thomas Burger (MIT Press, 1991), and Paul Gilroy, *The Black Atlantic: Modernity and Double Consciousness* (Harvard University Press, 1993). See also Nancy Fraser, ed., *Transnationalizing the Public Sphere* (Polity, 2014).

26. The archive of ghosts includes those not celebrated because few remember their names: the people caught in between the battle lines or the people at the edge of the battles whose homes are confiscated and ravaged. Such stories appear mythic in Ambrose Bierce's renderings. They are nonchalant and yet painful in the reminiscences and letters of those like Louisa Jacobs, the daughter of Harriet Jacobs, who lives through the conflicts in Washington, DC, and then works to pick up the pieces

with orphans and the displaced. See, for instance, Mary Maillard, *Whispers of Cruel Wrongs: The Correspondence of Louisa Jacobs and Her Circle, 1879–1911* (University of Wisconsin Press, 2020).

27. An optimistic assertion of "absolute equality" appears in this declaration: "The people of Texas are informed that, in accordance with a proclamation from the Executive of the United States, all slaves are free. This involves an absolute equality of personal rights and rights of property between former masters and slaves, and the connection heretofore existing between them becomes that between employer and hired labor," *Headquarters District of Texas, Galveston*, June 19, 1865. A reading of this legacy appears at the African American History Museum website: https://nmaahc.si.edu/explore/stories/historical-legacy-juneteenth.

28. See Benjamin Soskis and John Stauffer, *The Battle Hymn of the Republic: A Biography of the Song That Marches On* (Oxford University Press, 2013). They note that the melody was developed in conjunction with antebellum camp meeting songs and then became a campfire song celebrating John Brown's rebellion before Julia Ward Howe rewrote it.

29. See Brigitte Fielder, "Black Madness, White Violence and John Brown's Legacy" in *Abolition's Afterlives*, an online forum for *American Literary History* (Oxford University Press, 2021). She references David S. Reynolds and his recent work on John Brown in relation to Abraham Lincoln: *John Brown, Abolitionist: The Man Who Killed Slavery, Sparked the Civil War, and Seeded Civil Rights* (Vintage, 2005).

30. I was able to read Civil War diaries during a fellowship at the Huntington Library. These range from tiny fragments in very small notebooks to larger descriptions with notations about taking souvenirs. The quote about being "chuck full of ale" comes from an entry of March 11, 1864, in the diary of Charles Ort (HM68422). He goes on to mention on April 6 that he read a dime novel called "the Backwoodsman and the Bride"; on April 10 he "read a dime novel through called The Indian Princess." The circulating library of dime novels must have been an active part of camp life. The papers of John Burrud, notable for appearing in this fine blog from Huntington curator Olga Tsapina, also perversely perform a sort of "war as slavery tourism" view of the South. See https://huntington.org/verso/where-solomon-northup-was-slave. See also https://huntington.org/frontiers/2017-spring-summer/archiving-civil-wars-text-messages.

31. I read this 800-page handwritten manuscript at the Huntington Library, where it can be retrieved as HMmss 58109. It has since been analyzed and made available by Christopher Grasso. See Grasso, ed., *Bloody Engagements: John R. Kelso's Civil War* (Yale University Press, 2017). See also Christopher Grasso, *Teacher, Preacher, Soldier, Spy: The Civil Wars of John R. Kelso* (Oxford University Press, 2021).

32. Jonathan Elmer, *On Lingering and Being Last: Race and Sovereignty in the New World* (Fordham University Press, 2008), 5. In contrast to such a historically situated reading, a variant on critical race theory, have been such readings as that proposed by Stephen Best and Sharon Marcus in "Surface Reading: An Introduction," in *Representations* vol. 108, no. 1 (2009), 1–21. They promote "the truth to which a text bears witness," in opposition to what they call "symptomatic reading" (1).

33. Work that seeks to understand the literatures of the United States through political engagement includes Andy Doolen, *Territories of Empire: U.S. Writing from*

the Louisiana Purchase to Mexican Independence (Oxford University Press, 2014). Such work remains influenced by the collection edited by Amy Kaplan and Donald Pease, *Cultures of United States Imperialism* (Duke University Press, 1994). See also Amy Kaplan, *The Anarchy of Empire in the Making of U.S. Culture* (Harvard University Press, 2002).

34. Avery Gordon, *Ghostly Matters: Haunting and the Sociological Imagination* (University of Minnesota Press, 1997), xvi.

35. James Fenimore Cooper's *The Pioneers* (1821) contains a prescient lament for environmental carelessness and waste. For an eloquent account of environments and affect, see Monique Allewaert, *Ariel's Ecology: Plantations, Personhood, and Colonialism in the American Tropics* (University of Minnesota Press, 2013).

36. Royall Tyler's *The Contrast* (1787), a satire on American affectations, was the first American play written to be professionally staged in the United States.

37. See Jane Johnston Schoolcraft, *The Sound the Stars Make Rushing through the Sky*, ed. Robert Dale Parker (University of Pennsylvania Press, 2007). See also the story told by Sarah Winnemucca of navigating between settler colonial worlds and the Pyramid Lake Paiute among whom she was born. Born in 1844 in territory then claimed by Mexico and subsequently by the United States, she was an interpreter between these worlds. She knew several languages, yet her language cannot always convey the depredations, including the death of her mother, at the hands of US troops in 1865. See her *Life among the Piutes: Their Wrongs and Claims* (1883), at http://www.yosemite.ca.us/library/life_among_the_piutes/.

38. Mason Locke Weems's biography of George Washington presents many fabrications; perhaps for that reason it was quite popular and its stories lived on in schoolbooks. See *The Life of George Washington* (Philadelphia, 1800) at this site: https://archive.org/details/lifeofgeorgewashweem.

39. For an emphasis on how the nineteenth-century United States commemorated the corpses of children, see "The Death of a Child and the Replication of an Image," in Karen Sanchez-Eppler, *Dependent States: The Child's Part in Nineteenth-Century American Culture* (University of Chicago, 2005), 101–148. She notes that the "power that adheres in the figure of the dying child may be used to enforce a wide array of social issues" (101).

40. On libraries, see also Elizabeth McHenry, *Forgotten Readers: Recovering the Lost History of African American Literary Societies* (Duke University Press, 2002). She focuses on literary societies that operated between 1830 and 1940. For the development of a different written language in the period, see Ellen Cushman, *The Cherokee Syllabary: Writing the People's Perseverance* (Oklahoma University Press, 2013). She claims that the Cherokee language has a "completely indigenous writing system" that might also be part of the persistence of records about their displacement (6).

41. Franklin's *Autobiography* calls attention to "errata" as a motif indicating oddly superficial regrets for the occasions of betrayals and broken promises.

42. Many books have appeared on the ghosts of the Civil War (haunting battlefields, among other locations), but that process of reenacting Civil War battles on the fields where they first occurred suggests the repetition of haunting as a generational trauma that increases as it repeats. See, for instance, Rebecca Schneider, *Performing Remains: Art and War in Times of Theatrical Reenactment* (Routledge, 2011).

43. For an eloquent expansion of this concept, see Walter Johnson, *River of Dark Dreams: Slavery and Empire in the Cotton Kingdom* (Harvard University Press, 2017). A recent collection of essays proposes to understand a watery version of the Underground Railroad: *Sailing to Freedom: Maritime Dimensions of the Underground Railroad*, ed. Timothy Walker (University of Massachusetts Press, 2021).

44. For a vivid account of such statues, see Wendy Bellion, *Iconoclasm in New York: Revolution to Reenactment* (Pennsylvania State University Press, 2019).

45. These statues might refer obliquely to the cenotaph, holding the empty space that still ceremonially holds the remains of the memories we have of the dead. Compare the Tomb of the Unknown Soldier. See also Kirk Savage, *Monument Wars: Washington, D.C., the National Mall, and the Transformation of the Memorial Landscape* (University of California Press, 2011). In June 2021, the House of Representatives voted to remove Confederate statues from the Capitol building.

46. In the early nineteenth century, many developments emerged for reproducing images. The lithographs that copied photographs in magazines, initially colored by hand, were supplemented by the color lithograph. For consumers of portraits done by photographic techniques, the daguerreotype gave way to the sequential possibilities of the collotype, the collodion, and the wet-plate process. For those who could afford it, the stylized large-scale imperial supplemented the inexpensive *cartes de visite*, but all these processes reflected the slow extension of the self into a circulation on paper once unimaginable.

47. The famous example of Mary Todd Lincoln comforted by her deceased husband is a "spirit photograph," from the studio of William H. Mumler. Such an image extends the possibilities for photographers to claim they could see into hitherto inaccessible spaces of death. See Louis Kaplan, *The Strange Case of William Mumler, Spirit Photographer* (University of Minnesota Press, 2008).

48. See Ariella Azoulay, *The Civil Contract of Photography* (Zone Books, 2008). Azoulay draws on the work initiated by Carole Pateman in *The Sexual Contract* (1988) and replied to by Charles Mills in *The Racial Contract* (1997) to make an argument about the relation of vision to social contracts.

49. According to Shawn Michele Smith, "In the United States, race has been one of the cultural inscriptions most defined by a dynamic of revelation and obfuscation, of hypervisibility and invisibility." Compare *At the Edge of Sight: Photography and the Unseen* (Duke University Press, 2013), 14.

50. The famous photograph of the furrowed scars on the back of "Gordon" was widely reproduced as an illustration of the evils of slavery. The photograph I prefer instead presents him in the tattered clothing that concealed those scars and purports to show Gordon in April 1863 as he first arrived in a Union army camp based in the South after escaping from the plantation where he received the severe beating that disfigured his back. The photographs were originally taken by itinerant photographers and then reproduced by the studio of Mathew Brady and circulated as "*cartes des visite*," an interesting (to put it mildly) application of the technique for distributing photographs as calling cards. A version of the photograph was published in *Harper's Weekly* with an image of "Gordon" in uniform as a newly enlisted Union soldier. This image is on display at the National Museum of African American History. See https://www.loc.gov/item/2018648117/. The story has most recently been used as the basis

for the movie *Emancipation*. See https://www.theguardian.com/film/2022/dec/07/emancipation-will-smith-slavery-drama.

51. The legal concept of *partus sequitur ventrem* is simply that the child will follow the legal status of the mother. The North American version originated in Virginia in 1662 and opened the structure of Southern families to numerous abuses, including, often, the sale of children. See the chapter on "Slavery and the Law of Successions" in Thomas Morris, *Southern Slavery and the Law, 1619–1860* (University of North Carolina, 1996).

52. Rather unbelievably, when *Dred* was performed as a play in New York, the minor characters included Tom Thumb, borrowed from his appearances with P. T. Barnum. This production was reviewed in the *New York Tribune* on October 18, 1956. See https://lostmuseum.cuny.edu/archive/dred-at-the-museum-new-york-tribune-october.

53. Originally published in the *Atlantic Monthly* in June 1859, "The Stereoscope and the Stereograph" was reprinted by Oliver Wendell Holmes in *Soundings from the Atlantic* (Ticknor and Fields, 1864), 125–126.

54. See Susan Sontag, *Regarding the Pain of Others* (Farrar, Straus and Giroux, 2003), and Roland Barthes, *Camera Lucida: Reflections on Photography* (Hill and Wang, 1981). Notable writers on photography include Jonathan Crary, who, in *Techniques of the Observer: On Vision and Modernity in the Nineteenth Century*, asserted that the conditions for viewers to understand what it meant to see photographically predetermined its emergence as a technology (MIT Press, 1990). See also James Elkins, *The Object Stares Back: On the Nature of Seeing* (Harcourt, 1996). As his title suggests, Elkins has a fascination with objects that seem to look at the viewer. In *Burning with Desire: The Conception of Photography* (MIT Press, 1999), Geoffrey Batchen extends Crary's fascination with photography's preconditions. Shawn Michele Smith proposes that "the surface politics of the body" work to "establish social boundaries founded in the name of discursively naturalized interior essences"; see *American Archives: Gender, Race, and Class in Visual Culture* (Princeton University Press, 1999), 4–5.

55. Again performing a repetition and a haunting of that assassination, the play *Topdog / Underdog* (2001), by Suzan-Lori Parks, forces the brothers "Lincoln" and "Booth" to reenact murder on a nightly basis.

56. Holmes, 126.

57. See also the introduction to my edited collection *Race and Vision in the Nineteenth-Century United States* (Lexington Books, 2019).

58. This claim is made in Celeste-Marie Bernier, John Stauffer, and Zoe Trodd, eds., *Picturing Frederick Douglass: An Illustrated Biography of the Nineteenth Century's Most Photographed American* (Liveright, 2018).

59. From a speech by Frederick Douglass given at Tremont Temple in Boston, Massachusetts, on December 3, 1861. I quote from a transcription of his handwritten remarks that can be read at https://frederickdouglasspapersproject.com/item/9106. An earlier acoustic invention is juxtaposed with this visual one. Douglass contrasts Daguerre with Samuel Morse and the telegraph. By his account, Morse has the "glory of bringing the ends of the earth together, and of converting the world into a whispering gallery." Yet for Douglass it matters to noticethat there's also a class dynamic: "What was once the exclusive luxury of the rich and great is now within reach of all."

60. The British artist Isaac Julien has a compelling work titled *Lessons of the Hour* (commissioned by the Memorial Art Gallery in Rochester, New York, in 2019) that uses imaginative reconstructions of Douglass speaking these words. This work will be on display at the Smithsonian American Art Museum through 2026. See https://americanart.si.edu/exhibitions/isaac-julien. See also Maurice Wallace and Shawn Michelle Smith, eds., *Pictures and Progress: Early Photography and the Making of African American Identity* (Duke University Press, 2012).

61. Crary, 1, 3. Addressing the history of concepts of representation that precede photography, Crary considers effects within the first decades of photography's evolution; to move from the "one-off" daguerreotype to the collodion or "wet-plate" process of reproduction of image is to include attention to the overlaps between photography and other arts.

62. Many of these photographs were collected in photo albums that are now held at places such as the Library of Congress and Kroch Library at Cornell University. Some are held privately, by Stanley Burns, in an archive partly represented in the book *Shooting Soldiers: Civil War Medical Photography* (Burns Archive Press, 2011). For an example of Bontecou's own writing see the text written for surgeons, *What Class of Gunshot Wounds and Injuries Justify Resection, in Modern Warfare?* (1888) https://archive.org/details/101165124.nlm.nih.gov.

63. See Sarah Chinn, *Disability, the Body, and Radical Intellectuals in the Literature of the Civil War and Reconstruction* (Cambridge University Press, 2024).

64. "My Hunt after the Captain," *The Atlantic Monthly* (December 1862), 66. See also "Doings of the Sunbeam," *The Atlantic Monthly* (July 1863). For an account of Brady's studio see James Horan, *Mathew Brady: Historian with a Camera* (Crown, 1955), as well as Beaumont Newhall, *The History of Photography from 1839 to the Present Day* (New York, 1964).

65. Shawn Michele Smith and Laura Wexler have done significant work on the ideological force of photography. In *Tender Violence: Domestic Visions in an Age of U.S. Imperialism*, Wexler writes about Frances Benjamin Johnston, who, later in the century, took more than six hundred photographs at the Tuskegee Institute at the invitation of Booker T. Washington (University of North Carolina Press, 2000). Washington looks directly at the camera in the frontispiece to Johnston's book.

66. For insight on these matters, see Betsy Erkkila, *Whitman, the Political Poet* (Oxford University Press, 1996), and Peter Coviello, *Intimacy in America: Dreams of Affiliation in American Literature* (University of Minnesota Press, 2005).

67. The reference here is to Edward Baptist, *The Half Has Never Been Told: Slavery and the Making of American Capitalism* (Basic Books, 2016).

68. Maria Amparo Ruiz de Burton, *Who Would Have Thought It?* (Lippincott, 1872). In this convoluted novel, the visual matter of racial identification is at first contained within the body of a young girl who is thought to be "spotted," until the dye used to hide her white identity eventually wears off.

69. Walt Whitman, *Leaves of Grass* (Random House, 2000), 620. See Gillian Silverman, *Bodies and Books: Reading and the Fantasy of Communion in Nineteenth-Century America* (University of Pennsylvania Press, 2012).

70. Ellen Gruber Garvey explores scrapbooks in *Writing with Scissors: American Scrapbooks from the Civil War to the Harlem Renaissance* (Oxford University Press, 2012). Another and more disturbing thrill can come from something like the

handwriting of a plantation ledger, recording the names, ages, and dates of humans claimed as property. See http://rmc.library.cornell.edu/gettysburg150/exhibition/dedicated/index.html.

71. See Joan Cashin, ed., *War Matters: Material Culture in the Civil War Era* (University of North Carolina Press, 2018).

72. See, for example, Molly Rogers, *Delia's Tears: Race, Science, and Photography in Nineteenth-Century America* (Yale University Press, 2010). See also the extensive work done by Deborah Willis, especially *Envisioning Emancipation: Black Americans and the End of Slavery* (Temple University Press, 2017).

73. Carrie Mae Weems, "From Here I Saw What Happened and I Cried" (1995). See https://www.moma.org/learn/moma_learning/carrie-mae-weems-from-here-i-saw-what-happened-and-i-cried-1995/. See also *To Make Their Own Way in the World: The Enduring Legacy of the Zealy Daguerreotypes*, ed. Ilisa Barbash, Molly Rogers, and Deborah Willis (Aperture, 2020).

74. The decision written by Chief Justice John Marshall in *Cherokee Nation v. Georgia* (1831) uses this term to describe the limited authority that states had over inhabitants who were members of the Cherokee nation. See https://supreme.justia.com/cases/federal/us/30/1/.

75. Among several sources for the Louisiana Purchase agreement, see the historical examination of it in Jon Kukla, *A Wilderness So Immense: The Louisiana Purchase and the Destiny of America* (Knopf, 2004).

76. For the original wording of the Missouri Compromise of 1820, see this link from the Library of Congress: https://www.loc.gov/resource/llsalvol.llsal_003/?sp=587&r=-0.685,0.243,2.17,0.848,0.

77. For a transcript and commentary on the Kansas–Nebraska Act of 1854, see https://www.archives.gov/milestone-documents/kansas-nebraska-act.

78. Compare Bonnie Honig, "Declarations of Independence: Arendt and Derrida on the Problem of Founding a Republic," *American Political Science Review* vol. 85, no. 1 (March 1991), 97–113. Derrida's comments on the Declaration of Independence appeared in *Diacritics* in 1976. See also the references to Indians in the Compromise of 1820, cited earlier.

79. This sentence abbreviates references to two forces and events sometimes announced under different names. The Iroquois confederacy uses the French name for what are now known as the Haudenosaunee. The Cherokee removals has become the term used for what was once called the Trail of Tears. On the first topic, see Francis Jennings et al., eds., *The History and Culture of Iroquois Diplomacy: An Interdisciplinary Guide to the Treaties of the Six Nations and Their League* (Syracuse University Press, 1995), and Daniel Richter, *The Ordeal of the Longhouse: The Peoples of the Iroquois League in the Era of European Colonization* (University of North Carolina, 1992). For a history of resistance to "removal," see Sam Gwynne, *Empire of the Summer Moon: Quanah Parker and the Rise and Fall of the Comanches, the Most Powerful Indian Tribe in American History* (Scribner, 2011).

80. An extract from section six of the Fugitive Slave Act provides an absolute prohibition against admitting testimony from someone accused of escaping from slavery. These excerpts spell out some details: "That when a person held to service or labor in any State or Territory of the United States, has heretofore or shall hereafter escape into another

State or Territory of the United States, the person or persons to whom such service or labor may be due . . . may pursue and reclaim such fugitive person . . . with authority to such claimant . . . to use such reasonable force and restraint as may be necessary . . . to take and remove such fugitive person back to the State or Territory whence he or she may have escaped as aforesaid. In no trial or hearing under this act shall the testimony of such alleged fugitive be admitted in evidence; and the certificates . . . shall be conclusive of the right of the person or persons in whose favor granted, to remove such fugitive to the State or Territory from which he escaped, and shall prevent all molestation of such person or persons by any process issued by any court judge, magistrate, or other person whomsoever." The idea that "all molestation" will be prohibited encourages the use of fraud in pursuing humans who cannot testify to their own freedom.

81. For the original wording of the Fugitive Slave Act of 1850, see this link from the Library of Congress: https://www.loc.gov/resource/llsalvol.llsal_009/?sp=490.

82. For artifacts associated with secret resistance movements, see the Massachusetts Historical Society: https://www.masshist.org/features/boston-abolitionists/resisting-fugitive-slave-law.

83. Reflecting on these conditions in the preface to the new edition of *Scenes of Subjection* to the motives that had propelled her to compose it, Saidita Hartman says powerfully that she could have written the book as one sentence in the "past, present, and future tense" because temporal entanglement best articulates the still open question of abolition. For her, more than the violence of slavery practices, "to be interpellated as a subject before the law" became the performative subjection. *Scenes of Subjection: Terror, Slavery, and Self-Making in Nineteenth-Century America* (Norton, 2022), xxix, xxx.

84. As a senator in what was then called the Democratic Party (which included many Southern senators who were proslavery), Stephen Douglas added this provision to what was then called the Nebraska Act: "The act preparatory to the admission of Missouri into the Union . . . being inconsistent with the principle of non-intervention by Congress with slavery in the states and territories, as recognized by the legislation of eighteen hundred and fifty, commonly called the compromise measures, is hereby declared inoperative and void; it being the true intent and meaning of this act not to legislate slavery into any territory or state, not to exclude it therefrom, but to leave the people thereof perfectly free to form and regulate their domestic institutions in their own way, subject only to the Constitution of the United States." This provision caused widespread violence as protests led to bloodshed in both Kansas and Missouri. As Abraham Lincoln ran against Douglas for the Senate seat, they had a series of debates that have become renowned. See Alan Guelzo, *Lincoln and Douglas: The Debates That Defined America* (Simon and Schuster, 2009).

85. In the Kansas–Nebraska Act, section 10: "That the provisions of an act entitled 'An act respecting fugitives from justice, and persons escaping from the service of their masters,' . . . and the provisions of the act entitled 'An act to amend, and supplementary to, the aforesaid act,' . . . be, and the same are hereby, declared to extend to and be in full force within the limits of said Territory of Nebraska." See https://www.loc.gov/resource/llsalvol.llsal_010/?sp=299.

86. For the original wording of the Emancipation Proclamation, see this link from the Library of Congress: https://www.loc.gov/resource/llsalvol.llsal_010/?sp=299.

87. John Emerson, the enslaver who took Dred Scott to Wisconsin, was a US Army surgeon stationed on what was then considered the frontier, in an area later designated as Minnesota. The overlap of frontier battles and battles over states that determined identities as free and enslaved needs further attention. See, for example, Alaina Roberts, *I've Been Here All the While: Black Freedom on Native Land* (University of Pennsylvania Press, 2021).

88. For commentary and context, see Paul Finkelman, ed., *Dred Scott v. Sandford: A Brief History in Documents* (Bedford, 2016). The original court ruling, with two dissenting opinions, can be read at https://www.gutenberg.org/cache/epub/31425/pg31425-images.html.

89. For the original wording of the Dred Scott decision, see this link from the Library of Congress: https://www.loc.gov/item/usrep060393a/.

Chapter 2. Poetry and War: Emily Dickinson, Walt Whitman, and Abraham Lincoln

1. William Cullen Bryant, "Thanatopsis" (1818). See https://www.poetryfoundation.org/poems/50465/thanatopsis.

2. Philip Freneau, "The Indian Burying Ground." See https://www.poetryfoundation.org/poems/46094/the-indian-burying-ground.

3. All poem numbers are from Emily Dickinson, *Poems of Emily Dickinson*, ed. R. W. Franklin (Harvard University Press, 1998).

4. Walt Whitman, *Leaves of Grass* (Boston, 1860), 24.

5. Dickinson continues, "If I make the mistake—that you dared to tell me—would give me sincerer honor—toward you— / I enclose my name—asking you, if you please—Sir—to tell me what is true? / That you will not betray me—it is needless to ask—since Honor is it's [sic] own pawn—." Compare the reading of this letter/poem in Virginia Jackson, *Dickinson's Misery* (Princeton University Press, 2013).

6. Herman Melville, *Battle-Pieces and Aspects of the War* (Harper and Brother, 1866), 63.

7. Whitman, *Leaves of Grass*, 382.

8. See for instance, Betsy Erkkila, "Democracy and (Homo) Sexual Desire," in *Whitman the Political Poet* (Oxford University Press, 1989).

9. Doris K. Goodwin, *Team of Rivals: The Political Genius of Abraham Lincoln* (Simon & Schuster, 2005).

10. Lincoln's Second Inaugural Address is carved in stone across from the Gettysburg Address at the Lincoln Memorial. See https://www.nps.gov/linc/learn/historyculture/lincoln-second-inaugural.htm.

11. See the cartoon, attributed to Louis Maurer, at the following link: http://www.loc.gov/pictures/item/2003674571/. More information may be obtained in Bernard F. Reilly, ed., *American Political Prints, 1766–1876* (G. K. Hall, 1991), entry 1860-30.

12. Reprinted in Abraham Lincoln, *Speeches and Writings, 1859–1865: Speeches, Letters, and Miscellaneous Writings, Presidential Messages and Proclamations*, Don E. Fehrenbacher and Roy P. Basler, eds. (Literary Classics of the United States, 1989), 360.

13. Frederick Douglass, *Frederick Douglass: Selected Speeches and Writings*, ed. Philip S. Foner and Yuval Taylor (Lawrence Hill Books, 1999), 620.

14. Lincoln, *Speeches*, 361. See John Burt, *Lincoln's Tragic Pragmatism: Lincoln, Douglas, and Moral Conflict* (Belknap Press of Harvard University Press, 2013).

15. Lincoln, *Speeches*, 338.

16. Lincoln, *Speeches*, 35.

17. Lincoln, *Speeches*, 398, 636.

18. Lincoln, *Speeches*, 636, 637, 398.

19. Daniel Aaron, *The Unwritten War: American Writers and the Civil War* (University of Alabama Press, 2003).

20. Founded in 1857, *Harper's Weekly* became extremely popular and, through the political cartoons of Thomas Nast, possibly influenced both legislation and political careers. During the war, the journal used images from the battle at Gettysburg to sway public sentiment; in 1863, they reproduced an etching of the notorious photograph of "Gordon," a photograph that mobilized further support for abolitionists. See David Silkenat, "'A Typical Negro': Gordon, Peter, Vincent Colyer, and the Story behind Slavery's Most Famous Photograph," *American Nineteenth Century History* vol. 15, no. 2, 169–186. See also the account provided by Monica Huerta of another photograph reprinted in *Harper's Weekly* as "Learning Is Wealth. Wilson, Charley, Rebecca & Rosa. Slaves from New Orleans." Huerta points out that the resentful glare of Rosa in this sequence of imagining an equivalence between reading and "wealth" is also a commentary on photography's limits. See Monica Huerta, *The Unintended: Photography, Property, and the Aesthetics of Racial Capitalism* (New York University Press, 2023), xiii–xvii.

21. Political cartoons after the assassination showed Lincoln in relation to Washington, who was understood as the "father of his country." Not (quite) a son, Lincoln repeatedly refers to fathers. His own father was a problematic figure; Lincoln refused to travel to see him when he lay dying.

22. The recent movie *Civil War* has an oblique reference to this statue, as it shows the Lincoln Memorial blasted to pieces.

23. For the debates surrounding the commission for Vinnie Ream, see Gregory Tomso, "Lincoln's 'Unfathomable Sorrow': Vinnie Ream, Sculptural Realism, and the Cultural Work of Sympathy in Nineteenth-Century America," *European Journal of American Studies* vol. 6, no. 2 (2011). Some of the debates are reprinted in Glenn V. Sherwood, *A Labor of Love: The Life and Art of Vinnie Ream* (Sunshine Press Publications, 1997). The statue now stands in the US Capitol. Copies of the statue by Augustus Saint-Gaudens appear in several public places.

24. Quoted in John H. Dryfhout, *The Work of Augustus Saint-Gaudens* (University Press of New England, 2008), 158.

25. The gangly male figure of Brother Jonathan was developed as a caricature in relation to the rotund personification of the British John Bull. Both have visual representation in political cartoons produced during the American Revolution. The cozier, although still ungainly, figure of Uncle Sam has been traced to the War of 1812. For a humorous rendering, see James Kirke Paulding, writing as "Hector Bull-Us," *The Diverting History of John Bull and Brother Jonathan* (Philadelphia, 1827). This account can be read at https://archive.org/details/divertinghistor00paulgoog.

26. The melodramatic description of the three children distributed in the newspapers contained this plea: "It is earnestly desired that all papers in the country will draw attention to the discovery of this picture and its attendant circumstances, so that, if possible, the family of the dead hero may come into possession of it." *Philadelphia Enquirer*, October 19, 1863. The search for the children led not only to the distribution of their picture in newspapers, but also to poetry, sheet music, and fund raising for an orphanage where they were temporarily housed with their mother. See https://uniondb.com/products/the-children-of-the-battlefield-sheet-music-by-james-g-clark.

27. Alexander Gardner, *Gardner's Photographic Sketch Book of the Civil War* (repr. Dover, 1959).

28. Compare Ellen Gruber Garvey, *Writing with Scissors: American Scrapbooks from the Civil War to the Harlem Renaissance* (Oxford University Press, 2013).

29. Jason Frank, *Constituent Moments: Enacting the People in Postrevolutionary America* (Duke University Press, 2010).

30. Lincoln, *Speeches*, 29, 31, 32.

31. Whitman, *Sequel to Drum-Taps* (1865), 3.

32. Nathaniel Hawthorne, "Chiefly about War Matters," *Atlantic Monthly* vol. 10, no. 57 (1862), 43–62. The website for *The Atlantic* comments on the disputed items in Hawthorne's essay in italics. Compare http://www.theatlantic.com/magazine/archive/2012/02/chiefly-about-war-matters-by-a-peaceable- man/308816/. Letter to James T. Fields dated 23 May 23, 1862, Fields Collection, Huntington Library (FI 2287).

33. Frederick Douglass, *Frederick Douglass: Selected Speeches and Writings*, ed. Philip S. Foner and Yuval Taylor (Lawrence Hill Books, 1999), 620.

34. Archer Alexander had become well known because of a biography written by William Greenleaf Eliot. One of the founders of Washington University, he might be better remembered as the grandfather of T. S. Eliot. See *The Story of Archer Alexander: From Slavery to Freedom* (1863). Also at https://docsouth.unc.edu/neh/eliot/eliot.html.

35. See, again, the key analysis by Kirk Savage in *Standing Soldiers, Kneeling Slaves*. The competition for the statue included a model from the sculptor Harriet Hosmer, but her entry was deemed too expensive. Now it appears as a lost opportunity. See https://encyclopediavirginia.org/the-missed-opportunity-of-the-emancipation-monument/.

36. *Frederick Douglass*, 622.

37. Elizabeth Keckley, *Behind the Scenes: Or, Thirty Years a Slave and Four Years in the White House*, 1868 (repr. University of Illinois Press, 1988), 140, 130.

38. Walt Whitman, *Specimen Days* (David McKay, 1882), 79.

Chapter 3. Democratic Mourning: Louisa May Alcott, Elizabeth Stuart Phelps, and Harriet Beecher Stowe

1. August J. Evans, *Macaria, or the Altars of Sacrifice* was published in 1864 and was popular in the North as well as the South. Her earlier novel about Texas, *Inez*, was published when she was still a teenager. See Susan K. Harris, *Nineteenth-Century American Women's Novels: Interpretive Strategies* (Cambridge University Press, 1990).

2. Martha Schoolman, *Abolitionist Geographies* (University of Minnesota Press, 2014).

3. This landscape of dangerous water might be viewed in relation to crossing lakes in the landscapes of James Fenimore Cooper's Indians—or the territorial disputes along the Mississippi River that appear in the memoirs of Black Hawk.

4. Louisa May Alcott, "The Brothers," *Atlantic Monthly* (November 1863), 584–595.

5. Louisa May Alcott, "The Brothers," 584–595.

6. Frank Moore, *Women of the War; Their Heroism and Self-Sacrifice* (Scranton & Co., 1866).

7. Frank Moore, 529.

8. S. Emma E. Edmonds, *Unsexed; or, The Female Soldier. The Thrilling Adventures, Experiences, and Escapes of a Woman, as Nurse, Spy, and Scout, in Hospitals, Camps, and Battle-fields* (Philadelphia Publishing Company, 1864). https://archive.org/details/unsexedorfemales00edmo/page/n5/mode/2up?view=theater.

9. Edmonds, 299.

10. See DeeAnne Blanton and Lauren Cook, *They Fought Like Demons: Women Soldiers and the Civil War* (Baton Rouge: Louisiana State University Press, 2002). Their treatment looks at women from both Union and Confederate armies. They argue persuasively that, like male soldiers, women who passed as male soldiers were typically from "agrarian, working class or immigrant backgrounds"; in such circumstances, in addition to concealing their cross-dressing, they were even less likely to be literate and have left fewer traces of their war time experiences.

11. Angelina Grimke, *Appeal to the Christian Women of the South* (1836), 5.

12. *Philadelphia Enquirer*, October 19, 1863. A difficult distinction arises concerning the availability of photographs of children. Many losses may be traced through the ongoing reconstruction of the searches documented in the "Freedom on the Move" project, but little visual evidence remains. See https://freedomonthemove.org/.

13. Published in the United States without securing international copyright protection, the novel in various editions sold more than 100,000 copies on both sides of the Atlantic in the decades after its publication, making it one of the top novels of the nineteenth century. See Stephanie Palmer, *Transatlantic Footholds: Turn-of-the-Century American Women Writers and British Reviews* (Routledge, 2019). See also Desiree Henderson, *Grief and Genre in American Literature, 1790–1870* (Ashgate, 2001), 139–145.

14. The title page for the initial publication of *The Story of Avis* (James Osgood, 1877) calls attention to Phelps as "Author of 'The Gates Ajar,'" but it tells a story very far removed from it. In *The Story of Avis*, the woman's desire to be a writer is thwarted by her conventional marriage and no religious consolation appears.

15. The novel's project of consolation available through religion drew on a learned family background. Her mother's father, Moses Stuart, had been president of the Andover Theological Seminary. Her own father, Austin Phelps, was a minister who became president of the Andover Theological Seminary the same year that *The Gates Ajar* was published. With no current biography of Phelps, details on her life can be found in her autobiographical writing as well as in the multiauthored nineteenth-century illustrated tome *Our Famous Women*. The typically ornate subtitle is *An*

Authorized Record of the Lives and Deeds of Distinguished American Women of Our Times (A. D. Worthington, 1884).

16. For helpful readings of the novel, see Justine Murison, *The Politics of Anxiety in 19th-Century American Literature* (Cambridge University Press, 2011), and Elizabeth Duquette, *Loyal Subjects: Bonds of Nation, Race, and Allegiance in Nineteenth-Century America* (Rutgers University Press, 2010), 94. See also Elizabeth Young, *Disarming the Nation: Women's Writing and the American Civil War* (University of Chicago Press, 1999). Duquette pairs *The Gates Ajar* with John de Forest's *Miss Ravenel's Conversion from Secession to Loyalty* (1867). She reads both as examples of the "reunion romance," where political struggles are solved through a form of remarriage (85). See also Lisa Long, "'The Corporeity of Heaven': Rehabilitating the Civil War Body in *The Gates Ajar*," *American Literature* vol. 69, no. 4 (December 1997), 781–811, and Cindy Weinstein, "Heaven's Tense: Narration in *The Gates Ajar*," *Novel* vol. 45, no. 1 (2012), 56–70.

17. In "Reynolds' Political Map of the United States," a map produced in 1856 to show the importance of Kansas, the territory is presented as a blank white space in the midst of a series of states and territories marked by color as free or slave. Compare Library of Congress: http://memory.loc.gov/cgi-bin/query/h?ammem/gmd:@field%28NUMBER+@band%28g3701e+ct000604%29%29.

18. In particular, the speech that Lincoln gave in Peoria, Illinois, on October 16, 1854, has been understood as a turning point in his announced views on slavery and his work toward the presidency. Roy P. Basler, ed., *The Collected Works of Abraham Lincoln*, vol. II (Rutgers University Press, 1953), 275.

19. See Joanne Freeman, *The Field of Blood: Violence in Congress and the Road to Civil War* (Farrar, Straus and Giroux, 2018). Senator Charles Sumner, well known as an abolitionist politician, was beaten over the head with a cane by Preston Brooks, a Southern senator, on the floor of the Senate in 1856 and nearly killed. In retaliation, John Brown, who had arrived to carry out abolitionist agitation in Kansas in 1855, conducted several violent raids, dragging men suspected of slavery sentiments from their homes and killing them with swords. Compare Nicole Etcheson, *Bleeding Kansas: Contested Liberty in the Civil War Era* (University of Kansas Press, 2004). Compare also "Report of the Special Committee Appointed to Investigate the Troubles in Kansas" (1856). This report notes that territories inhabited by Indians have previously been barriers to settlers and anticipates that the troubles in Kansas have "endangered" the continued existence of the United States (2). This document is available through the American Memory project: http://quod.lib.umich.edu/cgi/t/text/text-idx?c=moa;idno=AFK4445.0001.001.

20. The language of compromise operates in conjunction with the language of "forever"—a language reiterated in the Emancipation Proclamation's words, "forever free." It also might suggest the way that the Declaration of Independence, as read by Derrida, establishes a moment of "becoming" built into the declarations of nation and state alike. Compare Jacques Derrida, "Declarations of Independence," in *Negotiations: Interventions and Interviews, 1971–2001* (Stanford University Press, 2002), 46–54. See Bonnie Honig, "Declarations of Independence: Arendt and Derrida on the Problem of Founding Republic," *American Political Science Review* vol. 85, no. 1 (March 1991), 97–113, and Jacques de Ville, "Sovereignty without Sovereignty: Derrida's Declarations of Independence," *Law and Critique* vol. 19, no. 2 (2008), 87–114.

That sense of both land and body as a process of becoming in relation to belonging emerges in several legal decisions of the antebellum period.

21. For an account of how this name was applied to the Sharps rifle supplied by the resistance movements fed by Henry Ward Beecher, brother of Harriet Beecher Stowe, and his congregation, see the article in the *New York Tribune* of February 8, 1856. Here's a link that talks about the "moral agency" of the rifle: https://www.kshs.org/kansapedia/beecher-bibles/11977.

22. See T. J. Stiles, *Jesse James: Last Rebel of the Civil War* (Vintage, 2003).

23. *Liberty: The Fair Maid of Kansas (1856)*. In the Library of Congress, Alfred Whittal Stern collection: https://www.loc.gov/pictures/item/2008661579/.

24. These are further details about the political cartoon called "The Fair Maid of Kansas in the Hands of the Border Ruffians" (1856). It has no signature, but based on its style it has been attributed as a drawing to John L. Magee, a drawing that was then turned into an extremely detailed lithograph. Many tiny figures appear in the background, but the foreground contains a fairly savage political commentary. The Library of Congress website identifies some of the controversial accounts, but I also include my own interpretation here. In the foreground of the image are the names of political figures identified from left to right as "MARCY—BUCHANAN—PIERCE—CASS—DOUGLAS." The Democratic incumbent in this presidential race of 1856 was Franklin Pierce, but the print also works to blame Stephen Douglas for consequences of the Kansas-Nebraska act—his is the figure holding aloft a bleeding scalp. The man who has been scalped is armed with a scythe and Douglas has apparently used a tomahawk to kill him. In the background, houses are burning and corpses lie along the far fields. See also the detailed account in Bernard F. Reilly, *American Political Prints, 1766–1876* (G. K. Hall, 1991).

25. See the "as told to" story by one of the raiders, John McCorkle and O. S Barton, *Three Years with Quantrell: A True Story* (Armstrong Herald Print, 1914). See also Duane Schultz, *Quantrill's War: The Life and Times of William Clarke Quantrill,1837–1865* (St. Martin's Press, 1996).

26. The date of the raid makes it possible to conjecture other dates in the novel and to understand that her daughter Grace was born close enough to the events of this raid as to leave some doubt about her paternity. *The Gates Ajar* (Fields, Osgood & Co., 1869), 60. Further references to this edition will be in parentheses.

27. See also Donald R. Hale, *We Rode with Quantrill: Quantrill and the Guerrilla War as Told by the Men and Women Who Were with Him, with a True Sketch of Quantrill's Life* (D. R. Hale, 1992), and Michael Fellman, *Inside War: The Guerilla Conflict in Missouri* (Oxford University Press, 1989). A contemporary book, John Edwards, *Noted Guerillas* (1867), appeared the year before *The Gates Ajar*. The full title is *Noted Guerrillas, or The Warfare of the Border. Being a History of the Lives and Adventures of Quantrell, Bill Anderson, George Todd, Dave Poole, Fletcher Taylor, Peyton Long, Oil Shepherd, Arch Clements, John Maupin, Tuck and Woot Hill, Wm. Gregg, Thomas Maupin, the James brothers, the Younger brothers, Arthur McCoy, and Numerous Other Well Known Guerillas of the West* (Thompson and Wakefield, 1877). See also Jay Monaghan, *Civil War on the Western Border, 1854–1865* (Little, Brown, 1955), and Thomas Goodrich, *Bloody Dawn: The Story of the Lawrence Massacre* (Kent State University Press, 1992).

28. Susan B. Warner, *The Wide, Wide World* (J. B. Lippincott & Co., 1862), 12–13. Ashley Barnes compares *Uncle Tom's Cabin* with *The Gates Ajar* in "The Word Made Exhibition: Protestant Reading Meets Catholic Worship in *Uncle Tom's Cabin* and *The Gates Ajar*," *Legacy* vol. 29, no. 2 (2012), 179–200.

29. Joseph Roach, *Cities of the Dead: Circum-Atlantic Performance* (Columbia University Press, 1996), 6.

30. Roach, 6.

31. Such doubling resembles that described by John Irwin's attention to William Faulkner's novels in his influential work *Doubling and Incest/Repetition and Revenge: A Speculative Reading of Faulkner* (Johns Hopkins University Press, 1996). See also Tavia N'yongo, *The Amalgamation Waltz: Race, Performance, and the Ruses of Memory* (University of Minnesota Press, 2009).

32. Rebecca Schneider, *Performing Remains: Art and War in Times of Theatrical Reenactment* (Routledge, 2011), 18.

33. On the first page of the novel, a week has passed since she found about her brother's death, but she has not yet opened the "yellow" packets, packets that never reappear in *The Gates Ajar*—these might be the stationery used by the government to send packets with his "effects." As she searches her desk for paper, the narrator finds a "poor little book" where she has previously kept "memoranda of the weather, and my lovers" (1).

34. *Essays of Elia*, first published in 1823, was quite popular in the United States. See https://www.gutenberg.org/cache/epub/10343/pg10343-images.html.

35. It also proposes what has been described as the "nonreproductive futurity" arising from unions not presumed to result in the birth of children. Compare Lee Edelman in *No Future: Queer Theory and the Death Drive* (Duke University Press, 2004), and Sarah Ensor, "Spinster Ecology: Rachel Carson, Sarah Orne Jewett, and Nonreproductive Futurity," *American Literature* vol. 84, no. 2 (2012), 409–435.

36. The words of Anne Hutchinson only survive as quoted by the judges at her trial. For that reason they bear something beyond the difficulty of oral history. The judges, according to John Winthrop's account, have their own agenda, but they also record a spirited defense including Hutchinson's insistence on the idea of "union with the person of the Holy Ghost . . . so as to amount to a personal union." John Winthrop, journal entry, October 25, 1636. Compare David Hall, ed., *The Antinomian Controversy, 1636–1638: A Documentary History* (Duke University Press, 1990). See also Amy Schrager Lang, *Prophetic Woman: Anne Hutchinson and the Problem of Dissent in the Literature of New England* (University of California Press, 1987). Thanks to Timothy Sweet for help with a discussion of this matter.

37. The attraction to beliefs about the "little bone" fits with the nineteenth-century attraction to comparative religions. The concept is that the tip of the coccyx is imperishable. Possibly Phelps found out about it from a translation of the Koran that was much discussed in the mid-nineteenth century: *The Koran: Commonly Called the Alcoran of Mohammed*, translated by George Sale (J. W. Moore, 1856). The commentary by Sale explains the coccyx as a "seed" for reincarnation: "as it was the first formed in the human body, it will also remain uncorrupted until the last day, as a seed from whence the whole is to be renewed" (54).

38. These are not literal footnotes, but rather embedded citations. For example, Aunt Winifred cites "Dr. Chalmers" on "spiritual materialism." He has given a sermon

on "New Heavens and Earth" and Winifred interrupts herself to say "which, by the way, you should read" (77). Compare Justine Murison, *The Politics of Anxiety*, on spiritualism and its relation to the Scottish "divine" Thomas Chalmers (140). Chalmers proposed that a body could be both spiritual and material.

39. As part of her lesson, Winifred quotes from Isaac Taylor, "Physical Theory of Another Life," in order to connect "argument from analogy" to "abstract reasoning" (89). Isaac Taylor wrote about "enthusiasm," noting "Some form of beauty, engendered by the imagination, or some semblance of dignity or grace, invests almost every object that excites desire." Works by Isaac Taylor can be read here: https://www.gutenberg.org/cache/epub/55988/pg55988-images.html.

40. Harriet Beecher Stowe, *Uncle Tom's Cabin*, ed. Elizabeth Ammons (Norton, 2012), 381.

Chapter 4. The Republic of Men at Sea: Nathaniel Hawthorne, Herman Melville, and Mark Twain

1. This magazine, familiarly known as the *Democratic Review*, was published from 1837–1859 and was an early venue for Nathaniel Hawthorne, among other writers. It promoted Jacksonian Democracy; its editor, John O'Sullivan, has been credited with the phrase "manifest destiny." Given her deep investment in the project of imperialist expansion, Cora Montgomery, discussed here, might also be responsible for the term.

2. "The King of Rivers," *United States Magazine and Democratic Review* vol. 25 (December 1849), 506–515. Cora Montgomery was the pseudonym of Jane Maria Eliza McManus Storm (1807–1878), also known as Jane Cazneau, a remarkably independent journalist who argued that the United States should annex Cuba when she republished this piece in pamphlet form in *The King of Rivers and the Queen of Islands* (1850). See Linda Hudson, *Mistress of Manifest Destiny: A Biography of Jane McManus Storm Cazneau, 1807–1878* (Texas State Historical Association, 2001).

3. William Wells Brown, *Clotel* (Partridge and Oakey, 1853), 166, 160.

4. Percival Everett rewrites the narrative, notably invoking the idea of linguistic passing as a ploy engaged to keep white listeners ignorant of the standard English use that they might associate with insolence. See *James: A Novel* (Doubleday, 2024).

5. See, for example, Anna Arabindan-Kesson, *Black Bodies, White Gold: Art, Cotton, and Commerce in the Atlantic World* (Duke University Press, 2021). A more traditional but nonetheless inspiring approach appears in Marcus Rediker, *The Slave Ship: A Human History* (Penguin, 2008). See also Cheryl Finley's wonderful volume *Committed to Memory: The Art of the Slave Ship Icon* (Princeton University Press, 2018).

6. Douglass, *Narrative*, 46.

7. "What to the Slave Is the Fourth of July?" Reprinted in *Narrative*, 120.

8. From *Life and Times of Frederick Douglass* (1892). Reprinted in *Narrative*, 104.

9. See the recent collection of essays *Sailing to Freedom: Maritime Dimensions of the Underground Railroad*, ed. Timothy Walker (University of Massachusetts, 2021).

10. See *Loophole of Retreat*. The work represented the United States at the 2020 Venice Biennale and was awarded the Golden Lion award. It has inspired other exhibitions. See, for instance, https://www.guggenheim.org/exhibition/hugo-boss-prize-2018.

11. *Recollections of an African Cruiser*, by Horatio Bridge, edited by Nathaniel Hawthorne (Wiley and Putnam, 1845).

12. The phrase is from Dorothy Ziesler-Vralstad, who cites Johnson: between 1800 and 1860 at least "875,000 American slaves were forcibly removed from the Upper South to the Lower South" by means of the Mississippi River. See *Rivers, Memory, and Nation-Building: A History of the Volga and Mississippi Rivers* (Berghahn Books, 2014), 5. See also Walter Johnson, *River of Dark Dreams: Slavery and Empire in the Cotton Kingdom* (Harvard University Press, 2017).

13. See Paul Gilroy, *The Black Atlantic: Modernity and Double Consciousness* (Harvard University Press, 1994), and Marcus Rediker, *Between the Devil and the Deep Blue Sea: Merchant Seamen, Pirates, and the Anglo-American Maritime World, 1700–1750* (Cambridge University Press, 1989). See also his *Villains of All Nations: Atlantic Pirates in the Golden Age* (Beacon, 2005).

14. An investigation of the settling of Liberia appears in David Kazanjian, *The Brink of Freedom: Improvising Life in the Atlantic World* (Duke University Press, 2016).

15. *Recollections of an African Cruiser*, 4–5.

16. This college class of 1825 also had Henry Wadsworth Longfellow, later to write the *Song of Hiawatha*, as a student.

17. This scene anticipates the opening of *The House of the Seven Gables*: "A little black fellow, whose sobriquet is Othello, manages the castanets."

18. The book's account of the voyage includes stories about emigrants to Liberia and how they are not suited, after slavery, to being independent.

19. See Susan Stewart, *On Longing: Narratives of the Miniature, the Gigantic, the Souvenir, the Collection* (Duke University Press, 1992). This book on the relation of social encounters at sea to the objects invoked can also be put into relation with works such as Arjun Appadurai, *The Social Life of Things: Commodities in Cultural Perspective* (Cambridge University Press, 1988), and Bruno Latour, *Reassembling the Social: An Inquiry into Modes of Existence* (Harvard University Press, 2013).

20. "*Huckleberry Finn* Chapter 1," ESL Lounge Student: https://www.esl-lounge.com/student/proficiency/cpe-069-huckleberry-finn-reading-multiple-choice.php.

21. Mark Twain, *The Adventures of Tom Sawyer* (University of California Press, 2010), 85.

22. Kerry Driscoll, *Mark Twain among the Indians and Other Indigenous Peoples* (University of California Press, 2018). Kerry Driscoll points out, for example, that Twain's brother, Orion Clemens, served as acting governor and ex officio superintendent of Indian affairs when the regional governor was absent (55). He wrote a "Sketch of the Black Hawk War and History of the Half Breed Tract," which he included in the Keokuk City Directory in 1856. Orion Clemens ran a print shop in Iowa, the Ben Franklin Book and Job Office, and Sam Clemens was his assistant (31). Orion Clemens praised Black Hawk as an "able and patriotic chief" (quoted, 33).

23. Published in 1834, the book known as *The Life of Makataimeshekiakiak, or Black Hawk* would certainly have been available to Twain. See Adam John Waterman, *The Corpse in the Kitchen: Enclosure, Extraction, and the Afterlives of the Black Hawk War* (Fordham University Press, 2021). To steal corpses for profit, whether selling them to doctors for dissection or interring skeletons in museums, brings us to the

present business of repatriation of bodily remains. Harvard has become notorious because of the photography associated with Louis Agassiz (the anthropologist who wanted visual demonstrations of racial inequity), but the practice of collecting corpses in their museum has more recently come to the fore. Only in Illinois, to bring us back to the other side of the Mississippi River, has the law finally intervened to declare that the communities in which these bones once resided when alive have the right to determine their destiny. See the "Human Remains Protection Act" at this site: https://www.ilga.gov/legislation/ilcs/ilcs3.asp?ActID=376&ChapterID=5&Print=True#:~:text=All%20non-Native%20American%20human,other%20arrangements%20have%20been%20established.

24. *Life on the Mississippi* (Harper and Bros., 1902). First published in *The Atlantic* in 1874; H. O. Houghton & Co. copyright 1883 by Samuel Clemens. There's an illustrated version, published in 1883 by James R. Osgood and Co., available as a free ebook: http://www.gutenberg.org/ebooks/245.

25. In general, Twain takes pleasure in mocking how civilization presents itself. Along the Mississippi, as he characterizes it, appear the artifices of homes that consider themselves settled. He notes that the music on the piano includes randomly assorted pieces such as "Battle of Prague; Bird Waltz; Arkansas Traveler; Tosin the Bow; Marseillaise Hymn . . . The Last Link is Broken; . . ." The art on the wall seems a deliberately ludicrous assortment: "Lithograph, Napoleon Crossing the Alps. Lithograph, The Grave at St. Helena. Steel-plates, Trumbull's Battle of Bunker Hill . . . Copper-plates, Moses Smiting the Rock, and Return of the Prodigal Son" (278–280). Resembling nineteenth-century museum practices, the house contains an absurd collection of artifacts: the "convention of dessicated bugs and butterflies pinned to a card" next to remainders of travel, quartz from California, bead moccasins from the "uncle who crossed the Plains" (280). Twain contrasts the stuffiness and datedness of the "best" home with the thrill of entering into the "home" of the steamboat, a "new and marvelous world" (282).

26. "Mark Twain's Life on the Mississippi," *Atlantic Monthly*, September 1883, 406.

27. Francis Parkman, *The Oregon Trail: Sketches of Prairie and Rocky-Mountain Life* (George P. Putnam, 1847).

28. See Howard Horwitz, "'Ours by the Law of Nature': Romance and Independents on Mark Twain's River," *Boundary 2* vol. 17, no. 1 (1990), 243–271. He says, "the river plays havoc with boundary lines and jurisdictions" (244).

29. Twain's childhood memories might appear in the small passage in his co-authored *Gilded Age*, when he depicts children noticing "All in an instant, a fierce eye of fire shot out from behind the cape and sent a long brilliant pathway quivering athwart the dusty water. The coughing grew louder and louder, the glaring eye grew larger and still larger, glared wilder and still wilder. A huge shape developed itself out of the gloom, and from its tall duplicate horns dense volumes of smoke, starred and spangled with sparks, poured out and went tumbling away into the farther darkness." *The Gilded Age: A Tale of Today*, by Mark Twain and Charles Dudley Warner (American Publishing Company, 1873), 37.

30. See also the steamboat race in William Wells Brown's *Clotel* (London: Partridge and Oakey, 1853). See https://docsouth.unc.edu/southlit/brown/summary.html.

31. See Thomas Buchanan, *Black Life on the Mississippi: Slaves, Free Blacks, and the Western Steamboat World* (University of North Carolina Press, 2004).

32. See Twain's account in "The Private History of a Campaign That Failed," included in *The American Claimant* (Harper and Brothers, 1892), 235–282.

33. See, for example, Basil Hall, *The Lieutenant and Commander* (Bell and Daldy, 1862); Frances Trollope, *Domestic Manners of the Americans* (Whittaker, Treacher & Co., 1832); and Captain Frederick Marryat, *Second Series of a Diary in America* (T. K. & P. G. Collins, 1840), 84. See also Timothy Flint, *The History and Geography of the Mississippi Valley* (Flint and Lincoln, 1832).

34. The massacre at Fort Pillow appears, for example, in Brian Steel Wills, *The River Was Dyed with Blood: Nathan Bedford Forrest and Fort Pillow* (University of Oklahoma Press, 2014). For a detailed account of Twain's relation to Civil War memories, see Neil Schmitz, "Mark Twain's Civil War: Humor's Reconstructive Writing," in Forrest Robinson, ed., *Cambridge Companion to Mark Twain* (Cambridge University Press, 1995), 74–92. Although Mr. Bixby has been head pilot of the Union fleet, his possibly heroic relation to warfare does not appear here (219). The interspersing of comic, tragic, and picturesque accounts of the river, including a poetic sunrise, shows the writer preparing for similar accounts, and possibly similar evasions, in the novel *Huckleberry Finn*. One of the key morbid scenes from that novel has a deflected presence as the narrator of *Life on the Mississippi* begins, "We were approaching Napoleon, Ark." (232). The sense of doom is enhanced and deflected by a tale of watching the dead in Germany. In that story, the corpse watcher who waits for a bell to ring to show that a corpse has moved (and might still be alive) has inspired Twain to arrive at a place of desolation. The sleight of hand shuffling in this account, however, makes him seem distracted, like a conjurer with a parlor trick that he has played before. The interspersed story is literally undercut when the boat turns out to be passing over the town where the events took place, a town now drowned under the river's waters.

35. Sometimes spelled Murrell, the pirate John Murel appears in several accounts. The stories contain half-truths as well as a grim history of a group called the Mystic Confederacy that sought to incite revolt for those held as slaves in order to steal them. For details, see the loquacious contemporary book credited to H. R. Howard: *The History of Virgil A. Stewart and His Adventure in Capturing the "Great Western Land Pirate" and His Gang, in Connexion with the Evidence; also of the Trials, Confession, and Execution of a Number of Murrell's Associates in the State of Mississippi in the Summer of 1835, and the Execution of Five Professional Gamblers by the Citizens of Vicksburg on the 6th July 1835* (Harper & Brothers, 1835).

36. Smith, 177. For the picturesque in these watery landscapes, see also Arne Smith, *Arcadian Waters and Wanton Seas: The Iconology of Waterscapes in Nineteenth-Century Transatlantic Culture* (Peter Lang, 2009). He discusses paintings such as Caleb Bingham, *Fur Traders Descending the Missouri*, and Winslow Homer, *The Gulf Stream*.

37. Smith, 181. It matters to remember the different myths and legends of the railroad, such as the story of John Henry as well as the humor of the "southwest" along the river, including "the big bear of Arkansas."

38. Quoted by Smith, 182.

39. The chapter titled "The Professor's Yarn" contains stories reminiscent of Melville's *Confidence-Man* and depicts a boat headed for California with gamblers aboard.

40. Benjamin Franklin crosses the Atlantic repeatedly; he does it at once to promote his own career and to escape financial difficulty. For the duel between Alexander Hamilton and Aaron Burr to take place, the participants had to leave New York and cross the water to New Jersey; the dying body then was rowed back to the island of Manhattan. But each had already crossed water to arrive at that duel—Hamilton had perhaps come the furthest from his origins in the Caribbean.

41. Black Hawk's *Autobiography* includes several scenes of crossing the Mississippi. See also Daniel Richter, *Facing East from Indian Country: A Native History of Early America* (Harvard University Press, 2001).

42. Herman Melville, *The Confidence-Man* (Dix, Edwards, and Co., 1857).

43. Anacharsis Cloots was the pseudonym of a French citizen who appeared before the National Constituent Assembly in Paris in 1790 declaring his support for the "Declaration of the Rights of the Man and of the Citizen of 1789" flanked by a gathering of foreigners. He met his fate at the guillotine in 1794.

44. The reference appears in Joshua Greenberg's *Bank Notes and Shinplasters: The Rage for Paper Money in the Early Republic* (University of Pennsylvania Press, 2020). Tracking the instabilities of identification and currency manipulation onto the situation of the fugitive and the displacements of genocide, his book mostly investigates the documents attached to land transactions, but it also briefly considers slavery. Especially significant is how to buy one's freedom in a time of fluctuating currency without the reliable assumption that a bank will accept the proffered piece of paper (66). The very display of familiarity with uncertainty could paradoxically make a person seem reliable: "bank notes served as conspicuous tools to display one's identity as free" (67). According to Greenberg, with each bank printing its own notes, "The fear of fake money permeated every transaction" (49). Also, parenthetically, "shaving" appears as a link between shaving off the value of money and an occupation as a barber, such as that pursued by William Wells Brown when he first escaped into Michigan. The delicate business of wielding a razor around a man's throat, brought vividly to life as Babo wields the razor in *Benito Cereno*, becomes the delicate business of shaving off value from a bank note as it travels from bank to bank.

45. James Kirke Paulding, *The History of a Little Frenchman and His Bank Notes: Rags! Rags! Rags!* (Edward Earle, 1815).

46. The story "The Indian Hater" appears in James Hall, *Legends of the West* (Harrison Hall, 1832); reprinted in *The Indian Hater and Other Stories by James Hall*, ed. Edward Watts (Kent State University Press, 2009).

47. Somewhat unbelievably, given its lurid bloodletting, *Nick of the Woods* was also a popular dramatic performance in the early nineteenth century and featured actors like Edwin Forrest who had made a career playing Metamora, another white man playing Indian. See also Philip Deloria, *Playing Indian* (Yale University Press, 1998).

48. See, for example, Randolph C. Randall, *James Hall: Spokesman of the New West* (Oklahoma State University Press, 1964).

Chapter 5. Women at Home: Charlotte Perkins Gilman, Harriet Jacobs, Lucy Larcom, and Frances Harper

1. Some controversy exists about the right text to use when reading the classic short story by Charlotte Perkins Gilman. The manuscript version of "The Yellow Wallpaper" has been compared with its first appearance in 1892 in *The New England Magazine* and a reasonably strong case has been made for following the manuscript, still extant, in the author's hand. Arguments for and against this conclusion, as well as both versions of this very short story, are to be found in *"The Yellow Wallpaper": by Charlotte Perkins Gilman: A Dual Text Critical Edition*, ed. Shawn St. Jean (Ohio University Press, 2006), 48, 50. Page numbers to this edition will be given in parentheses throughout the text.

2. Kate Chopin, *The Awakening* (H. S. Stone, 1899), and Charlotte Perkins Gilman, *Herland* (published serially in 1915). More recently these works have been challenged for their implicit racial bias, but they became key literary texts in the late-twentieth-century feminist movement.

3. Charlotte Perkins Gilman, *Women and Economics: A Study of the Economic Relation between Men and Women as a Factor in Social Evolution* (Small, Maynard & Co., 1898). Further references will be given parenthetically as "Women."

4. Karen Sanchez-Eppler declares provocatively that "Dying is what children do most and do best in the literary and cultural imagination of nineteenth-century America." The tears of children hover at the edge of accounts like that of *The Gates Ajar*; they do not become very visible, however, while the tears of women dominate. Karen Sanchez-Eppler, *Dependent States: The Child's Part in Nineteenth-Century American Culture* (University of Chicago Press, 2005), 101.

5. S. Weir Mitchell, physician and author, wrote the story "The Case of George Dedlow" for the *Atlantic Monthly* in 1866. Showing the aftereffects of amputation and war, the story focuses on a soldier who loses his limbs; it was apparently read as a true story. The relation between gender ambiguity and amputation that appears here connects with the PTSD strategies promoted by S. Weir Mitchell and with the complicated ways that the bodies of Civil War soldiers and women seem to trade positions as part of the prone passivity promoted by the "rest cure."

6. Charlotte Perkins Gilman, *The Home: Its Work and Influence* (McClure, Phillips & Co., 1903).

7. *The Man-Made World; or, Our Androcentric Culture* (Charton Co., 1911).

8. Nancy Cott, *The Bonds of Womanhood: "Woman's Sphere" in New England, 1780–1835* (Yale University Press, 1997).

9. See, for example, Teresa Anne Murphy, *Ten Hours' Labor: Religion, Reform, and Gender in Early New England* (Cornell University Press, 1992), and Timothy Duerden, *Lewis Hine: Photographer and American Progressive* (McFarland & Co., 2018).

10. The photography of Lewis Hine showed children working in mills, especially poignant in Jacob Riis's *How the Other Half Lives* (1890). Rebecca Harding Davis shows the conditions for immigrant women working in "Life in the Iron Mills" (1861, in *Atlantic Monthly*). Her novel *Margaret Howth* has a main character who works in a woolen mill. See also Elizabeth Oakes Smith (1806–1893), who wrote about women

and economic circumstances. Her "Woman and Her Needs" was published as a pamphlet by Fowler and Wells in 1851. Harriet Jacobs can also be read as interrogating the conditions of work available to women, whether held in conditions of slavery or recently freed.

11. Larcom (1824–1899) went to work at age 11 in 1835. Her sister started a literary newspaper similar to the *Lowell Offering*, based on Lydia Maria Child's *Juvenile Miscellany*. Larcom worked at a loom in a mill on the Merrimack River, as does the subject of her poem.

12. Lucy Larcom, "Weaving," reprinted in Faith Barrett and Christanne Miller, eds. *"Words for the Hour": A New Anthology of American Civil War Poetry* (University of Massachusetts, 2005). For her work in the *Lowell Offering*, see Larcom's autobiography *A New England Girlhood, Outlined from Memory* (Houghton Mifflin, 1889).

13. "The Lady of Shalott," a poem by Alfred, Lord Tennyson, retells the Arthurian legend.

14. Edward Taylor, "Upon a Spider Catching a Fly," *The Poems of Edward Taylor*, ed. Donald E. Stanford (Yale University Press, 1960).

15. Lydia Maria Child, "Slavery's Pleasant Homes." First published in *The Liberty Bell*, an antislavery publication produced for the 1843 Anti-Slavery Fair in Boston.

16. Critical attention to Harriet Jacobs and the "loophole of retreat" continues to inspire artists and performers. See especially the conference engaged with the work of the artist Simone Leigh at the recent Venice Biennale: https://simoneleighvenice2022.org/loophole-of-retreat/.

17. See Carroll Smith-Rosenberg, *Disorderly Conduct: Visions of Gender in Victorian America* (Oxford University Press, 1986).

18. See Jean Fagan Yellin, *Harriet Jacobs: A Life* (Civitas, 2005).

19. Paula Whitacre, *A Civil Life in an Uncivil Time: Julia Wilbur's Struggle for Purpose* (University of Nebraska, 2017). Living in Virginia and Washington, DC, after the war, Wilbur kept a diary from 1844 until 1873. Her papers at Haverford College have mostly been transcribed. They include tidbits such as going to see President Lincoln and observing that Sojourner Truth has been denied entrance: "When I said it was too bad, she said 'never mind honey. I don't mind it.' It did not occur to me until too late that I should have gone directly in & told the President. I would like to know what he wd. have said. I cannot think it was done by his orders." She observes that Frederick Douglass is received by Lincoln and speaks with Harriet Tubman.

20. From "Diary of Julia Wilbur, 1865," transcribed May 2015. See https://www.alexandriava.gov/uploadedFiles/historic/info/civilwar/JuliaWilburDiary1865.pdf.

21. Lucy Colman, *Reminiscences* (H. L. Green, 1891). She recounts that she "was once advertised to speak in a place. . . . A colored lady was speaking in the State at the same time, and no one of the getters-up of the meeting knew whether the name Colman belonged to the white woman or the colored. I arrived at the station after nightfall. . . . At last a man, a little more bold than some of the others in waiting, propounded the important question: 'Mrs. Colman, we do not know whether you are colored or white. We know there is a colored lady in the lecture field; will you please tell us which you are?' I felt a little mischievous, and so said: 'If you are not able to tell a white person and a colored, one from the other, why should you care? If I am colored, and pass for white, I may gain a little among the people who are prejudiced;' and so

I refused to tell them. Not one of the audience was able, positively, to decide. The morning light gave them the much-desired answer" (51).

22. Frances E. W. Harper, *Iola Leroy, or Shadows Uplifted* (Garrigues Brothers, 1892), 39.

23. The question of passing preoccupies early-twentieth-century writers who consider racial identification. For example, in Nella Larsen's *Passing* (1929), one character fears having a second child because her husband might find her out by the child's appearance. A different example appears in Angelina Weld Grimke's play *Rachel* (1920), in which the titular character refuses to marry because she refuses to have children who might die violently because of the racism that surrounds her.

24. See, for example, Kirsten Silva Gruesz, *Ambassadors of Culture: The Transamerican Origins of Latino Writing* (Princeton University Press, 2001).

25. That would be John William de Forest, who wrote *Miss Ravenel's Conversion from Secession to Loyalty* (1867), in an attempt to capture Civil War romance while intertwining battle scenes. He declared in 1868 that *Uncle Tom's Cabin* came closest to the national greatness that he invoked because of its "picture of American life." Dismissively, he asserts that Stowe then "shrank into her native shell of New England" in her later novels. See "The Great American Novel," *The Nation* vol. 9 (January 1868), http://utc.iath.virginia.edu/articles/n2ar39at.html.

26. A recent collection of "literatures of the Civil War" provides a deliberately mixed genre of speeches, poetry, diaries, and newspaper entries. These documents include Southern perspectives as well as Northern ones and emphasize the uncertainty of the outcome expressed during the early years of the war. See *The Civil War: The First Year, Told by Those Who Lived It*, ed. Brooks D. Simpson et al. (Library of America, 2011); *The Civil War: The Second Year, Told by Those Who Lived It*, ed. Stephen W. Sears (Library of America, 2012); *The Civil War: The Third Year, Told by Those Who Lived It*, ed. Brooks D. Simpson (Library of America, 2013), and *The Civil War: The Final Year, Told by Those Who Lived It*, ed. Aaron Dean-Sheehan (Library of America, 2014). Perhaps unsurprisingly, most of the writers included in these volumes are male.

27. I wrote about Menken in *Facing America*, 111–115. Subsequently I found this letter in an "extra illustrated" book at the Huntington Library. The "extra" of the illustrations was the inclusion of photographs by Napoleon Sarony, the famed photographer of the theatrical scene, in a book by Adah Isaacs Menken titled *Infelicia* (1868). The letter, catalogued separately, was once inserted in the book and is mentioned in the catalogue entry for the auction of Augustin Daly's large collection of books. On Menken, see Renee Sentilles, *Perfoming Menken: Adah Isaacs Menken and the Birth of Modern Celebrity* (Cambridge University Press, 2012). On "extra illustrated books," otherwise known as "grangerized," see Erin Blake, *Extending the Book: The Art of Extra-Illustration* (Folger Shakespeare Library, 2010).

28. Adah Menken's performance as Mazeppa, cross-dressing as a man riding a horse in Byron's drama, drew audiences in both the United States and Europe to view her as a titillating spectacle. See Kari Weil, "Purebreds and Amazons: Saying Things with Horses in Late-Nineteenth-Century France," *differences: A Journal of Feminist Cultural Studies* vol. 11, no. 1 (1999), 1–37.

29. Some of Sarony's photographs can be viewed in this post: http://civilwaref.blogspot.com/2013/06/adah-isaacs-menken-born-june-15-1835.html.

30. Adah Isaacs Menken, "Pro Patria," *Infelicia* (J. B. Lippincott & Co., 1868).

31. Menken, "Pro Patria."

32. Frances Harper, *Forest Leaves* (1843). See the wonderful account of discovering this early collection, once thought lost, by Johanna Ortner: "Lost No More: Recovering Frances Ellen Watkins Harper's Forest Leaves," https://commonplace.online/article/lost-no-more-recovering-frances-ellen-watkins-harpers-forest-leaves/.

Afterword: The History of the Present

1. George Saunders, *Lincoln in the Bardo* (Random House, 2017).

2. Rebecca Schneider, *Performing Remains: Art and War in Times of Theatrical Reenactment* (Routledge, 2011). Suzan-Lori Parks, *Topdog/Underdog* (Theatre Communications Group, 2001).

3. *Father Comes Home from the Wars* (parts 1, 2, and 3), (Theatre Communications Group, 2015).

4. For more on Ream and this commission, see https://www.aoc.gov/explore-capitol-campus/art/vinnie-ream.

5. The execution was covered by the *New York Times* in disturbing detail in Stephen Riggs, "The Indian Executions: An Interesting Account, from Our Special Correspondent," Friday, December 26, 1862: http://m.startribune.com/dec-26-1862-38-dakota-men-executed-in-mankato/138273909/. See also the exhibition that took place at the National Museum of the American Indian: http://nmai.si.edu/explore/exhibitions/item/?id=947. Gary Anderson has an extensive evaluation of the remark supposedly made by Andrew Myrick in August 1862, a remark some blamed as instigation for the bloodshed that followed, in the online *Minnesota History Magazine*. See "Myrick's Insult," in *Minnesota History* (Spring 1983), 198–206, http://collections.mnhs.org/MNHistoryMagazine/articles/48/v48i05p198-206.pdf.

6. See also Scott Berg, *38 Nooses: Lincoln, Little Crow, and the Beginning of the Frontier's End* (Pantheon Books, 2012).

7. Joel Whitney, a pioneer in photography, operated his studio in St. Paul from 1851–1867. For more of his images, see https://collections.theautry.org/mwebcgi/mweb.exe?request=record;id=PE65213;type=701.

8. Roland Barthes, *Camera Lucida: Reflections on Photography* (Hill and Wang, 1981).

9. Susan Stewart, *Crimes of Writing: Problems in the Containment of Representation* (Duke University Press, 1994).

10. Claudia Rankine, *Citizen: An American Lyric* (Greywolf, 2014); Christina Sharpe, *In the Wake: On Blackness and Being* (Duke University Press, 2016); and Alexander Weheliye, *Habeas Viscus: Racializing Assemblages, Biopolitics and Black Feminist Theories of the Human* (Duke University Press, 2014).

11. There are copies of the engravings in several places, including the resources of the Library of Congress: http://www.loc.gov/pictures/item/2003672892/.

12. I refer here to Kimberle Crenshaw's influential term. See *Critical Race Theory: The Key Writings That Formed the Movement* (New Press, 1996).

13. A controversial statue of Lincoln at Bennington College in Vermont was defaced with a spray-painted "38." The work *Scaffold* presented a large wooden

platform at the Walker Art Center in Minneapolis expressly designed as a protest against the execution authorized by Abraham Lincoln. Confronted with outrage, the artist authorized the destruction of his own creation. On Sam Durant, see https://www.artnews.com/art-news/news/sam-durant-wins-decordova-sculpture-parks-25000-rappaport-prize-8761/.

14. Ariella Azoulay, *The Civil Contract of Photography* (Zone Press, 2004), 17. The books with which she engages are Carole Pateman, *The Sexual Contract* (Stanford University Press, 1988), and Charles Mills, *The Racial Contract* (Cornell University Press, 1999).

15. Isaac Heard, *History of the Sioux Wars and Massacres of 1862 and 1863* (Harper Bros., 1863). Before the Dakotas had been claimed as states, and while the Dakota nation had a precarious alliance with the Sioux, in one of several "last stands" against what they perceived as the treachery of Bureau of Indian Affairs (BIA) agents, the uprising ended in a series of massacres. Traders on the frontier had engaged in suspect transactions with the BIA through which they diverted most of the promised hundreds of thousands of dollars in compensation that had been promised in return for the transfer of millions of acres of western land. The attacks that began in August 1862 probably meant the deaths of hundreds of white settlers, which explains the initial bloodthirsty call to execute all of the four hundred warriors who were rounded up after troops were diverted from the Civil War battlefields to fight on the frontier. The eventual execution of thirty-eight was a significant reduction from the original possibility.

16. The title that Kara Walker gave to her enormous installation provides a label with "homage" to the "unpaid and overworked Artisans," although I wonder if she would have included my ancestor among the workers who have "refined our Sweet tastes." For images and the title, see http://creativetime.org/projects/karawalker/. I have one tiny photograph that claims to show my great great grandfather working as a foreman on the Havemeyers and Elder building in 1879. For an extensive account of the building (written as a preservation report for the City of New York in 2007), and one that mentions Thomas Winslow as a builder, see https://www.nyc.gov/html/records/pdf/govpub/3311domino.desigrep.pdf.

17. The stories told in Louise Erdrich's many novels remind me of the barely recorded life of my grandmother's father, Sidney Winslow, who worked in the "ax handle factory" in Bemidji, Minnesota, in the early twentieth century before abandoning his family and heading to the lumber mills of the northwestern United States. Bemidji was a boom town because of lumber while bordering several reservations, including the Red Lake, the White Earth, and the Leech Lake. The complications that ensue with such consideration are broached in a recent book: Megan Kate Nelson, *The Three-Cornered War: The Union, The Confederacy, and Native Peoples in the Fight for the West* (Scribner, 2021).

18. Thomas Crawford (1822–1857) made the plaster version from which the bronze statue, known as *The Statue of Freedom*, was cast. The statue was erected on top of the US Capitol in 1863, soon after the hangings in Mankato, Minnesota. The statue, facing east, is more than 19 feet high and weighs 15,000 pounds. In spite of the official explanations that call attention to Greek and Roman antecedents, the stated intent of the sculptor was to allude to Indian identity in the Americas.

Ironically, as it turned out, then Secretary of War Jefferson Davis resisted the idea of a "liberty cap" for the statue because it suggested emancipation. The response from the sculptor was to design a crested version of a Roman helmet, "the crest of which is composed of an eagle's head and a bold arrangement of feathers, suggested by the costume of our Indian tribes." This design was approved by Jefferson Davis in April 1856. Thomas Crawford died before his plaster model could be shipped to the United States, and the casting of the statue was carried out by Clark Mills, famous for the Andrew Jackson statue that still stands near the White House. He was assisted by a formerly enslaved man, Philip Reid, who had been newly freed by the Emancipation Proclamation. See http://www.visitthecapitol.gov/Exhibitions/online/the-capitol-story/statue-of-freedom/1337-clark-mills-sculptor.html. See also https://www.aoc.gov/explore-capitol-campus/art/thomas-crawford and https://www.aoc.gov/explore-capitol-campus/art/statue-freedom.

BIBLIOGRAPHY

Primary Texts

Alcott, Louisa May. “The Brothers.” *Atlantic Monthly*. November 1863.

———. *Hospital Sketches*. 1863.

———. *Little Women*. 1868.

Bird, Robert Montgomery. *Nick of the Woods*. 1837.

Black Hawk. *The Life of Black Hawk, or, Ma-ka-tai-me-she-kia-kiak: Dictated by Himself*. 1833.

Brown, William Wells. *Clotel*. 1853.

Burton, Maria Amparo Ruiz de. *Who Would Have Thought It?* 1872.

Cooper, James Fenimore. *Home as Found*. 1838.

. *The Pioneers*. 1821.

Davis, Rebecca Harding. *Life in the Iron Mills*. 1861.

De Forest, John William. *Miss Ravenel’s Conversion from Secession to Loyalty*. 1867.

Dickinson, Emily. *Poems*, ed. R. W. Franklin. Harvard University Press, 1999.

Douglass, Frederick. *Frederick Douglass: Selected Speeches and Writings*, eds. Philip S. Foner and Yuval Taylor. Lawrence Hill Books, 1999.

———. *Narrative*. 1845. Reprinted as *Narrative of the Life of Frederick Douglass, An American Slave, Written by Himself*, ed. William Andrews and William S. McFeely. W. W. Norton, 1997.

Evans, Augusta. *Inez*. 1855.

———. *Macaria*. 1864.

Gardner, Alexander. *Photographic Sketch Book of the War*. Philp & Solomons, 1866.

Gilman, Charlotte Perkins. *Herland*. 1915.

———. *The Home: Its Work and Influence*. McClure, Philips, and Co., 1903.

———. *The Man Made World: Our Androcentric Culture*. Charlatan Co., 1911.

———. *Women and Economics: A Study of the Economic Relation Between Men and Women as a Factor in Social Evolution*. Small, Maynard, and Co., 1898. http://digital.library.upenn.edu/women/gilman/economics/economics.html.

———. “Why I Wrote the Yellow Wallpaper.” http://www.library.csi.cuny.edu/dept/history/lavender/whyyw.html.

[Gilman] Stetson, Charlotte Perkins. “The Yellow Wall-paper. A Story.” *New England Magazine* vol. 11, no. 5, January 1892.

Harper, Frances. *Forest Leaves*. 1843.

———. *Iola Leroy, or, Shadows Uplifted*. 1892.

Hawthorne, Nathaniel. “Chiefly about War Matters.” *Atlantic Monthly* vol. 10, no. 57 (1862), 43–62.

———. *The Scarlet Letter*. 1850.

Higginson, Thomas Wentworth. *Army Life in a Black Regiment*. 1870.

———. “Letter to a Young Contributor.” *Atlantic Monthly*. April 1862.

Holmes, Oliver Wendell. “Doings of the Sunbeam.” *Atlantic Monthly*. July 1863.

Jacobs, Harriet. *Incidents in the Life of a Slave Girl.* 1861.

Jefferson, Thomas. *Notes on the State of Virginia.* 1785.

Keckley, Elizabeth. *Behind the Scenes: Or, Thirty Years a Slave and Four Years in the White House.* 1868; University of Illinois Press, 1988.

Larcom, Lucy. *A New England Girlhood, Outlined from Memory.* Houghton Mifflin, 1888.

Lincoln, Abraham. *Speeches and Writings, 1859–1865: Speeches, Letters, and Miscellaneous Writings, Presidential Messages and Proclamations,* ed. Don E. Fehrenbacher and Roy P. Basler. Literary Classics of the United States, 1989.

Longfellow, Henry Wadsworth. *The Song of Hiawatha.* 1855.

Marsh, E. S. *Memoir of the Centennial Exhibition of 1876.* J. H. Coates, 1876.

Melville, Herman. *Battle Pieces and Aspects of the War.* Harper Bros., 1866.

——. *Billy Budd.* 1891; 1924.

——. *The Confidence Man.* Dix, Edwards, & Co., 1857.

——. *Moby-Dick.* 1852.

——. *Typee: A Peep at Polynesian Life.* 1846.

Menken, Adah Isaacs. *Infelicia.* 1868.

Mitchell, S. Weir. *Injuries of Nerves and Their Consequences.* 1872.

Parkman, Francis. *The Oregon Trail: Sketches of Prairie and Rocky-Mountain Life.* 1847.

Phelps, Elizabeth Stuart. *The Gates Ajar.* 1868.

——. *The Story of Avis.* 1877.

Piatt, Sarah. *Palace Burner: The Selected Poetry of Sarah Piatt,* ed. Paula Bennett. University of Illinois Press, 2005.

Poe, Edgar Allan. *The Narrative of Arthur Gordon Pym, of Nantucket.* 1838.

Ridge, John Rollin. *The Life and Adventures of Joaquin Murieta, The Celebrated California Bandit.* 1871.

Riis, Jacob. *How the Other Half Lives.* 1890.

Schoolcraft, Henry Rowe. *Algic Researches: Comprising Inquiries Respecting the Mental Characteristics of the North American Indian.* Harper & Bros., 1839.

——. *Personal Memoirs of a Residence of Thirty Years with the Indian Tribes on the American Frontiers.* Philadelphia, 1851.

Stone, John Augustus. *Metamora; or, The Last of the Wampanoags.* 1829.

Stowe, Harriet Beecher. *Dred.* 1856.

——. *Uncle Tom's Cabin; or, Life among the Lowly.* 1852.

Thoreau, Henry David. *On the Duty of Civil Disobedience.* 1849.

——. *Walden.* 1854.

Twain, Mark. *The Adventures of Huckleberry Finn.* 1885.

——. *Life on the Mississippi.* 1883.

Walker, David. *Appeal.* 1829.

Warren, Mercy Otis. *History of the Rise, Progress, and Termination of the American Revolution.* 1805.

Whitman, Walt. *Complete Poetry and Collected Prose.* Literary Classics of the United States, 1982.

——. *Leaves of Grass.* 1855.

——. *Specimen Days.* 1882.

Winnemucca, Sarah. *Life among the Piutes: Their Wrongs and Claims.* Putnam's, 1883.

Historical and Critical Works

Azoulay, Ariella. *The Civil Contract of Photography*. MIT Press, 2008.

Baptist, Edward. *The Half Has Never Been Told: Slavery and the Making of American Capitalism*. Basic Books, 2014.

Barthes, Roland. *Camera Lucida: Reflections on Photography*, trans. Richard Howard. Hill and Wang, 1981.

Beach, Caitlin Meehye. *Sculpture at the Ends of Slavery*. University of California Press, 2022.

Bellion, Wendy. *Citizen Spectators: Art, Illusion, and Visual Perception in Early National America*. University of North Carolina Press, 2011.

———. *Iconoclasm in New York: Revolution to Reenactment*. Pennsylvania State University Press, 2019.

Bergland, Renee. *The National Uncanny: Indian Ghosts and American Subjects*. University Press of New England, 2000.

Berlant, Lauren. *The Female Complaint: The Unfinished Business of Sentimentality in American Culture*. Duke University Press, 2008.

Bernier, Celeste-Marie, John Stauffer, and Zoe Trodd, eds. *Picturing Frederick Douglass: An Illustrated Biography of the Nineteenth Century's Most Photographed American*. Liveright, 2018.

Bernstein, Robin. *Racial Innocence: Performing American Childhood from Slavery to Civil Rights*. New York University Press, 2011.

Best, Stephen. *The Fugitive's Properties: Law and the Poetics of Possession*. University of Chicago Press, 2004.

Bonner, Christopher. *Remaking the Republic: Black Politics and the Creation of American Citizenship*. University of Pennsylvania Press, 2020.

Burt, John. *Lincoln's Tragic Pragmatism: Lincoln, Douglas, and Moral Conflict*. Harvard University Press, 2013.

Byrd, Jodi. *The Transit of Empire: The Indigenous Critique of Colonialism*. University of Minnesota Press, 2011.

Cliff, Nigel. *The Shakespeare Riots: Revenge, Drama, and Death in 19th-Century America*. Random House, 2007.

Cohen, Lara Langer. *The Fabrication of American Literature: Fraudulence and Antebellum Print Culture*. University of Pennsylvania Press, 2011.

Coviello, Peter. *Intimacy in America: Dreams of Affiliation in American Literature*. University of Minnesota Press, 2005.

Cox, Karen. *Dixie's Daughters: The United Daughters of the Confederacy and the Preservation of Confederate Culture*. University Press of Florida, 2019.

Davidson, Cathy. *Revolution and the Word: The Rise of the Novel in America*. Oxford University Press, 2004.

Debord, Guy. *The Society of the Spectacle*, trans. Donald Nicholson-Smith. Zone, 1994.

Deloria, Philip. *Playing Indian*. Yale University Press, 1999.

Dillon, Elizabeth Maddock. *New World Drama: The Performative Commons in the Atlantic World, 1649–1865*. Duke University Press, 2014.

Dinius, Marcy. *The Camera and the Press: American Visual and Print Culture in the Age of the Daguerreotype*. University of Pennsylvania Press, 2012.

Driscoll, Kerry. *Mark Twain among the Indians and Other Indigenous Peoples*. University of California Press, 2018.

Duquette, Elizabeth. *Loyal Subjects: Bonds of Nation, Race, and Allegiance in Nineteenth-Century America*. Rutgers University Press, 2010.

Elmer, Jonathan. *On Lingering and Being Last: Race and Sovereignty in the New World*. Fordham University Press, 2008.

Erkkila, Betsy. *Whitman, the Political Poet*. Oxford University Press, 1989.

Flint, Timothy. *The History and Geography of the Mississippi Valley*. Flint and Lincoln, 1832.

Freeman, Joanne. *The Field of Blood: Violence in Congress and the Route to the Civil War*. Farrar, Straus and Giroux, 2018.

Frydd, Vivien Green. *Art and Empire: The Politics of Ethnicity in the United States Capitol, 1815–1860*. Ohio University Press. 2001.

Garvey, Ellen Gruber. *Writing with Scissors: American Scrapbooks from the Civil War to the Harlem Renaissance*. Oxford University Press, 2013.

Gilroy, Paul. *The Black Atlantic: Modernity and Double Consciousness*. Verso, 1993.

Golden, Catherine. *The Captive Imagination: A Casebook on The Yellow Wallpaper*. Feminist Press, 1992.

Goodwin, Doris K. *Team of Rivals: The Political Genius of Abraham Lincoln*. Simon & Schuster, 2005.

Green, Vivien. "Hiram Powers's Greek Slave: An Emblem of Freedom." *American Art Journal*, 1982: 31–39.

Gruesz, Kirsten Silva. *Ambassadors of Culture: The Transamerican Origins of Latino Writing*. Princeton University Press, 2001.

Habermas, Jurgen. *The Structural Transformation of the Public Sphere: An Inquiry into a Category of Bourgeois Society*. MIT Press, 1989.

Hall, Stuart. *Selected Political Writings*. Duke University Press, 2017.

Hardt, Michael, and Antonio Negri. *Empire*. Harvard University Press, 2001.

Hartman, Saidiya. *Scenes of Subjection: Terror, Slavery, and Self-Making in Nineteenth-Century America*. Oxford University Press, 1997.

Hendler, Glenn, and Bruce Burgett. *Keywords for American Cultural Studies*. New York University Press, 2014.

Holland, Sharon, and Tiya Miles, eds., *Crossing Waters, Crossing Worlds: The African Diaspora in Indian Country*. Duke University Press, 2006.

Huerta, Monica. *The Unintended: Photography, Property, and the Aesthetics of Racial Capitalism*. New York University Press, 2023.

Insko, Jeffrey. *History, Abolition, and the Ever-Present Now in Antebellum American Writing*. Oxford University Press, 2019.

Jackson, Virginia. *Dickinson's Misery: A Theory of Lyric Reading*. Princeton University Press, 2005.

James, C. L. R. *Mariners, Renegades, and Castaways: The Story of Herman Melville and the World We Live In*. Published by the author, 1953.

Johnston, Patricia, ed. *Seeing High and Low: Representing Social Conflict in American Visual Culture*. University of California Press, 2006.

Kaplan, Amy. *The Anarchy of Empire in the Making of U.S. Culture*. Harvard University Press, 2002.

Kazanjian, David. *The Brink of Freedom: Improvising Life in the Nineteenth-Century Atlantic World*. Duke University Press, 2016.

———. *The Colonizing Trick: National Culture and Imperial Citizenship in Early America*. University of Minnesota Press, 2003.

Krieger, Murray. *Ekphrasis: The Illusion of the Natural Sign*. Johns Hopkins University Press, 1991.

Loughran, Trish. *The Republic in Print: Print Culture in the Age of U.S. Nation Building, 1770–1870*. Columbia University Press, 2007.

Lowe, Lisa. *The Intimacies of Four Continents*. Duke University Press, 2016.

Luciano, Dana. *Arranging Grief: Sacred Time and the Body in Nineteenth-Century America*. New York University Press, 2007.

Marrs, Cody. *Not Even Past: The Stories We Keep Telling about the Civil War*. Johns Hopkins University Press, 2020.

Mathiessen, F. O. *The American Renaissance: Art and Expression in the Age of Emerson and Whitman*. 1941; repr. Oxford University Press, 1968.

McHenry, Elizabeth. *Forgotten Readers: Recovering the Lost History of African American Literary Societies*. Duke University Press, 2002.

Mitchell, Koritha. *From Slave Cabins to the White House: Homemade Citizenship in African American Culture*. University of Illinois Press, 2021.

Mitchell, W.J.T. *Iconology: Image, Text, Ideology*. University of Chicago Press, 1987.

Moody, Richard. *The Astor Place Riot*. Indiana University Press, 1958.

Morrison, Toni. *Playing in the Dark: Whiteness and the Literary Imagination*. Harvard University Press, 1992.

Mulvey, Laura. "Visual Pleasure and Narrative Cinema." *Screen* vol. 16, no. 3 (1975), 6–18.

Murison, Justine. *The Politics of Anxiety in 19th Century American Literature*. Cambridge University Press, 2011.

Nelson, Charmaine. *The Color of Stone: Sculpting the Black Female Subject in 19th-Century America*. University of Minnesota Press, 2007.

Nelson, Dana. *Commons Democracy: Reading the Politics of Participation in the Early United States*. Fordham University Press, 2016.

Nelson, Megan Kate. *The Three-Cornered War: The Union, the Confederacy, and Native Peoples in the Fight for the West*. Scribner, 2021.

Nudelman, Franny. *John Brown's Body: Slavery, Violence, and the Culture of War*. University of North Carolina Press, 2004.

Nyong'o, Tavia. *The Amalgamation Waltz: Race, Performance, and the Ruses of Memory*. University of Minnesota Press, 2009.

Pascoe, Peggy. *What Comes Naturally: Miscegenation Law and the Making of Race in America*. Oxford University Press, 2009.

Patterson, Orlando. *Slavery and Social Death: A Comparative Study*. Harvard University Press, 1982.

Rankine, Claudia. *Citizen: An American Lyric*. Greywolf, 2014.

Richter, Daniel. *Facing East from Indian Country: A Native History of Early America*. Harvard University Press, 2001.

Rifkin, Mark. *When Did Indians Become Straight? Kinship, The History of Sexuality, and Native Sovereignty*. Oxford University Press. 2010.

Roach, Joseph. *Cities of the Dead: Circum-Atlantic Performance*. Columbia University Press, 1996.

Samuels, Shirley. *The Cambridge Companion to Abraham Lincoln*. Cambridge University Press, 2012.

———. *Facing America: Iconography and the Civil War*. Oxford University Press, 2004.

———. *Romances of the Republic: Women, the Family, and Violence in the Literature of the Early American Nation*. Oxford University Press, 1996.

Savage, Kirk. *Standing Soldiers, Kneeling Slaves: Race, War, and Monument in Nineteenth-Century America*. Princeton University Press, 2018.

Schoolman, Martha. *Abolitionist Geographies*. University of Minnesota Press, 2014.

Schulten, Susan. *Mapping the Nation: History and Cartography in Nineteenth-Century America*. University of Chicago Press, 2012.

Seelye, John. *Beautiful Machine: Rivers and the Republican Plan, 1755–1825*. Oxford University Press, 1991.

Sharpe, Christina. *In the Wake: On Blackness and Being*. Duke University Press, 2016.

Smith, Shawn Michelle. *American Archives: Gender, Race, and Class in Visual Culture*. Princeton University Press, 1999.

Smith, Thomas Ruys. *River of Dreams: Imagining the Mississippi before Mark Twain*. University of Louisiana Press, 2007.

Stewart, Susan. *On Longing: Narratives of the Miniature, the Gigantic, the Souvenir, the Collection*. Duke University Press, 1992.

Thompson, Erin. *Smashing Statues: The Rise and Fall of America's Public Monuments*. Norton, 2023.

Wallace, Maurice, and Shawn Michelle Smith, eds. *Pictures and Progress: Early Photography and the Making of African American Identity*. Duke University Press, 2012.

Waterman, Adam John. *The Corpse in the Kitchen: Enclosure, Extraction, and the Afterlives of the Black Hawk War*. Fordham University Press, 2021.

Weheliye, Alexander. *Habeas Viscus: Racializing Assemblages, Biopolitics, and Black Feminist Theories of the Human*. Duke University Press, 2014.

Young, Elizabeth. *Disarming the Nation: Women's Writing and the American Civil War*. University of Chicago, 1999.

FURTHER READING

Aaron, Daniel. *The Unwritten War: American Writers and the Civil War*. Knopf, 1973.

Allen, Thomas. *A Republic in Time: Temporality and Social Imagination in Nineteenth-Century America*. University of North Carolina Press, 2008.

Armstrong, Nancy. *Fiction in the Age of Photography: The Legacy of British Realism*. Harvard University Press, 1999.

Barrett, Faith. *To Fight Aloud Is Very Brave: American Poetry and the Civil War*. University of Massachusetts Press, 2012.

Bernstein, Iver. *The New York City Draft Riots*. Oxford University Press, 1990.

Brooks, Daphne. *Bodies in Dissent: Spectacular Performances of Race and Freedom, 1850—1910*. Duke University Press, 2006.

Chinn, Sarah. *Disability, the Body, and Radical Intellectuals in the Literature of the Civil War and Reconstruction*. Cambridge University Press, 2024.

Cobb, Jasmine Nichole. *Picture Freedom: Remaking Black Visuality in the Early Nineteenth Century*. New York University Press, 2015.

Crary, Jonathan. *Techniques of the Observer: On Vision and Modernity in the Nineteenth Century*. MIT Press, 1990.

Dain, Bruce R. *A Hideous Monster of the Mind: American Race Theory in the Early Republic*. Harvard University Press, 2002.

Diffley, Kathleen. *Where My Heart Is Turning Ever: Civil War Stories and Constitutional Reform, 1861–1876*. University of Georgia Press, 1992.

Drinnon, Richard. *Facing West: The Metaphysics of Indian-Hating and Empire Building*. Minnesota, 1980.

Du Bois, W. E. B. *Black Reconstruction in America, 1860–1880*. Harcourt, Brace, and Co., 1935.

Everett, Percival. *James: A Novel*. Doubleday, 2024.

Fahs, Alice. *The Imagined Civil War: Popular Literature of the North and South, 1861–1865*. University of North Carolina Press, 2002.

Fahs, Alice and Joan Waugh, eds., *The Memory of the Civil War in American Culture*. University of North Carolina Press, 2004.

Faust, Drew Gilpin. *This Republic of Suffering: Death and the American Civil War*. Alfred A. Knopf, 2008.

Fielder, Brigitte. *Relative Races: Genealogies of Interracial Kinship in Nineteenth-Century America*. Duke University Press, 2020.

Finseth, Ian Frederick. *Shades of Green: Visions of Nature in the Literature of American Slavery, 1770–1860*. Athens: University of Georgia Press, 2009.

Foster, Frances Smith. *Written by Herself: Literary Productions by Afro-American Women, 1746—1892*. Indiana University Press, 1993.

Frydd, Vivien Green. *Art and Empire: The Politics of Ethnicity in the U.S. Capitol, 1815–1860*. Yale University Press, 1992.

Gillman, Susan. *Blood Talk: American Race Melodrama and the Culture of the Occult.* Chicago University Press, 2003.

Goddu, Teresa. *Selling Antislavery: Abolition and Mass Media in Antebellum America.* University of Pennsylvania Press, 2020.

Goldberg, Shari. *Quiet Testimony: A Theory of Witnessing from Nineteenth-Century American Literature.* Fordham University Press, 2013.

Goldsby, Jacqueline. *A Spectacular Secret: Lynching in American Life and Literature.* University of Chicago Press, 2006.

Greiman, Jennifer. *Democracy's Spectacle: Sovereignty and Public Life in Antebellum American Writing.* Fordham University Press, 2010.

Gustafson, Sandra. *Imagining Deliberative Democracy in the Early American Republic.* University of Chicago Press, 2012.

Hudson, Linda. *Mistress of Manifest Destiny: A Biography of Jane McManus Storm Cazneau, 1807–1878.* Texas State Historical Association, 2001.

Huerta, Monica. *Unintended: Photography, Property, and the Aesthetics of Racial Capitalism.* New York University Press, 2023.

Levine, Robert, and Samuel Otter, eds. *Frederick Douglass and Herman Melville: Essays in Relation.* University of North Carolina Press, 2012.

Morgan, Jennifer. *Reckoning with Slavery: Gender, Kinship, and Capitalism in the Early Black Atlantic.* Duke University Press, 2021.

Rael, Patrick. *Eighty-Eight Years: The Long Death of Slavery in the United States, 1777–1865.* University of Georgia Press, 2015.

Richardson, Heather Cox. *How the South Won the Civil War: Oligarchy, Democracy, and the Continuing Fight for the Soul of America.* Oxford University Press, 2020.

Rosenheim, Jeff. *Photography and the American Civil War.* Metropolitan Museum, 2013.

Samuels, Shirley, ed. *Companion to American Fiction, 1780–1865.* Blackwell, 2004.

Sanchez-Eppler, Karen. *Dependent States: The Child's Part in Nineteenth-Century American Culture.* University of Chicago Press, 2005.

Silber, Nina. *Daughters of the Union: Northern Women Fight the Civil War.* Harvard University Press, 2011.

Sinha, Manisha. *The Slave's Cause: A History of Abolition.* Yale University Press. 2016.

Smith, Thomas Ruys. *Blacklegs, Card Sharps, and Confidence Men: Nineteenth Century Mississippi River Gambling Stories.* Louisiana State University Press, 2010.

Spillers, Hortense. *Black, White, and in Color: Essays on American Literature and Culture.* University of Chicago Press, 2003.

Spires, Derrick. *The Practice of Citizenship: Black Politics and Print Culture in the Early United States.* University of Pennsylvania Press, 2023.

Stewart, Matthew. *An Emancipation of the Mind: Radical Philosophy, the War over Slavery, and the Refounding of America.* Norton, 2023.

Stewart, Susan. *Crimes of Writing: Problems in the Containment of Representation.* Duke University Press, 1994.

Stoler, Ann Laura, ed., *Haunted by Empire: Geographies of Intimacy in North American History.* Duke University Press, 2006.

Sweet, John Wood. *Bodies Politic: Negotiating Race in the American North, 1730–1830.* Baltimore: Johns Hopkins University Press, 2003.

Sweet, Timothy. *Traces of War: Poetry, Photography, and the Crisis of the Union.* Johns Hopkins University Press, 1990.

Trouillot, Michel-Rolph. *Silencing the Past: Power and the Production of History.* Beacon Press, 1995.

Weierman, Karen Woods. *One Nation, One Blood: Interracial Marriage in American Fiction, Scandal and Law, 1820–1870.* University of Massachusetts Press, 2005.

Wells, Cheryl A. *Civil War Time: Temporality and Identity in America, 1861–1865.* University of Georgia Press, 2005.

Wilson, Edmund. *Patriotic Gore: Studies in the Literature of the American Civil War.* Oxford University Press, 1962.

Wilson, Ivy. *Specters of Democracy: Blackness and the Aesthetics of Politics in the Antebellum U.S.* Oxford University Press, 2011.

Yao, Xine. *Disaffected: The Cultural Politics of Unfeeling in Nineteenth-Century America.* Duke University Press: 2021.

Yellin, Jean Fagan. *Women and Sisters: The Antislavery Feminists in American Culture.* Yale University Press, 1989.

INDEX

A NOTE ON THE TYPE

THIS BOOK has been composed in Miller, a Scotch Roman typeface designed by Matthew Carter and first released by Font Bureau in 1997. It resembles Monticello, the typeface developed for The Papers of Thomas Jefferson in the 1940s by C. H. Griffith and P. J. Conkwright and reinterpreted in digital form by Carter in 2003.

Pleasant Jefferson ("P. J.") Conkwright (1905–1986) was Typographer at Princeton University Press from 1939 to 1970. He was an acclaimed book designer and AIGA Medalist.

The ornament used throughout this book was designed by Pierre Simon Fournier (1712–1768) and was a favorite of Conkwright's, used in his design of the *Princeton University Library Chronicle*.